THE FIRST
SOUTH PACIFIC
CAMPAIGN

THE FIRST SOUTH PACIFIC CAMPAIGN

PACIFIC FLEET STRATEGY | December 1941–June 1942

JOHN B. LUNDSTROM

Naval Institute Press
Annapolis, Maryland

This book has been brought to publication with the generous assistance of Marguerite and Gerry Lenfest.

Naval Institute Press
291 Wood Road
Annapolis, MD 21402

First Naval Institute Press paperback edition published in 2014.
ISBN: 978-1-59114-417-5 (paperback)
ISBN: 978-1-61251-352-2 (eBook)

Library of Congress Catalogue Card No. 76-23507 (hardcover)

♾ Print editions meet the requirements of ANSI/NISO z39.48-1992 (Permanence of Paper).
Printed in the United States of America.

22 21 20 19 18 17 16 15   9 8 7 6 5 4

o my parents

"The 'defensive-offensive' may be paraphrased as 'hold what you've got and hit them when you can,' the hitting to be done, not only by seizing opportunities, but making them."

Admiral Ernest J. King to
Secretary of the Navy Frank Knox,
February 8, 1942

Contents

Preface

Few periods of the Pacific War seem so easy to comprehend in terms of strategy and command decisions as the first seven months. The Pacific Fleet suffered a devastating blow at Pearl Harbor which evidently made its leaders cautious and wary, not anxious to commit themselves. For the next several months the United States apparently contented itself with a few offensive jabs at insignificant island bases while Japan eagerly gobbled up the Netherlands East Indies and Southeast Asia. Then in the spring of 1942, American naval intelligence discovered Japanese plans for the capture of Port Moresby, and the Pacific Fleet commander decided to commit his carriers in the South Pacific to lop off one of the Japanese tentacles inching toward northeastern Australia. Supposedly he had to time his operations carefully in order to meet the real Japanese main thrust across the Central Pacific. In desperation then, the United States committed its fleet reluctantly to defend Midway from overwhelming forces, winning subsequently what one historian aptly called an "incredible victory" and reversing the tide of Japanese conquest in the Pacific. So goes the standard view of United States Pacific Fleet participation in the early campaigns in the Pacific.

Newly declassified documents reveal a totally new picture of Pacific Fleet operations during the first several months of the Pacific War. The South Pacific served as the one area where the United States expanded its control to meet the Japanese and protect the supply line to Australia. Far from shunning decisive battle with the Japanese carrier force, by late April 1942 the Pacific Fleet sought a major engagement in the South Pacific where it appeared to Admiral Ernest J. King and Admiral Chester W. Nimitz that the Japanese would commit up to seven carriers in invasions of New Guinea and the Solomon Islands. Admiral King approved of the use of all currently available American carriers for the South Pacific because he believed the defense of the South Pacific was absolutely vital to the Allies. Admiral Nimitz welcomed the impending South Pacific battles as the first opportunity to deal a crippling blow to Japanese carrier strength. This study is intended as a strategic overview of the first seven months in the Pacific as it concerned the high commands and fleet commanders of the navies of the United States and Japan. For the first time it is possible by utilizing the actual text of deciphered Japanese messages to begin to assess the impact of radio intelligence on United States operations in the Pacific. Equally important is the availability of extremely important new Japanese sources which allow a better understanding of the Japanese operations in the South Pacific.

The author would like to express his great appreciation for the kind assistance and encouragement given to him by the following people. Rear Admiral Edwin T. Layton (Retired) provided great insights into naval intelligence and the manner in which it was utilized by Admiral Nimitz. He read an earlier version of the present manuscript and offered many valuable comments and emendations. Ota Tatsuyuki translated large portions of the new Japanese official history covering South Pacific operations. The search for documentation was greatly facilitated through the courtesy and competence of Dr. Dean C. Allard and Mrs. Kathleen Lloyd of the Classified Operational Archives, Naval History Division. Captain Roger Pineau, Director of the Navy Memorial Museum, made several visits to Washington much richer with his friendship and interest in this work. William F. Surgi, Jr. of the Battle of the Coral Sea Association was of enormous help, especially in his friendship and enthusiasm for researching the Battle of the Coral Sea. Another Coral Sea veteran who must be acknowledged here for his assistance and hospitality is Kenneth Crawford. Rear Admiral Phillip Fitzgerald (Retired) kindly lent the author a copy of his diary which he wrote while on board the heavy cruiser *New Orleans* which served under Rear Admiral Thomas C. Kinkaid at the Battle of the Coral Sea. LIC Milton Spearbraker, USN (Retired), who is the Milwaukee Public Museum's printer, provided information of his experiences as a printer in the Office of Naval Communication. Mr. Takeshita Takami of the War History Office in Tokyo responded fully to the author's inquiries. The War History Office also kindly provided the photographs of Japanese commanders. It is unlikely that this book would have been written had it not been for Dr. David Healy, the author's academic advisor, who had the interest and patience in seeing the original thesis brought to its conclusion.

A number of people helped directly in producing this work. Cheryl Castelli undertook the arduous task of typing the manuscript. Ronald Mazurkiewicz drew the maps. Two photographers, Robert T. Maciolek and Janice Mahlberg, reproduced the maps and photographs for use in the book. Constance MacDonald edited the final text, and Beverly Baum of the Naval Institute Press patiently weathered a number of delays in gathering necessary materials for inclusion in the book.

The facts and ideas contained in this work came from many sources and individuals, but responsibility for errors and interpretations must fall solely on the author.

Special Note

All Japanese individuals mentioned in the text have their names written surname first, then given name. This is proper Japanese usage. The West has rendered this courtesy to the Chinese, but not usually to the Japanese. Every author writing on the Pacific War has trouble with the international date line in giving exact dates. In every instance in the text, the author has striven in citing dates to indicate the location to which the specific date pertains. All distances are given in nautical miles.

Introduction to the Paperback Edition

You hold in your hands a newly reprinted little gem of a book, one that has languished in relative obscurity for far too long. I am, admittedly, somewhat biased in my assessment, in that I consider John Lundstrom both a good friend and a mentor. Yet I am genuine in my affection for this book, having tracked down a used copy back in 1999 for *way* too much money, which I subsequently had autographed for a *second* time by the author (the first having been inscribed to a former co-worker of John). Ask any historian (or the spouse of one) and you will hear that there are some books that are worth having, no matter the price. For me, this was one.

The book's title, *The First South Pacific Campaign*, is doubly fitting, in that it also represents John's first serious campaign into the field of Pacific War history. This is a subject area to which John has made substantial contributions over the course of nearly forty years, in the form of many splendid books. *The First South Pacific Campaign* established precisely why John would go on to earn a reputation as a heavyweight in the field. First was his capacity for conducting wide-ranging, exhaustive research in the archival materials. He is truly a researcher's researcher, always willing to pull that last box of files that might contain a hidden prize that no one has seen for decades. His passion for uncovering the evidence is truly formidable.

John's other trademark has always been his dedication to incorporating Japanese source materials into his work, so as to more accurately portray the Japanese perspective on their wartime operations. In the case of *The First South Pacific Campaign*, sections taken from the multi-volume official Japanese war history series (the Boeicho Boeikenshujo Senshibu, referred to in the trade as "BKS" or "Senshi Sōsho") form the core of the book's Japanese account. John had gone to the trouble to have translated substantial portions of the Senshi Sōsho volume dealing with early war operations in the south Pacific. In 1976, that was truly unprecedented. Senshi Sōsho was relatively hot off the presses, and most American historians didn't even know it existed. Even if they had, most of them would have found it too daunting to use—thick, opaque, and written in a semi-archaic academic style that even many modern Japanese cannot read. These difficulties did not daunt John, and his willingness to overcome such obstacles set him apart from his contemporaries.

One of the other things I find intriguing about *The First South Pacific Campaign* is its contrast with two of John's middle period books—*The First Team: Pacific Air Combat from Pearl Harbor to Midway* and *The First Team and the Guadalcanal Campaign*. These later volumes comprise an intimate look at naval fighter combat during the pivotal first year of the war. The *First Team* books are known among Pacific War students as what one might call "blow-by-blow" accounts. If you want to know who shot down whom over Guadalcanal on a given date, *First Team Guadalcanal* is the first book you reach for. Yet the point that often gets missed is that John always had a fine appreciation of the larger context that he was writing about and never failed to incorporate it in his detailed works. That sense of the "big picture" is clearly presented in *The First South Pacific Campaign*, which focuses on the strategic and operational decisions that shaped the first sixth months of the war. What makes this surprising is that one typically equates synthesis and depth of analysis with the experience that comes with being a more mature author. Yet John was just twenty-eight years old when this book was first published.

All in all, nearly forty years after its first publication, *The First South Pacific Campaign* remains a concise, readable, and cogent analysis of the initial phases of the Pacific War. I am delighted that it is more easily available once again, so that it can continue educating another generation of students of this crucial conflict.

Jonathan B. Parshall

Maps

Errata

Plate 1: The correct spelling is Vice Admiral Inoue Shigeyoshi.

Page 9, paragraph 3: The correct spelling is Vice Admiral Inoue Shigeyoshi.

Page 17, paragraph 2: Fletcher was to reach Wake on 24 December.

Page 69, paragraph 1: Hara planned to reach Truk on 28 April.

Page 75, paragraph 1: Joseph J. Rochefort's rank was commander.

Page 76, paragraph 2: John R. Redman ran Section G.

Page 79, paragraph 3: OP-20-G was Redman's Negat office in Washington.

Page 90, paragraph 3: Rochefort's rank was commander.

Page 90, paragraph 3: The message likely went to Commander Redman's Negat office.

Page 98, paragraph 2: Takagi's rank was vice admiral. He was promoted on 1 May.

Page 98, paragraph 4: Takagi's rank was vice admiral.

Page 104, paragraph 4: Fletcher believed the Japanese invasion convoy would arrive off Port Moresby by 10 May.

Page 106, paragraph 2: Takagi was a vice admiral and Hara was a rear admiral.

Page 138, paragraph 3: Rochefort's rank was commander.

Page 143, paragraph 2: Takagi's rank was vice admiral.

Page 150, paragraph 1: Layton was a lieutenant commander and Rochefort was a commander.

Page 234, left column: The correct spelling is Inoue, Vice Admiral Shigeyoshi.

Page 238, left column: Reference to Safford, Commander Laurence J. should be Redman, Commander John R.

Page 238, left column: Rochefort's rank was commander.

Page 238, right column: Takagi's rank was vice admiral.

Abbreviations and Code Names

AAF	Army Air Forces
ABDA	American–British–Dutch–Australian
AF	Japanese code designation for Midway
AIF	Australian Imperial Forces
AlNav	Message address for all U.S. Naval Commands
ANZAC	Designation for area encompassing Australian and New Zealand waters; from the World War I acronym for Australian and New Zealand Army Corps
Arcadia	Code name for Allied conference held from 24 December 1941 to 14 January 1942 in Washington, D.C.
Belconnen	United States Naval Radio Intelligence Unit at Melbourne
Bleacher	Code name for Tongatabu

Bolero	Code name for Army plan for sending troops to Britain for an early invasion of France
Cast	United States Naval Radio Intelligence Unit at Corregidor; evacuated to Australia and redesignated Belconnen
CCS	Combined Chiefs of Staff
CinCAF	Commander-in-Chief, Asiatic Fleet
CinCLant	Commander-in-Chief, Atlantic Fleet
CinCPac	Commander-in-Chief, Pacific Fleet
CinCPac–CinCPOA	Commander-in-Chief, Pacific Fleet and Commander-in-Chief, Pacific Ocean Areas
CinCUS	Commander-in-Chief, U.S. Fleet (superseded by ComInCh)
CNO	Chief of Naval Operations
ComAirSoPac	Commander, Air Forces, South Pacific Area
ComANZAC	Commander, ANZAC Area
Comb	Combined Addresses (intelligence radio network)
Com 14	Commander, 14th Naval District (originator of Hypo messages)
ComInCh	Commander-in-Chief, U.S. Fleet
ComSoPac	Commander, South Pacific Area
ComSoWesPac	Supreme Commander, Southwest Pacific Area
ComSoWesPacFor	Commander, Southwest Pacific Forces (naval command)
CTF	Commander, Task Force
Fantan	Code name for the Fiji Islands
Gymnast	British plan for invading Northwest Africa
Hypo	Code name for Combat Intelligence Unit, 14th Naval District
JCS	Joint Chiefs of Staff
MI Operation	Japanese designation for the invasion of Midway

MO Operation	Japanese designation for the attack on Port Moresby
Negat	Code name for Section G. Communication Security Section within Office of Naval Communications; also known as OP-20-G
OpD	Operations Division within the War Department
OpNav	Chief of Naval Operations
Poppy	Code name for New Caledonia
Roses	Code name for Efate
Roundup	Army plan for full-scale invasion of France in 1943
RY Operation	Japanese designation for the invasion of Ocean and Nauru islands
RZP	Japanese code designation for Tulagi
SecNav	Secretary of the Navy
Sledgehammer	Army plan for the emergency invasion of France in August or September 1942
SoPac	South Pacific Area
Straw	Code name for Samoa
SWPA	Southwest Pacific Area
Torch	Final plan for the invasion of Northwest Africa
USAFFE	U.S. Army Forces in the Far East
USAFIA	U.S. Army Forces in Australia
WPD	War Plans Division within War Department (superseded by OpD)

Admiral Yamamoto Isoroku

Rear Admiral Ugaki Matome

Captain Tomioka Sadatoshi

Vice Admiral Nagumo Chuichi

Vice Admiral Tsukahara Nishizo

Vice Admiral Inoue Shigemi

Note: ranks cited are those in 1942. Japanese photographs courtesy of the War History Office.

Rear Admiral Takagi Takeo

Rear Admiral Hara Chuichi

Rear Admiral Goto Aritomo

Rear Admiral Kajioka Sadamichi

Rear Admiral Shima Kiyohide

Major General Horii Tomitaro

Admiral Ernest J. King

Admiral Chester W. Nimitz

Admiral Harold R. Stark

Admiral Husband E. Kimmel

Vice Admiral William S. Pye

Vice Admiral William F. Halsey

Rear Admiral Frank Jack Fletcher

Rear Admiral Raymond A. Spruance

Rear Admiral Aubrey W. Fitch

Rear Admiral Thomas C. Kinkaid

General George C. Marshall

Lieutenant General H. H. Arnold

General Douglas MacArthur

Brigadier General Dwight D. Eisenhowe

Lieutenant General Delos C. Emmons

Lieutenant General George H. Brett

Lieutenant Commander Edwin T. Layton
(Photograph taken in late 1944 as a Captain).

THE FIRST
SOUTH PACIFIC
CAMPAIGN

PART I

THE
STRATEGIC
SITUATION

1
Japan Plans for War in the Pacific

Imperial Japan decided to go to war with the Allied powers in order to secure the raw materials and population resources of the Netherlands East Indies and Southeast Asia. The basic war plan envisioned a limited war, one in which Japan would quickly conquer the holdings of the colonial powers in the Far East, establish an impregnable defense perimeter on both flanks and then repulse expected counterattacks, hopefully to the extent that the Allies would accept the Japanese *fait accompli* and negotiate peace on that basis. Such a war was the only way Japan could hope to challenge the industrial might of the United States, Britain, and the associated powers of the Commonwealth. To assist them, the Japanese depended upon Germany to defeat or tie down Britain and the Soviet Union, especially until conditions freed the Imperial Army to deal with Soviet holdings in the Far East.

The military might of the Japanese empire rested with the Imperial Army and the Imperial Navy, each with its own air arm. The rivalry between the Army and the Navy was proverbial. Competing for a limited defense budget, each sought to justify its basic strategy. The outlook of the Army was primarily continental. Army leaders were largely responsible for the current Japanese involvement in China and maintained strong forces in Manchuria to counter Soviet forces in the region. Premier Tojo Hideki, also an Army general, agitated for war to smash the so-called ABCD Encirclement by the Allies. War would give them the opportunity to capture the rich economic areas in Southeast Asia and render Japan independent of political control from without. War with the Allies would also allow the Army to capture key areas surrounding Nationalist China in order to prevent the reinforcement of that country by the Allies. The Army's concept for war envisioned attacks on the Philippines and Southeast Asia to evict the American, Dutch, and British troops there. Secondly, they would exploit the newly acquired resources for the enlarged war effort. Finally, the Army planned to withdraw most of their forces from a crippled China and launch a massive offensive against the Soviet Union. The fighting in the Pacific they would leave to the Navy. It was axiomatic among the Army leaders to veto any plans which would require the use of large numbers of Army troops other than for the above-mentioned outline. This prohibition included most operations in the Pacific for which the Navy might require troops.[1]

If the Army had laid the burden on them for waging war in the Pacific, the Navy accepted it without great reservations. For nearly 20 years before 1941 the Navy planned for what they thought was the inevitable encounter with the U.S. Fleet, which they believed to be their most dangerous opponent. In keeping with the distinction of having in Tsushima one of the truly decisive naval victories in history, the Japanese Navy planned for an equally decisive battle with the U.S. Fleet. By the early thirties the Japanese had deduced the essentials of the basic American war plan, which called for a step-by-step advance across the Pacific beginning with the seizure of the Marshall Islands. The Japanese Navy expected the decisive battle to occur there, after aircraft and submarines had reduced the strength of the American fleet. Most Japanese naval leaders still considered the battleship to be the prime weapon, although the Navy possessed one of the finest carrier fleets in the world. By 1941 the naval planners saw the impending war as a quick dash to the south to capture the key economically rich regions and a redeployment to the east to deal with the expected American counteroffensive.[2]

The Japanese high command structure was known as Imperial General Headquarters, divided into twin Army and Naval Sections. Each section in turn consisted of a general staff responsible for strategic planning and operations and a ministry for administrative and logistical duties. Decisions in grand strategy came about through agreement between the respective chiefs of the Army and Naval General Staffs. This agreement often occurred after intense debate, as the two services usually pursued conflicting strategic policies. After reaching a decision, Imperial General Headquarters through the two sections issued orders to the major commands of the Army and the Navy. Regarding direction from above, the two chiefs of the general staffs worked closely with the army and naval ministers, and at staff meetings directly advised the emperor. As the emperor did not take an active part in determining strategy, fundamental grand strategy rested with them. There was also the Imperial General Headquarters–Government Liaison Conference, comprising the premier, the army, naval, and foreign ministers, and the two chiefs of the general staffs. Because of its composition, this body allowed wide latitude to Imperial General Headquarters for strategic policy.[3]

Because of the nature of fighting in the South Pacific, the Imperial Army did not participate actively in early 1942 in any great numbers; but as the Imperial Navy did, it is necessary to note its basic organization.[4] The Navy consisted of nine naval stations in the homeland area, the China Area Fleet, and, most importantly, the Combined Fleet. The Combined Fleet was the mobile or "mission" force encompassing the main body of the Navy. Because its strategic area was confined largely to the Pacific Ocean, it was roughly equivalent to the U.S. Pacific Fleet, but at the beginning was considerably larger than the latter. In early 1942 the Combined Fleet consisted of five mobile fleets comprising the principal striking forces and three localized or area fleets serving in a particular region. The ones most concerned with South Pacific operations were mobile fleets: First Fleet (battleships and cruisers), Second Fleet (cruisers), Sixth Fleet (submarines), First Air Fleet (carriers), and Eleventh Air Fleet (land-based aircraft). Each fleet possessed escort and support vessels in addition to the major types of warships. The one localized fleet was Fourth Fleet, based in the Mandated Islands. It consisted of a mixture of light cruisers, destroyers, submarines, auxiliary vessels, bases forces, and an air flotilla.

The Imperial Navy utilized an elaborate dual administrative-tactical designation system. Each fleet commander also had a specific operational title. All the tactical titles ended with the Japanese word butai, which meant "force," as in the U.S. Navy's usage of the designation "task force." The administrative designation was, as given above, the word "fleet," in Japanese, kantai. The only exception was Combined Fleet, which embodied both attributes. Thus the operational or tactical titles of the mobile fleets listed above were respectively, First Fleet (Main Force), Second Fleet

(Advance or Scouting Force), Sixth Fleet (Advance Expeditionary Force), First Air Fleet (Striking Force), and Eleventh Air Fleet (Base Air Force). The commander of Fourth Fleet utilized the operational title "South Seas Force" for his units. When units were detached for operational purposes to a force commander, they remained administratively under their own fleet, but received operational orders from the force to which they were attached. In practice, references to the two titles, administrative and tactical, were often interchangeable.

Planning for war accelerated in the Navy after Admiral Nagano Osami assumed command of the Naval General Staff in April 1941. Nagano favored the classic operations to the south to conquer the rich areas of Southeast Asia. Consequently the Naval General Staff, together with the Army General Staff, undertook detailed planning for the opening phase of the war. As evolved by early autumn 1941, the basic war plan provided for an initial period, "First Operational Stage," in which most of the conquests would take place. That period was divided into three phases, the first of which comprised attacks on the Philippines, Malaya, Borneo, the Celebes, Timor, Sumatra, and Rabaul in the Bismarck Archipelago. The second phase was to find the Japanese converging on Java from both the east and west flanks, leading to the capture of that large and important island. In addition, the second phase allowed for the Army's invasion of southern Burma. The third and final phase of the "First Operational Stage" called for the conquest of all of Burma, followed by the pacification and defense of the new areas comprising the "Great East Asian Co-Prosperity Sphere."[5]

There was little planning beyond the opening moves. Admiral Nagano briefly covered the subject of future operations during a conference held on 6 September 1941. He acknowledged that Japan would be in trouble if the war turned into a lengthy contest of attrition, but he indicated that with the resources of the Far East at its disposal, Japan would be able to make the defensive perimeter impregnable to Allied counteroffensives. Nagano was a member of the "huge battleships and big guns faction" of the Navy, who felt they could defeat the U.S. Fleet in decisive battle. It is paradoxical that the Navy did not heed the cries of those commanders urging heavy fortification beyond the development of airfields of the Mandated Islands. Perhaps Nagano never considered in detail the possibilities for a war of attrition and the detrimental consequences should the conflict turn that way.[6]

Admiral Yamamoto Isoroku, perhaps the most popular leader in the Navy, commanded the Combined Fleet. Under the aggresve Yamamoto and his staff, Combined Fleet gained considerable power in planning future operations, supposedly the prerogative of the Naval General Staff. With his prestige Yamamoto succeeded in gaining approval for a desperate plan of his own, a surprise carrier strike on Pearl Harbor with the intention of destroying or neutralizing the battleships and aircraft carriers of the Pacific Fleet. Yamamoto knew precisely the industrial potential of the United States and hoped to forestall as long as possible the anticipated American counteroffensive in the Pacific. He felt the only way to do this was to strike a heavy blow at the fleet as quickly as possible. He succeeded in persuading a cautious Nagano to let him risk the heart of Japan's carrier force, six fleet carriers, in the operation. Imperial General Headquarters issued final orders to all commands in early November 1941 and scheduled the opening of the war for December 1941 (Tokyo time).[7]

Contained in the orders were references to places to be "occupied or destroyed as speedily as operational conditions permit." These included eastern New Guinea, New Britain, Fiji, Samoa, the Aleutians, Midway, and "strategic points in the Australian area."[8] There was no detailed planning for these operations other than to say they would comprise the "Second Operational Stage." From the listing of the areas, it is clear that the Japanese were interested in the South Pacific as vital to the security of the defense perimeter. Indeed, prewar estimates of Allied reactions to a Japanese offensive in Southeast Asia stressed the fact that the Allies, when they finally completed mobilization, could be expected to begin their counteroffensive in the South or Central Pacific. The island chains stretching along the east-west axis of the South Pacific provided a useful series of actual or potential air bases which would support such a counteroffensive. If the Allies did not seek an early decisive battle, however, Japanese planners thought that the Americans would reinforce their supply lines with Australia and utilize that area for a base for their counteroffensive. Such an offensive coming from northern Australia could go in two different directions, straight north toward the Caroline Islands and northwest into the Netherlands East Indies.[9]

Vice Admiral Inoue Shigemi directly perceived the threat from Australia for it was his Fourth Fleet/South Seas Force which was responsible for the defense of the Mandates, the center of Japan's eastern defense perimeter. The Australian base at Rabaul on the northeastern tip of New Britain was only about 700 miles south of the major Japanese installations at Truk Atoll in the Carolines. An Allied counteroffensive striking north from Rabaul would

)

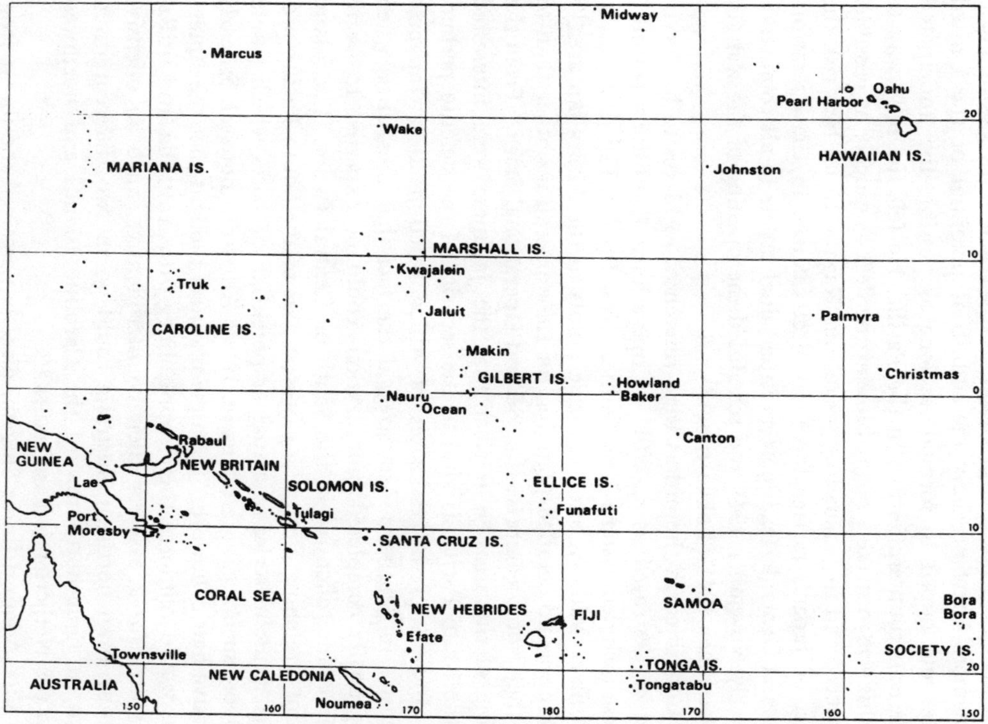

Midway
Marcus
Oahu
Pearl Harbor
Wake
HAWAIIAN IS.
MARIANA IS.
Johnston
MARSHALL IS.
Kwajalein
Truk
Jaluit
Palmyra
CAROLINE IS.
Makin
GILBERT IS.
Howland
Baker
Christmas
Nauru
Ocean
Canton
NEW GUINEA
Rabaul
NEW BRITAIN
SOLOMON IS.
ELLICE IS.
Lae
Funafuti
Port Moresby
Tulagi
SANTA CRUZ IS.
CORAL SEA
NEW HEBRIDES
FIJI
SAMOA
Bora Bora
Efate
SOCIETY IS.
Townsville
TONGA IS.
NEW CALEDONIA
Tongatabu
AUSTRALIA
Noumea
20
10
0
10
20
150
160
170
180
170
160
150

The Area of Confrontation

eatly flank the whole of the defensive positions built in the Mar-
all Islands. In prewar planning Fourth Fleet staff stressed that
 was vital to occupy points on New Britain, Lae and Salamaua
n the northeastern New Guinea coast, and Tulagi in the Solomon
lands, if only to safeguard the important hold on Rabaul. The
apture of positions in New Guinea and the Solomons would thrust
ae Japanese directly into the South Pacific and help forestall an
llied build-up in the region.[10]

Imperial General Headquarters deliberated upon the proposals
f Fourth Fleet, but considering the need to take the Dutch East
ndies first of all, they provided only for the seizure of Rabaul,
Vake Island, Guam, and Makin Atoll in the Gilberts as Fourth
leet's contribution to the First Operational Stage. There was a
efinite policy among the Army planners to limit the allocation
f troops for operations so far beyond what they considered was
neir proper area of concern. Consequently the Army provided only
ne reinforced infantry regiment (5,000 men) for the Fourth Fleet's
mphibious attacks. This was the "South Seas Detachment," com-
aanded by Major General Horii Tomitaro and organized around
ne 144th Infantry Regiment, with attached artillery, engineer,
econnaissance, antiaircraft, and supply troops. Horii communi-
ated directly with Imperial General Headquarters; cooperation
vith the Navy's South Seas Force came about through mutual
greement between Inoue and Horii, based on broad directives
rom above. Thus Inoue did not have complete control over the
ctivities of South Seas Detachment. Fourth Fleet possessed a few
attalions of Special Naval Landing Forces, but most of these naval
round troops were tied up in garrison duty.[11]

At the beginning of the war, South Seas Force launched simul-
aneous attacks on Guam, Wake Island, and Makin. The seizure
f Guam took only one day, 10 December, as Horii's troops and
aval landing forces forced the surrender of the island. Likewise
Makin fell with ease. A small force of naval troops and laborers
ccupied the atoll on 10 December and set about building a sea-
lane base at Butaritari, one of the islands in Makin Atoll. Wake
sland was a much tougher assignment. The combined Marine
Corps–Navy garrison repulsed one landing attempt on 11 Decem-
er, sinking two destroyers. Vice Admiral Inoue had to call for
arrier support from Combined Fleet, which responded with the
wo carriers, the *Soryu* and the *Hiryu*, from the Pearl Harbor
ttack force. The carriers pounded the island on 21 and 22 De-
ember, and on the twenty-third, the day the island was invaded
y naval landing forces from South Seas Force. The Wake attack

nearly brought about the first major encounter between the Japanese and U.S. carrier forces, as a relief expedition from the U.S. Pacific Fleet was not far from the island. His tasks in the Central Pacific completed, Inoue looked to the capture of Rabaul in January, Japan's first advance into the South Pacific.

2

The U.S. Navy
and the
Opening Moves
of the Pacific War

From the turn of the century, planners within the U.S. Navy had looked suspiciously across the length of the Pacific toward the growing naval might of Imperial Japan. After World War I removed Germany as the only other definitely hostile naval power, the U.S. Navy concentrated almost exclusively on the possibility of war in the Pacific as the basis for long range strategic planning. In the 1920s and 1930s, the Navy devised a number of strategic plans known collectively as the "Orange Plans," after the color assigned to represent Japan. In general, the Orange Plans envisioned war only between the United States and Japan, freeing America to concentrate most of the fleet in the Pacific. Indeed, beginning in 1922 the United States did station most of its warships in the Pacific. The basic idea was for the U.S. Fleet to advance to the Marshalls and Carolines to seize them as advance bases in anticipation of seeking decisive battle with the Japanese fleet. Given the relatively low steaming radius of capital ships before underway-refueling was perfected in the late 1930s, the step-by-step advance through island bases was the only way a fleet could even make its way toward the enemy, given the wide expanses of the Pacific.[12]

By the end of the 1930s, the U.S. Navy had to acknowledge possible commitments in the Atlantic Ocean, particularly in 194 after the defeat of France by Germany. In January 1941 during the ABC-1 (American-British Conversations) meetings in Washington, the British representatives proposed that strategic cooperatio between the two countries center around the concept that they mus defeat Germany first. The possible war in the Pacific against Japa should, according to the British, remain a defensive one unt forces could be spared from Europe. The British sought to gai American support for the defense of their Far Eastern holding especially the key naval base at Singapore.[13]

The U.S. Navy was already leaning in the direction of increase effort in the Atlantic. On 1 February 1941, the command know as the "United States Fleet" under one commander-in-chief (abbre viated CinCUS) was abolished. In its place came three separat fleet commands, the Atlantic Fleet under Admiral Ernest J. King the Pacific Fleet under Admiral Husband E. Kimmel, and the As atic Fleet under Admiral Thomas C. Hart. Hart's forces operate out of the Philippines. The Navy's top officer was Admiral Harol R. Stark, Chief of Naval Operations. The bulk of the Navy's force remained in the Pacific. President Franklin D. Roosevelt intende to use the strength of the Pacific Fleet as a deterrent to Japan' ambitions to the south. Indeed, the basing of the Pacific Fleet a Pearl Harbor, begun in May 1940, instead of at San Diego an San Pedro/Long Beach in southern California, provided dramati evidence of Roosevelt's strong line against the Japanese. More that one naval leader protested the exposure of the fleet in such an ad vanced base as Pearl Harbor. It was the opposition of Admira James O. Richardson, the outgoing CinCUS, to keeping the flee at Pearl Harbor which caused Roosevelt and Stark to call for hi relief from command.[14]

In May 1941, the Joint Board, a combined War Department-Navy Department planning group for Army-Navy operations, pro duced the basic war plan under which the Navy would fight Dubbed with the multicolor appellation "Rainbow Five" because it involved wars of more than two opposing countries, the war plan specified that the principal American war effort would be directed toward Europe in order to defeat Germany first. Initial operations in the Pacific were to be defensive, primarily concerned with hold ing the so-called Malay Barrier, a line extending from Malaya through the Netherlands East Indies to northern Australia. While the major American emphasis was to be in the European theater,

aval planners secured Army agreement that the Navy's first con-
ern should be the Pacific. The plan called for the Pacific Fleet to
ndertake the capture of the Marshalls and Carolines when circum-
tances proved favorable. In addition, the Pacific Fleet was to sup-
ort the defense of Commonwealth holdings east of longitude 155°
ast, or roughly westward from Hawaii to the center of the Coral
ea. Thus there were no definite plans for the commitment of
American forces into the South Pacific.[15]

As a result of the adoption of the policy of Europe first, in the
pring of 1941 the Pacific Fleet lost several strong units to the At-
antic Fleet, especially the carrier *Yorktown* and three battleships.
This weakened the striking power of the Pacific Fleet. Admiral
Kimmel spent the autumn of 1941 strengthening the outlying bases,
notably Wake Island, Midway Island, Palmyra, and to a lesser ex-
ent the only American holding in the South Pacific, Samoa. In
eneral, Naval Intelligence was aware of the impending Japanese
moves to the south, but as is well known, the Japanese concealed
their intentions for a strike on Pearl Harbor very well. The Pearl
Harbor attack on 7 December (8 December, Tokyo time) crippled
he battleship force by sinking or damaging five battleships. Very
ortunately all three carriers in the Pacific were elsewhere at the
ime of the attack. Task Force 8, centered around the carrier *Enterprise*, was returning to Hawaii after delivering fighters to the Wake
garrison. The task force had reached a point about 200 miles west
of Oahu when its commander, Vice Admiral William F. Halsey,
received word of the attack. Task Force 12 (Vice Admiral Wilson
Brown) with the carrier *Lexington* was executing a similar mission
or Midway. Brown was about 500 miles southeast of Midway. The
hird carrier, the *Saratoga*, was in port at San Diego. Rear Admiral
Aubrey W. Fitch flew his flag from that ship. Thus the essential
triking capability of the Pacific Fleet was not impaired, except in
he minds of battleship-oriented strategists.[16]

Admiral Kimmel received orders on 7 December to execute the
Rainbow Five war plan (WPL-46) against Japan.[17] His first order
of business was to regroup his forces after the shattering experience
of the Pearl Harbor surprise. There was a confused attempt at
pursuit of the retreating Japanese carriers which fortunately did
not overtake them. Kimmel shuttled Halsey's Task Force 8 in and
out of Pearl Harbor on 8 December and moved to deploy his two
available carriers in covering position to the west of Hawaii. The
Saratoga sailed west from San Diego. There came welcome news
in the form of a message from Admiral Stark detaching the *York-

town and three battleships from the Atlantic Fleet for duty in th
Pacific. These ships were expected to reach Hawaii in early Januar
1942.[18]

On 9 December the Joint Board issued new instructions regarc
ing Rainbow Five, altering the role of the Pacific Fleet greatl}
Admiral Stark ordered Admiral Kimmel to delete from WPL-4
the provisions calling for the capture of the Marshalls and Carc
lines and support for the Commonwealth holdings south of th
equator to longitude 155° east. Henceforth and until further notic
the Pacific Fleet was to confine its activities to the protection o
areas east of the 180th meridian.[19] The next day Kimmel and hi
staff produced an estimate of the situation. Primary mission fo
the fleet was the security of Hawaii and the line of communicatioı
to Samoa. Kimmel decided to form his mobile striking forces intc
three carrier task forces, each of one carrier, two or three heav\
cruisers, and six to nine destroyers. They were to be kept at se:
most of the time because Pearl Harbor was not deemed secure fron
a second Japanese attack. The plan was to deploy one task forc
north of Oahu and one in the Midway area to protect Hawaii
Kimmel decided to rotate the task forces one at a time, by succes
sively relieving each with the third task force. Thus one task forc
would be in the Hawaiian area at all times, either in port or iı
transit to or from the two patrol stations. The idea was to use the
task forces to support outlying bases, especially Wake and Mid
way.[20] Guam fell on 10 December, and Wake was under virtuaı
siege from Japanese aircraft based in the Marshalls. Carrier task
forces were to intercept and destroy Japanese raiding forces pene
trating the area east of the 180th meridian as well.

The Pacific Fleet considered its first course of action to be the
reinforcement of the Wake Island garrison. On 12 December Ad
miral Kimmel decided to employ the *Lexington* and the *Saratoga*
in the operation.[21] As refined, the plan was for Vice Admiraı
Brown's Task Force 11 (designation changed from Task Force 12)
with the *Lexington* to raid the island of Jaluit in the Marshalls,
while Task Force 14 under Rear Admiral Frank Jack Fletcheı
would reinforce Wake with aircraft and equipment. Fletcher based
his force around the *Saratoga*, with Rear Admiral Fitch as air
commander. Brown sailed on 14 December, and Fletcher left Oahu
two days later. Vice Admiral Halsey with the *Enterprise* (Task
Force 8) was to be used in general reserve in the Midway area. He
was scheduled to sail from Pearl Harbor on 19 December.

During the first three weeks of the war, the naval high command underwent a drastic shakeup, but one which substantially

produced the leadership which would fight successfully through the rest of the war. It was inevitable that Admiral Kimmel would be replaced as Commander of the Pacific Fleet because of Pearl Harbor. Vice Admiral William S. Pye took over temporary command in Hawaii on 17 December, pending the arrival in late December of the new Commander-in-Chief, Pacific Fleet (CinCPac), Admiral Chester W. Nimitz.[22] President Roosevelt and Admiral Stark felt that the post of Commander-in-Chief, U.S. Fleet (abbreviated CinCUS, later ComInCh) must be filled. On 18 December Roosevelt defined the duties of the Navy's two highest posts. The Commander-in-Chief, U.S. Fleet was to have supreme command over the Navy's "operating forces," that is, strategic control over the activities of the three fleets and other forces afloat. He was to keep Admiral Stark informed of logistical and other needs of the operating forces. Stark, as Chief of Naval Operations (abbreviated CNO or, as a command, OpNav), had the duty of keeping the operating forces supplied. Under OpNav was also a department engaged in long-range planning for strategy. On 20 December Roosevelt named Admiral King as the new Commander-in-Chief, U.S. Fleet. King officially assumed command ten days later, organizing his headquarters in Washington at the Navy Department.[23]

Vice Admiral Pye continued with the Wake Island relief expedition, but with increasing trepidation. Deciphered radio intercepts of Japanese messages on 17 December revealed the association of Japanese carrier forces, specifically the 2nd Carrier Division, with the Fourth Fleet in the Marshalls. On 20 December word came from Wake that enemy carrier planes were attacking the island. Pye called off the attack on Jaluit and ordered Brown to move north to support Fletcher. He slowed the timetable to allow the two task forces to move into mutual support range. Fletcher was to reach Wake on 25 December, local time. Pye and the CinCPac staff were especially worried about the fuel situation and ordered Fletcher to fuel before he approached the island. On 23 December the Japanese invaded Wake Island and captured it in less than a day. In Hawaii the staff deliberated as to whether Task Force 14 should continue to Wake to hit the enemy invasion forces. In the final analysis Pye concluded the risk of loss was too high for possible objectives achieved. He ordered the two task forces to retire in the direction of Hawaii and deployed Halsey's Task Force 8 to cover their retreat. It was a strong blow to the morale of the Pacific Fleet.[24]

During the panic immediately following the attack on Pearl Harbor, the planners in Washington were not sure that Midway

Island, only 1,130 miles from Oahu, could be held against the un expectedly powerful Japanese carrier forces. They reaffirmed thei desire to hold Johnston, Palmyra, and Samoa if at all possible.² On 14 December, Admiral Stark indicated in a message to Kimme that the Japanese would attempt the capture of key South Pacifi island groups and had to be stopped at Samoa and Palmyra. H suggested that reinforcements be sent to Samoa and proposed tha the 8th Marine Regiment and the 2nd Defense Battalion be con voyed there from the West Coast. Escorting them would be the York town and other forces newly arrived from the Atlantic. On 1" December Stark outlined the tasks for the Pacific Fleet. As expected the major emphasis was on protecting Hawaii and preserving the fleet, but Stark warned CinCPac to expect increasing demands fo shipping and escort for the South Pacific and Australia.²⁶

Pye responded to Stark's message on 21 December. He recom mended that the Samoan reinforcements be sent in increments and advised instead that the Yorktown reach Hawaii as soon as possible She could ferry aircraft from the West Coast on her trip out. The Pacific Fleet staff spelled out their course of action in a lengthy situation estimate dated 24 December.²⁷ In it they emphasized that the main task of the fleet was to defend the Hawaiian Islands and the outlying bases, particularly Midway, Palmyra, and Johnston islands. It was necessary to secure the fleet base until the fleet became strong enough to assume the strategic offensive. There was the possibility of a direct attack on Oahu, but more probable, they thought, were carrier raids on the peripheral bases and attempts to capture Samoa and Fiji. Recommended action was the immediate build-up of forces in the Hawaiian Islands and the outlying bases. The principal offensive action of the fleet was to encompass raids on enemy communications and bases with a "judicious choice of objectives" to divert the enemy and try to destroy weaker forces. Later there were to be offensive sweeps with two carrier task forces operating in conjunction with each other. Also participating would be battleship task forces, "as supporting 'strong points' on which the fast groups could retire."²⁸ The only problem was selecting the proper targets to raid, as it would be very risky to attack any base where meaningful results could be obtained. Clearly the Pacific Fleet wished to keep its forces in the Central Pacific, deployed so that they could meet any Japanese threat to Hawaii. The staff was not interested in scattering their task forces throughout the wide expanse of the South Pacific. Reflecting this concern, on 27 December, Pye called off a proposed raid by Task Force 11 on the Marshalls or the Gilberts, citing the risk involved in damaging a carrier

18

at that time. Compensating for this, Pye agreed to full reinforcements for Samoa to be escorted by the *Yorktown.*

Admiral Nimitz took formal command of the Pacific Fleet on 31 December. He found waiting for him a 30 December directive from Admiral King. King instructed CinCPac to cover and hold the line Hawaii to Midway. As important, Nimitz was to maintain the line of communication between the United States and Australia by holding the string of bases between Hawaii and Samoa. King added that the Pacific Fleet should extend its control westward to the Fiji Islands as soon as practicable.[29] On 31 December King informed Admiral Hart, commanding the Asiatic Fleet, that basic Allied strategy in the Far East encompassed the defense of the Malay barrier with special concern for holding the two flanks, Burma and Australia.[30] King's two directives to his fleet commanders foreshadowed his interest in using the Pacific Fleet for more than merely static defense of the eastern Pacific. He recognized the enormous strategic importance of defending the line of communication to Australia, in contrast to the prevalent feeling within the Pacific Fleet. As early as 24 December, King called for a major fueling base for the South Pacific to support fleet operations there. His staff favored Bora Bora for the site, as it was not as exposed as Samoa and other forward areas.[31]

Galvanized into action by the swift Japanese advance, the Allies convened on 22 December in Washington a meeting of the chiefs of staff of the United States and Britain to decide grand strategy for the first period of the war. Prime Minister Winston S. Churchill also attended the conference, which was known as Arcadia.[32] The Allied military leaders reaffirmed the basic policy of Germany first, and the British advocated two operations for the European area, the despatch of troops to the United Kingdom and the invasion of North Africa (Gymnast). Regarding the Pacific, the planners advocated a defensive posture, "maintaining only such positions in the Eastern theatre as will safeguard vital interests."[33] The conference decided, however, that it was necessary to secure "points of vantage from which an offensive against Japan can be eventually developed."[34] The main result of the conference was the decision to organize the ABDA (American-British-Dutch-Australian) Command under General Sir Archibald Wavell to unify the defense of the Malay barrier west of Australia. Wavell was to assume command on 15 January. The basic strategy for ABDA envisioned a rapid build-up of air power in the area to seize air superiority and hold the Japanese at bay until other reinforcements could arrive. Unfortunately the planners overestimated the air strength they could send to the ABDA area and greatly underrated the potential of Japanese air power, particularly as Japan operated with interior lines.

The subject of the defense of the South Pacific came up in the agenda of items discussed. On 2 January 1942, American representatives expressed their desire to help defend Australia and New Zealand if the Commonwealth military forces were unable to do so. Several days later War Department planners indicated they were going to reinforce with service troops the command U.S. Army Forces in Australia (USAFIA), set up in December. The object was to build USAFIA into the major supply base for the Philippines and the Southwest Pacific. On 11 January Admiral King brought up the importance of New Caledonia, stressing its economic importance and strategic position across the direct line of communications to Australia. King requested that the Army consider the need to garrison New Caledonia with troops. Army Chief of Staff General George C. Marshall agreed, allocating a division-sized Army force for immediate shipment there. It would arrive at Noumea in March. The conference also proposed the creation of an air and naval command for the area east of Australia to be called the ANZAC Command, but they postponed the idea as yet. On 12 January the Combined Chiefs of Staff agreed to garrison the air ferry bases on the route between Hawaii and Australia.[35]

The Arcadia Conference lasted until 14 January and was extremely important in outlining Allied strategy for the Pacific, because it indicated a definite American commitment to assist in the defense of the South Pacific. The main discovery for all participants was the acute lack of shipping, which prevented in large measure the accomplishment of tasks in both oceans at the same time. At first the Army planners were willing to provide troops and aircraft to shore up the defenses in the Pacific, but they were able to offer no overall plans of their own as to what should be done. Certainly they did not like their first real taste of wartime coalition planning among several powers. Because the Army was in the process of a massive expansion in manpower and aircraft, the War Department had only a few units capable of immediate movement. The Army began to balk at committing these to the Pacific or in a British-sponsored descent on Northwest Africa as Churchill wanted. As of yet the Army planners from Marshall on down were not sure what they wanted to do, only that they did not want to disperse their forces under U.S. naval or overall British command.[36]

The naval planners under Admiral King stressed the necessity of securing "points of vantage" as outlined in the Arcadia Conference in order to facilitate the eventual offensives in the Pacific. They began to emphasize the need to develop a series of island bases in the South Pacific to serve as air and support bases for large scale fleet movements into enemy zones. Unfortunately neither the Navy nor the Marine Corps had adequate men or aircraft to serve as garrisons for the islands they needed to hold. The Marine Corps especially was loathe to use its amphibious troops for garrison duty. Also important was the need for shipping and the necessity to allocate adequate amounts of tonnage for a large number of tasks. Thus the Navy had to obtain the use of Army troops, air units, and shipping to carry out its strategic plans. Mid-January 1942 found the beginning of an intense debate between Navy and Army planners over basic American strategy in the Pacific.

Meanwhile Admiral Nimitz proceeded with the reinforcement of Samoa. At the end of December, Admiral Stark suggested that CinCPac plan a diversionary or covering raid into the Gilberts to coincide with the passage of the Samoa convoy south from the West Coast. Admiral King vigorously seconded that proposal on 2 January. In response to this, the staff worked on a plan which would have Vice Admiral Brown's Task Force 11 attack positions in the Marshalls sometime around 13 and 14 January, while Task Force 8 raided the Gilberts three or four days later. Task Force 14 with the *Saratoga*, under the command of Rear Admiral Herbert Fairfax Leary, was to support the attacks from a central position. Rear Admiral Fletcher received orders to fly to San Diego and organize the new Task Force 17 around the *Yorktown*. The Samoa convoy with Task Force 17 in escort sailed from the West Coast on 6 January.[37]

By 8 January, it was evident that the Samoa reinforcement would be the primary task of the Pacific Fleet in January. CinCPac decided to hold off on the raids until after the landing of the troops at Samoa, expected to be about 20 January. Then Task Force 8 and Task Force 17 could combine for simultaneous strikes against Japanese positions in the Gilberts, timed for the first week of February. Task Force 11 and Task Force 14 would remain in the Central Pacific to cover Hawaii. Unfortunately the Pacific Fleet lost the services of a carrier, when on 11 January the Japanese submarine I-6 torpedoed the *Saratoga* in the vicinity of Johnston Island. The *Saratoga* returned on 13 January to Oahu, and two days later Admiral Nimitz decided to return her to the West Coast for repairs and modernization. The *Saratoga* remained inactive until the end of May. It was a very serious blow to the striking power of the Pacific Fleet.[38]

Aside from the damage to the *Saratoga,* the next two weeks proceeded smoothly for the carrier task forces. Vice Admiral Halsey's Task Force 8 with the *Enterprise* departed from Oahu on 11 January to cover the right flank of the convoy by sailing toward Samoa. Admiral King on 19 January provided an inkling of the effort he would later demand of CinCPac in the South Pacific. Sketching the plans following the Samoa operation, King stated that he was considering the occupation of Funafuti in the Ellice group to serve as an outpost for Samoa and Fiji against Japanese incursions from the Gilberts. In this capacity, King added, Funafuti became a "linkage post" between the eastern Pacific bases and the Solomons. Ominously for CinCPac planners King noted:

> Foregoing factors combine to make it advisable early consideration of keeping suitable and available forces constantly in the area embracing Canton, Funafuti, Samoa, Fiji, Bobcat [Bora Bora].[39]

Thus King contemplated stationing one or possibly more task forces in the South Pacific to protect the area from Japanese attack, rather than relying on sporadic raids from carriers based in the Central Pacific.

Admiral Hart's Asiatic Fleet consisted of a number of cruisers and destroyers and a large submarine force based in the Philippines. Within a few days after the outbreak of the war, Japanese air strikes forced the fleet to evacuate the waters around the Philippines for the sanctuary of Java. Only General Douglas MacArthur's U.S. Army Forces in the Far East (USAFFE) remained in the Philippines, besieged in the Bataan peninsula. Admiral Hart's warships came under the ABDA Command when it was set up on 15 January 1942. December and January found ABDA clearly in trouble, with Japanese landings on Borneo to the west and Celebes and Ambon to the east, not to mention the advance on Singapore.[40]

3
Initial Planning for the Port Moresby Operation

Even before he embarked upon operations south of Truk, Vice Admiral Inoue impressed upon Imperial General Headquarters the need to advance beyond Rabaul to secure the approaches to that vital base. On 8 January 1942, Fourth Fleet staff submitted a proposal to Tokyo to invade eastern New Guinea, seizing the Australian air strips at Lae and Salamaua. "Air" was the keyword in Inoue's mind. Long acknowledged as one of the most vocal proponents of naval aviation, Inoue more than most realized the power of aviation and the potential of mutually supporting island air bases. In 1940–1941 before taking command of Fourth Fleet, Inoue served as chief of the Naval Aeronautical Department and even advocated the virtual conversion of the Navy into an air force. "Who commands the air commands the sea,"[41] was one of his aphorisms. Inoue apparently had more familiarity and experience with land-based air than carrier aviation. He believed that air superiority in the South Pacific hinged on controlling a web of fortified island air bases through which the air units could shift quickly to points of danger.

The Rabaul invasion was the first direct thrust into the South Pacific for South Seas Force. In early January, aircraft from the

24th Air Flotilla based at Truk began bombing raids on Australian positions at Rabaul. Imperial General Headquarters on 4 January issued the specific directive for the Rabaul attack. Major General Horii's South Seas Detachment embarked on transports and sailed south from Guam. Combined Fleet arranged for the participation of Vice Admiral Nagumo's Striking Force to cover the descent upon Rabaul. Nagumo's force numbered four fleet carriers, two battleships, three cruisers, with destroyers in escort. Vice Admiral Inoue provided a scouting force of four heavy cruisers and screen. Nagumo's carriers pounded Rabaul on 20 and 21 January with powerful air strikes, then stood off north of the island to watch for the approach of any Allied task forces. The invasion convoy reached the waters off Rabaul after dark on 22 January, and landed troops the next day. There was only a small Australian garrison, and the Japanese captured all the vital installations the same day. As there was no evidence of major Allied naval forces in the area, Nagumo took his carriers into the Dutch East Indies to support the Japanese offensives in that region. Seven days after the landing, the first Japanese aircraft flew down from Truk to operate from Rabaul. Vice Admiral Inoue arranged to place two naval air groups at Rabaul, one with 36 medium bombers and 27 fighters, and the other with 24 big patrol bombers. The units actually sent never reached the strength figures quoted above for them, because the Imperial Navy was chronically short of aircraft of all types. Failure to amass adequate air power would plague the Japanese throughout the First South Pacific Campaign.[42]

In the latter half of January, but especially after the easy conquest of Rabaul, Imperial General Headquarters deliberated as to the strategic locations which South Seas Force should capture to ensure the security of Rabaul. Prewar strategic planning had highlighted the necessity of capturing Lae and Salamaua in New Guinea to utilize the airstrips there as air outposts for Rabaul. Tulagi with its excellent natural harbor and at least rudimentary base facilities dominated the southeastern approaches to Rabaul. A Japanese force planted there would control the Solomon Islands. In addition to these previous objectives, the planners in Tokyo advocated the capture of the important Australian base at Port Moresby on the southern coast of Papua. Taking their cue from Vice Admiral Inoue's thoughts on the power of aviation, the naval planners pointed out the impressive strategic position of Port Moresby as an air base. In Allied hands it served as a means to project Allied air power into the Rabaul area and beyond, allowing heavy bombers to patrol as far north as Truk. It was a definite menace to Japanese naval operations south of the Carolines.

Conversely, under Japanese control, Port Moresby would serve as the focus for searches deep into the Coral Sea. The Imperial Navy had long believed that the U.S. Fleet would most likely approach the empire from the southeast, that is, toward the triangle connecting Port Moresby–Tulagi–Rabaul. Air searches covering the southern Coral Sea would give the Japanese time to prepare a suitable welcome for Allied naval forces. In addition, Japanese land-based air units at Port Moresby could undertake strikes against Allied air bases in northern Australia and neutralize them. Because Port Moresby was beyond normal Allied fighter range from Australia, the Japanese would be spared a long air battle of attrition over their own bases. Port Moresby also provided a link to air bases in the Netherlands East Indies, allowing direct staging of bombers along the whole length of the defensive perimeter. Thus, the decision to capture Port Moresby involved two related objectives, to deny a strategic location to the Allies and to utilize an important air base for the defense of the perimeter surrounding Japan's Pacific holdings.[43]

On 29 January Imperial General Headquarters issued Naval Directive Number 47, instructing Combined Fleet to carry out operations against "British New Guinea" and the Solomon Islands according to the terms of the Army-Navy Central Agreement just concluded in Tokyo.[44] The order specified that the Navy, with the cooperation of the Army's South Seas Detachment, was to occupy Lae and Salamaua as soon as possible. Then the Navy alone would seize Tulagi. Ultimately the two services working together were to undertake the invasion of Port Moresby after the occupation of Lae and Salamaua. Imperial General Headquarters instructed the two commands, South Seas Force and South Seas Detachment, to do the detailed planning themselves. On 2 February the Army Section sent an identical order to Major General Horii, then in Rabaul, instructing him to cooperate with South Seas Force in the seizure of the aforementioned strategic points.[45]

Under the original orders, Inoue would have only the resources of South Seas Force itself, in cooperation with the Army's South Seas Detachment, to execute his mission. Inoue had no aircraft carriers in his command capable of active operations against the enemy. On 1 February he received the services of the newly commissioned light carrier *Shoho*, but for ferry purposes only. Otherwise air power for the operations south of Rabaul resided in units

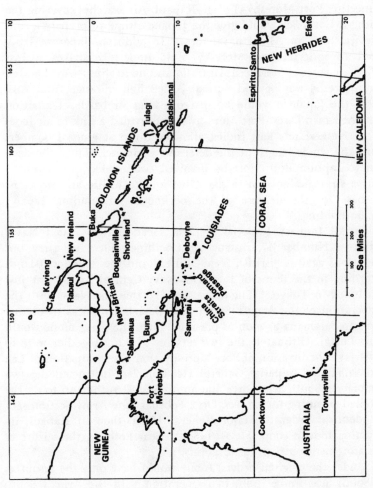

The Coral Sea

of the 24th Air Flotilla. Regarding warship strength, South Seas Force controlled four heavy cruisers, two light cruisers, a destroyer squadron, a submarine squadron, and a minelayer squadron, with a considerable number of naval auxiliary vessels such as gunboats, minesweepers, tankers, and transports to support them. It certainly was not an overwhelming force, but the planners of South Seas Force thought it sufficient for the task. Lulled by the easy successes the Japanese experienced in capturing Rabaul and positions in the East Indies, Imperial General Headquarters did not see the need in supplying carrier support for what they considered a secondary theater. At least for the present, Inoue saw no reason to ask for additional forces. Planning proceeded quickly and by 16 February, South Seas Force's basic plans were complete. On that date Inoue's staff signed the "Army-Navy Local Agreement" with South Seas Detachment. The agreement called for the invasion of Lae and Salamaua in early March, the Army to provide one infantry battalion as its share of the landing force. Inoue further stated that he planned to attack Port Moresby and Tulagi early in April, after he had a chance to develop Lae and Salamaua as advanced air bases for the 24th Air Flotilla's medium bombers and fighters.[46]

Imperial General Headquarters provided another task for Inoue and South Seas Force. On 27 February the Naval Section issued a directive instructing South Seas Force to capture the British islands of Ocean and Nauru. These positions, south of the Marshalls and west of the Gilberts, would provide another link in the chain of island air bases to protect the flank of South Seas Force. Air searches from there would assist in covering the area between the Marshalls and the Gilberts as well as the Rabaul area to detect raids by Allied naval forces. In addition, the islands possessed great economic resources, for they were rich in phosphates which would greatly benefit Japanese agriculture. It was not thought that the Allies had much of a garrison on Ocean and Nauru because of their exposed location. Therefore no Army troops would be needed for their capture. Inoue decided to seize the two islands after the Port Moresby Operation.[47]

4
Allied Reaction
to the Fall of Rabaul

The Allied strategic situation in the Pacific took a definite turn for the worse on 23 January, when the Japanese stormed ashore at Rabaul and expelled the small Australian garrison. The way to the south seemed open to Japan. Highlighting this weakness was a 15 January British situation estimate which stated that the defense of the area must rest in the hands of the U.S. Pacific Fleet.[48] The estimate noted that Fiji and New Caledonia were the next likely targets. The Australian government under Prime Minister John Curtin felt the loss of Rabaul left open the door for a direct assault on northern Australia. The Australians were particularly worried because four of their best divisions were abroad, three in the Middle East and one in Malaya. Already on 21 January Curtin had become restive and disagreed with Churchill's ideas of using two Australian divisions from the Middle East for the defense of Burma. Curtin wanted to withdraw them for the direct defense of Australia and also requested additional fighters for Australia and Port Moresby.[49]

While the Japanese exerted pressure on the Bismarck archipelago with powerful fleet units, the Pacific Fleet continued with the Samoa operation. Naval Intelligence noted the Japanese build-up to the south of Truk, and Admiral King believed it allowed a fine opportunity for the Pacific Fleet to raid outer enemy bases with little risk of encountering heavy opposition. On 20 January he suggested to Nimitz that proposed raids by Halsey and Fletcher be speeded up and also that another task force attack Wake. The next day Nimitz radioed to Brown with Task Force 11 that he should raid Wake. Because Brown's fuel situation would be critical after a high-speed approach to the target, CinCPac arranged to have him rendezvous with the fleet oiler *Neches* 600 miles west of Johnston on 27 January after the raid. The *Neches* sailed on 22 January from Pearl Harbor. The oiler was to pick up an escort on the morning of 23 January, but a Japanese submarine sank her just after midnight in a position about 135 miles west of Oahu.[50] It speaks eloquently of CinCPac's shortage of destroyers that one could not be found to escort the slow tanker through waters known to contain Japanese submarines. As a result, Nimitz had to recall Task Force 11 short of the objective. Task Force 8 and Task Force 17 received orders to attack Japanese bases as soon as the troops had disembarked at Samoa. It was hoped that after so may setbacks the Pacific Fleet would be able to undertake its first offensive sorties against the Japanese.[51]

Admiral King reacted to the news of the fall of Rabaul with characteristic dispatch. On 24 January he proposed that plans for a naval command in the waters east of Australia, the ANZAC Area, be implemented under the command of an American flag officer. He eventually chose Rear Admiral Leary, who received the three stars of a vice admiral on 27 February. Leary's command was to be an air and sea one only, not controlling land defense. The area comprised the eastern coast of Australia and the waters east to Fiji and Tongatabu. The Allies formally activated the ANZAC Area on 7 February. King instructed Admiral Nimitz on 26 January to detach one heavy cruiser or new light cruiser plus two new destroyers to the ANZAC command. Nimitz chose the heavy cruiser *Chicago*. Also joining Leary's force was the Australian Squadron of two cruisers under Rear Admiral John G. Crace, Royal Navy. Leary's force was to serve as a deterrent to any Japanese moves into the waters south of Rabaul. Admiral King retained the ANZAC Area under direct ComInCh control.[52]

Aside from detaching a few ships, Admiral King expected direct support for the South Pacific from CinCPac. On 27 January he radioed Nimitz underlining exactly how dangerous was the "serious enemy threat to communications with Australia."[53] Pacific Fleet planners themselves estimated on 25 January that the next Japanese move in the area would be attacks either on New Caledonia or Port

Moresby, or both. King's message precipitated a sharp debate on 28 January at Pearl Harbor. The central question was the nature of Pacific Fleet support to the ANZAC Area should the Japanese continue attacking south from Rabaul. Brown's Task Force 11 with the *Lexington* had returned to Pearl Harbor after the abortive Wake raid and could be used immediately. The other two task forces, Halsey's Task Force 8 and Fletcher's Task Force 17, were proceeding with attacks on the Marshalls and Gilberts, scheduled for 1 February. Vice Admiral Pye, serving as an advisor to CinCPac, proposed to the staff that Task Force 17 head directly to Suva in the Fijis, there to be joined by Task Force 11 rushing south from Hawaii. The two carriers would then oppose any enemy advances in the direction of New Caledonia. Plans Division of the Pacific Fleet staff, headed by Captain Lynde D. McCormick, opposed the extension of CinCPac responsibility so far to the southwest. They felt it would interfere with the fleet's essential mission of protecting Hawaii. McCormick recommended that Task Force 11 conduct a raid on Wake or the Marshalls once more to help divert Japanese forces from the Dutch East Indies.[54]

Admiral King temporarily ended the debate. On 29 January and 31 January in two separate messages he proposed that the Pacific Fleet eventually commit strong forces to the South Pacific. The second message ordered Nimitz to provide a carrier task force in early February to cover the passage of several important convoys headed through the South Pacific. Task Force 11 would have to go, as both Halsey and Fletcher were to return to Pearl Harbor for supplies after the 1 February raids. King also informed Nimitz that he would have to supply two heavy cruisers and four destroyers for protection of the Samoa area. They would supplement the escort for convoys and should remain there until further notice.[55]

On 1 February came the long-awaited first offensive move against Japan by the Pacific Fleet. Vice Admiral Halsey with Task Force 8 attacked the northern islands of the Marshall group. The *Enterprise* launched several air strikes against Kwajalein, Wotje, and Taroa. The aircraft sank three gunboats and a freighter and damaged ten other ships, including a light cruiser. Losses amounted to five aircraft. The *Enterprise* and the heavy cruiser *Chester* sustained light damage from Japanese air attacks. Cruisers and destroyers also bombarded Wotje and Taroa. Rear Admiral Fletcher's Task Force 17 hit Jaluit and Mille in the southern Marshalls and also struck Makin in the Gilberts. The *Yorktown* flyers faced bad weather and low visibility. They bombed Japanese shore installations and damaged several auxiliary vessels, but lost eight aircraft in the process. The raids provided a tremendous boost to the morale of the Pacific Fleet. Task Force 8 reached Pearl Harbor on 5 February, followed by Task Force 17 the next day.[56]

By early February 1942, Admiral King and the Navy were under tremendous pressure from the Allies to do something in the Pacific to take the heat off the ABDA Area. In quick and alarming succession the Japanese attacked Singapore and converged from two directions toward Java. General Wavell daily radioed his doubts that he could hold the Japanese. Allied strategy of reinforcing the Malay barrier with aircraft to gain air superiority had failed miserably. Allied air strength dribbled into the fight piecemeal and fell prey to defeat in detail by powerful Japanese concentrations of land- and carrier-based aircraft. On 4 February General MacArthur inquired from the Philippines as to the actions of the Pacific Fleet. He wanted to know why they were not attacking the long Japanese line of communication from the homeland to the South Seas. He felt a frontal defense against the Japanese thrusts into the Dutch East Indies would fail. General Marshall replied on 8 February that the Pacific Fleet was too weak to effect such an offensive through the maze of interlocking Japanese bases in the Central Pacific islands.[57]

On 5 February King requested Nimitz' opinion on whether the Pacific Fleet should send reinforcements to the ABDA Area or make diversionary raids with carriers and even battleships to draw Japanese strength away from the East Indies. Even before receiving a reply, King modified his orders regarding Task Force 11, and on 6 February he ordered CinCPac to detach Task Force 11 to the ANZAC Area to cooperate in the defense of New Caledonia.[58] Intelligence reports indicated that the Japanese were planning a general advance along the Southwest Pacific line, including New Caledonia and the New Hebrides. Nimitz answered King's inquiry on 7 February, stating that the Pacific Fleet possessed insufficient strength to detach anything to ABDA or conduct any offensive operations other than small raids. He suggested that of the two remaining carrier task forces currently available, one should cover Samoa while the other remained in reserve in the Central Pacific.

At the same time Nimitz and the CinCPac staff recommended to ComInCh that they suspend the carrier raids temporarily. The staff had still not resolved the basic strategic question, "Are we going to gamble all upon securing Australia as a base of future operations against the enemy and leave our Pacific Area open to attack . . .?"[59] Plans Division much preferred keeping its strength in the Central Pacific, perhaps executing "bold operations" in that area to attack the Japanese left flank and arrest their southward advance. Already ComInCh had detached one-third of CinCPac's available carrier strength, and there was the distinct possibility that another carrier task force might be sent to the South Pacific. On 5 February, they recommended a combined carrier-battleship raid on Truk. If ComInCh persisted in detaching light forces to ANZAC and the Samoan area, they opted instead for a carrier raid against the Marianas.

On 9 February, King replied to CinCPac's communication suggesting a temporary moratorium on raids. He disagreed and ordered "a continuous effort to damage ships and bases."[60] The planners in Hawaii then attempted to determine the correct combination of circumstances in which the diversion would be meaningful but not too risky. This was difficult because of increasing fleet detachments of cruisers, destroyers, oilers, and auxiliaries to protect and service convoys to the South Pacific. There were proposals to raid Rabaul, Wake, Eniwetok, and even Tokyo. On 11 February, CinCPac decided to form the *Enterprise* and the *Yorktown* into one large Task Force 13 under Halsey to raid Wake and Eniwetok or Marcus Island. Nimitz feared that this would not be much of a diversion, but it was all he could do at present. The next day word came from submarines reconnoitering the Central Pacific that there was little observable activity at Wake and none at Eniwetok. Halsey sailed on 12 February from Pearl Harbor. CinCPac changed the designation of his task force to Task Force 16. He took with him the *Enterprise* only and her escorts, and his objective had not yet been chosen. Fletcher remained in port for the time being.[61]

In the South Pacific, Vice Admiral Brown decided he would operate in the waters between Fiji and New Caledonia until given a specific objective. On 12 February, Admiral King ordered Brown and Leary to conduct offensive operations with Task Force 11 and the ANZAC Squadron in the Solomons area. King had arranged to fly 12 Army B-17's down from Hawaii to cooperate with the offensive. Two days later Brown suggested to Leary that the two task forces raid Rabaul. Informed of this proposal, King quickly agreed and instructed Brown, who was senior to Leary, to take charge of operations in the northern sector of the ANZAC Area. Brown received temporary control over the ANZAC Squadron, while Leary coordinated the raid with the B-17's flying from Townsville. On 16 February, Brown radioed King and Leary that he would attack Rabaul on 21 February. He planned to make a dawn air strike and follow up with a bombardment if the aircraft were successful in taking command of the air.[62]

By 15 February, with the fall of Singapore and attacks on Java, it became evident that the ABDA Area would not long survive. Consequently King eased the requirements for immediate offensive action by the Pacific Fleet. On that day he instructed CinCPac to deploy Task Force 17 in the Canton Island area. Fletcher sailed the next day. Little did he know it would be 101 days and one major battle before he returned to Pearl Harbor. Task Force 17 from its central position was to serve as a reserve for the two offensive actions taking place at about the same time. Halsey received orders on 15 February to attack Wake Island, while Brown completed preparations for his descent upon Rabaul. The strength of the three task forces was as follows: Vice Admiral Brown's flagship was the *Lexington* with a screen of four heavy cruisers and nine destroyers. The associated ANZAC Squadron under Rear Admiral Crace numbered two heavy cruisers, two light cruisers, and two destroyers. Task Force 16's commander, Vice Admiral Halsey, controlled the carrier *Enterprise*, two heavy cruisers, and seven destroyers. Rear Admiral Fletcher's Task Force 17 comprised the carrier *Yorktown*, two heavy cruisers, and six destroyers. Each carrier had about 70 combat planes, so the three task forces had among them around 210 carrier aircraft. On 20 February CinCPac received the good news that the new carrier *Hornet* with two heavy cruisers was to leave the East Coast about 1 March bound for the Pacific.

Task Force 11 was the first group to approach its objective. On the morning of 20 February Brown had closed to a point within 500 miles northeast of Rabaul, when Japanese patrol bombers made contact with him and reported his location to 24th Air Flotilla headquarters at Rabaul. Brown realized that he could not surprise Rabaul and did not think he had the fuel to spare for high speed maneuvers which might ensue if he continued the raid. He decided to steam in the direction of Rabaul until sundown and then reverse course. Such a feint would keep the Japanese guessing as to his intentions and maximize what remained of the diversionary impact of the raid on Japanese strategy. In Rabaul, the Japanese commander decided to launch an air strike immediately even though the target was out of fighter escort range. He wanted to attack the carrier force before it closed to within carrier plane attack radius. Consequently the 24th Air Flotilla launched a strike force of 17 medium bombers armed with bombs for horizontal bombing instead of the preferred torpedoes, because no aerial torpedoes were available yet at Rabaul. In a running battle, the *Lexington*'s fighters shot down 13 of the 17 Japanese bombers and forced two others to ditch. In return the task force sustained no damage, but lost two fighters shot down.[63]

Vice Admiral Halsey's attack on Wake Island went much more smoothly. He reached launch position at dawn on the morning of 24 February and sent a strike group of the *Enterprise*'s planes to pound the island. Rear Admiral Raymond A. Spruance, Halsey's cruiser commander, led the two cruisers and accompanying destroyers in close to the island to bombard shore installations. The *Enterprise*'s flyers found no air opposition and lost only one dive bomber to antiaircraft fire. Spruance's task group destroyed two gunboats. It was a highly successful operation for the very light losses taken by the attackers. American carrier raids on both flanks of their Central Pacific island bases would give the Japanese pause to think that a further advance to the south might weaken their outer bases. At any rate this was how the Pacific Fleet hoped they might react.[64]

5
Landing Operations in Eastern New Guinea

The abortive 20 February carrier raid toward Rabaul did indeed give Vice Admiral Inoue cause to reflect. The 24th Air Flotilla lost 15 medium bombers out of the 18 currently at Rabaul and most of its experienced crews. Rear Admiral Goto Eiji, commanding the 24th Air Flotilla, found it necessary to fly into Rabaul nine medium bombers from Tinian and nine from the Marshalls to enable his air units to provide some semblance of support for the upcoming landings in Papua. Goto also sent aircraft from the Marshalls to Wake Island after the carrier raid of 24 February. To allow time for the necessary deployments, Inoue postponed the New Guinea invasion five days to 8 March. He concentrated at Rabaul most of the mobile naval strength available to South Seas Force, including seaplane tenders, transports, auxiliaries, and a guard force of heavy cruisers and destroyers to cover them. The *Shoho,* the Fourth Fleet's only assigned carrier, was not available for active operations, as the ship was still working up and was used for ferrying aircraft only. Inoue depended on these same ships to execute in April the capture of Tulagi and Port Moresby.[65]

As the replacement aircraft arrived, Rear Admiral Goto began sporadic raids on 24 February against targets in New Guinea. On

28 February, the 24th Air Flotilla attacked Port Moresby with 1´ medium bombers and six fighters. The Lae-Salamaua Attack Force sailed from Rabaul on 5 March. The mixed force of Army and Navy transports assembled off the two Papuan villages during the night of 7 March. At daylight the next day one infantry battalion from the South Seas Detachment and a battalion of naval landing forces attacked Lae and Salamaua and quickly drove off the small Australian garrisons. The guard force, consisting of four heavy and three light cruisers with destroyers in escort, steamed across the strait separating eastern New Guinea and the island of Bougainville. They established a temporary anchorage at Queen Carola Inlet on the west coast of Buka. Inoue had reason to feel pleased over the smooth progress of the invasion operations. Aside from a few raids by Allied aircraft, there had been no interference. On 9 March, naval engineers succeeded in restoring to operational condition the airstrip at Lae. Goto prepared to despatch fighters from the 24th Air Flotilla to Lae in the next few days.

For once, Allied naval forces were deployed to do something to spoil the Japanese advance in the Southwest Pacific. Vice Admiral Brown had been impressed by the Japanese response to his attempted raid on Rabaul. He did not realize that the 24th Air Flotilla had about expended all of its medium bomber strength to deter his continued advance. Consequently, on 24 February Brown recommended that another carrier task force join him in the South Pacific. The next day, Admiral Nimitz agreed with Admiral King that it would be advantageous for Task Force 17 to combine with Task Force 11 for operations in the New Guinea–Solomons area. Rear Admiral Fletcher, operating in the Canton Island area, received orders to rendezvous with Brown as quickly as possible. Nimitz cautioned King that fleet logistics could not presently support for long two carrier task forces in the South Pacific. One task force would have to retire to Hawaii soon after the operation.[66] Brown confused matters the next day when he signaled Nimitz that he now did not think that two carriers could successfully raid Rabaul, given the excellent air search patrol surrounding the base. Yet Brown would soon have two-thirds of the Pacific Fleet's carrier strength and would have to find the most efficient use for its strike capability.[67]

On 26 February, King issued a general directive encompassing operations in the South Pacific.[68] He instructed Leary to remain ashore to coordinate with naval forces the U.S. Army and Australian aircraft based in Australia and Port Moresby, as well as control the activities and supply of the naval forces under his command. King greed that single carrier task forces should not undertake raids without air support and decried "offensive sweeps" where there was no evidence that the enemy was planning to do something. He saw as the proper targets Japanese mobile forces, particularly carriers, cruisers, and transports. Destroying ships was much preferred over raids on shore installations, which damage the Japanese could easily repair. King added that either Task Force 11 or Task Force 17, but ideally both, should remain in the ANZAC Area at least until Army troops destined for New Caledonia reached there in the middle of March. This, however, depended upon fleet logistics, and King requested Nimitz's advice on the matter. Also important, King noted, were reconnaissance patrols by Allied aircraft in the Bismarcks-Solomons area, and naval operations depended heavily on the information gathered in this way. Finally, he suggested that American fighters be based at Port Moresby "to protect this very important airfield."[69]

Vice Admiral Halsey with Task Force 16 pulled off another raid in the Central Pacific, this time against Marcus Island, only about a thousand miles from Tokyo. After the Wake raid on 24 February, Halsey withdrew to fuel and then headed northwest, skirting the air patrols from Wake, to approach Marcus unseen. On the morning of 4 March he launched an air strike from long range, 175 miles. There was no air opposition at the island, or ships, and the bombers inflicted some damage to the installations on shore at the cost of one aircraft shot down by antiaircraft fire. Halsey retired at high speed and returned directly to Pearl Harbor, arriving on 10 March. It was an important diversion, as will be seen later.[70]

The Pacific Fleet staff decided on 27 February that two carriers were capable of attacking Rabaul successfully. Because Task Force 11 had been at sea longer and needed reprovisioning, Admiral Nimitz determined the same day that he would withdraw Brown's force by the middle of March. The preparations for joining the *Lexington* and the *Yorktown* into one carrier task force proceeded quickly. Fletcher departed from the Canton area and arranged to join Brown on 6 March at a location about 300 miles north of Noumea. On 2 March, King ordered Brown to attack enemy positions in the New Britain–Solomons area about 10 March and then return Task Force 11 to Hawaii. Brown's operation would serve as a cover for the arrival of the Army garrison for New Caledonia. When Brown and Fletcher met, they decided to make combined air and cruiser raids against the Japanese air bases at Rabaul and Gasmata on New Britain. While steaming north to attack the two objectives, Brown learned on 8 March that the Japanese had landed in strength at Lae and Salamaua on the north Papuan coast.[71] Brown determined that the best course of action was to attack Japanese shipping lying off Lae and Salamaua. He proposed to send his aircraft from a point in the Gulf of Papua across the Owen Stanley Mountains to the target, a distance of 125 miles. He flew two officers from the *Lexington* to Townsville to arrange through Vice Admiral Leary's headquarters a simultaneous strike on Lae and Salamaua by Army B-17 heavy bombers. On 10 March the *Lexington* and the *Yorktown* sent a combined strike force of 104 aircraft and took the Lae-Salamaua Attack Force completely by surprise. The carrier planes sank two large transports and two auxiliaries and heavily damaged two destroyers, a seaplane tender, a minelayer, and a light cruiser. Four other vessels sustained light damage. The aviators had claimed a much higher total: the sinking of five transports, two heavy cruisers, one light cruiser, and one destroyer, illustrating the understandable inaccuracy of estimated damage inflicted on the enemy by aircraft. As will be shown, this was a common fault among the aircrews of both powers. Brown was pleased with the raid and wrote in his report:

> It seems probable that our appearance off Rabaul on February 20 and our overwhelming attack at Salamaua on March 10 has caused them [the Japanese] to proceed with caution quite apart from the losses they have suffered in ships and planes.[72]

CinCPac was surprised when Brown radioed the location of his attack and its target. On 11 March, the *Greybook* commented, "Even with the damage inflicted, it is doubtful if the enemy will be greatly retarded."[73] The analyst could not have been more wrong.

6
Japanese Strategic Planning for the Second Operational Stage

The American 10 March carrier strike against the shipping off Lae and Salamaua shocked both Vice Admiral Inoue and Major General Horii and delayed for a month the attack on Port Moresby and the Solomons. To Inoue it became obvious that his South Seas Force could no longer carry out the original plan of invading Tulagi and Port Moresby in April. South Seas Force had operated with relatively weak naval forces, and these suffered substantial damage in the air strike. Task Forces 11 and 17 sank or damaged 13 of the 18 Japanese vessels directly involved in the Papuan landings. Several had to return to the homeland for extensive repairs, and Inoue did not have ships to replace them. The raid caused the heaviest damage yet inflicted on the Imperial Navy during the war, but successes in the East Indies overshadowed it. It began to appear to Fourth Fleet staff that the Americans were stationing at least one carrier in the South Pacific. Combined with this was an increase in the number of Allied aircraft encountered over New Guinea. General Horii was extremely worried over the possibility of his troops being caught at sea by an air strike of such intensity as at Lae and Salamaua. South Seas Force could no longer undertake the Port Moresby–Solomons operation with its own resources.

A few days after the Lae-Salamaua disaster, Inoue requested carrie support for the operation from his superiors in Combined Flee headquarters.[74]

Vice Admiral Inoue's request for aircraft carriers from Combinec Fleet raised the status of the Port Moresby–Tulagi invasion from a local operation to a matter intimately involved with grand strat egy formulated in Tokyo. This happened because Combined Flee placed a premium on the services of the six fleet carriers of Vice Admiral Nagumo's Striking Force. Inoue would have to plan his operations according to the exigencies of available carrier support and devise his timetable in accordance with schedules worked out by the Naval General Staff and Combined Fleet. This brought Inoue and his staff into closer contact with the various factions in the high command, each of which was pressing for the adoption of its own special plan. Inoue would not find this to his liking.

The principal problem facing the Japanese planners in January 1942 was the question of what to do next. The First Operational Stage unfolded more easily than their wildest dreams. The Naval General Staff had the responsibility of strategic planning, and within that body the most active faction was the so-called Australia-first group, headed by Captain Tomioka Sadatoshi, Chief of the Plans Division in the First (Operations) Section. Based on the general premise held by most of the planners that the Navy must remain on the offensive, Tomioka argued that Australia represented the greatest strategic threat to Japan's holdings in the South Pacific because of its potential as a base for an Allied counteroffensive. The Australian mainland also possessed economic possibilities which would be most valuable to Japan in the event of its capture. Tomioka wanted first of all to invade and capture Australia, thereby denying it totally to the Allies. Because of this, Tomioka was friendly to Fourth Fleet's plans for expansion in the Solomons–New Guinea area, as these operations served as the necessary first steps required for landings on the Australian mainland.[75]

Tomioka's position in turn received considerable support from Vice Admiral Inoue's staff. Rear Admiral Yano Shikazo, the chief of staff, later related the views of the staff held in early 1942. They recognized fully the danger that the Allies would pour unlimited amounts of men and material into Australia to turn it into the feared offensive base for stabs against Japan's southern defensive perimeter. Attacks from Australia would directly threaten Japanese holdings in New Guinea, the Bismarcks, and Truk itself. Fourth Fleet would have liked nothing more than to knock Australia out of the war.[76]

In February, members of the Naval Staff brought up the question of invading Australia to their colleagues in the Army General Staff. The Army was appalled at the proposal. They quickly pointed out that such a mammoth undertaking would require ten to twelve infantry divisions which the Army, because of commitments on the Asian mainland, could not furnish. Even if the troops could be found, Army leaders argued, how would they be supplied? Nowhere in the empire could there be spared the shipping necessary to maintain such a large force so far from Japan. Lieutenant General Tanaka Shinichi, chief of the First (Operations) Bureau of the Army General Staff, summed up the Army's objections. He stated that the Army General Staff had initially opposed the Navy's advance into the Bismarcks and the planned invasion of Port Moresby, but finally acquiesced because of strategic reasons even though these holdings were difficult to supply. Now the Navy wanted to proceed farther and establish Japanese troops in Australia. Tanaka absolutely refused to consider such a course of action. The Army could be counted on to oppose any plan which deflected effort from their goal of consolidation and further conquests on the mainland of Asia.

Faced with such vehement opposition on the part of the Army General Staff, Tomioka's group had no recourse but to back down. Thus in March the Naval General Staff began to develop an overall plan for isolating and neutralizing Australia through the acquisition of key island bases along the line of communication from the United States to Australia. They hoped to interpose an interlocking web of fortified air and submarine bases along the supply route to Australia. Vital areas for the execution of this plan were eastern New Guinea, the Solomons, New Caledonia, Fiji, and Samoa. Because they expected little Allied ground opposition in the South Pacific region, the Navy calculated that few Army troops would be required, easing Army objections to the plan. In its preliminary form, the Naval General Staff's strategic plan for the Second Operational Stage called for the invasions of New Caledonia, Fiji, and Samoa to begin after the completion of the Port Moresby–Solomons operation. Timing was not so definite as it was contingent on the course of the preliminary operations, but the Naval General Staff tentatively scheduled the invasions for June or early July.[77]

Thus Inoue's request for carrier support arrived in Tokyo at a time when the Naval General Staff was acutely interested in operations in the South Pacific. On 13 March Captain Miwa Shigeyoshi from Combined Fleet staff flew to Truk to confer with Admiral Inoue. During the subsequent meeting the two officers determined that the Port Moresby Operation required the attachment of at least one carrier division (two carriers) to South Sea Force as air support. At that time Striking Force had other tasks and the only available fleet carrier, the *Kaga*, was under repair in Japan. Miwa, however, assured Inoue that the major impetus of the Second Operational Stage would occur in the South Pacific. Aside from increased naval forces, the majority of Eleventh Air Fleet (Base Air Force) would be sent there as well. The two officers agreed that they should quickly set the dates for the Port Moresby–Solomons operations. Consequently, on 4 April Rear Admiral Yano announced his chief's decision postponing the Port Moresby invasion until the end of May. This would allow South Seas Force to take advantage of the availability of a carrier division at least from Striking Force. Inoue knew that by that time Nagumo's carriers would have completed current commitments and refitted and would be ready for another operation.[78]

Tomioka's faction in the Naval General Staff failed to take into account the power of another group in determining what strategy the Navy would follow in the Second Operational Stage. This group was Admiral Yamamoto's Combined Fleet staff under chief of staff Rear Admiral Ugaki Matome. Yamamoto felt strongly that the Navy must retain the initiative and cautioned against complacency. As yet he did not know what the Navy should do, but he always acknowledged the American Pacific Fleet as his chief foe. In January 1942, Ugaki at his chief's direction began informal planning for possible courses of action in the Second Operational Stage. Combined Fleet theoretically took second place to the Naval General Staff in strategic planning, but the aggressive Yamamoto and the equally intense Ugaki often managed to get their way.[79]

Ugaki considered a number of options. Taking Yamamoto's cue that the Pacific Fleet was Japan's greatest enemy, he looked for a means to strike at it. His initial idea was the capture of Midway, Johnston, and Palmyra as advanced bases for an eventual landing in the Hawaiian Islands. Such an advance would be sure to draw out the Pacific Fleet for an engagement which could be decisive. Combined Fleet's overwhelming strength in battleships and carriers would, according to Yamamoto and Ugaki, win out in any full-scale encounter with the enemy. Ugaki had to reject his proposal when he realized that the Hawaiian Islands would be most difficult to capture because of their size and American strength in land-based aircraft and troops. They were too much for Combined Fleet to handle.

The next operation considered by Combined Fleet was an offensive to the west into the Indian Ocean to destroy the British Eastern Fleet, capture Ceylon, and extend Japanese air power over the Central Indian Ocean. The plan had the value of safeguarding the western flank of the East Indies and could free Japanese forces to deal with American forces in the Pacific. In late February, Combined Fleet presented the plan to the Naval General Staff, which in turn brought it to the attention of the Army. In mid-March, Imperial General Headquarters considered the plan. The Army protested, citing the same reasons they had used to torpedo the invasion of Australia. Army leaders claimed that no infantry divisions were available to seize and garrison Ceylon. Actually Army planners favored the idea of moving east to sweep the British from the Indian Ocean and cooperate with the Germans in the Middle East. However, they thought the move toward Ceylon was premature and feared that if they approved it, tacitly admitting that troops were available, the Navy might siphon off the resources for Pacific operations.

Because of the Army's objections and a lack of response from Germany for strategic cooperation in the region, Imperial General Headquarters decreed that offensive operations in the Indian Ocean would be confined to a massive raid by Striking Force and Vice Admiral Kondo Nobutake's Scouting Force. The *Kaga*, which had run aground with moderate damage during operations in the East Indies, would return to the homeland for repairs. Kondo and Nagumo were to conduct in early April air strikes on Ceylon and destruction of shipping in the Bay of Bengal. The operation would tie up five of Nagumo's six fleet carriers until the end of April, when at least three, the *Akagi*, the *Soryu*, and the *Hiryu*, would have to return to the homeland for normal upkeep and refitting. Thus not before the end of May could Striking Force sortie once more at full strength for another operation. Combined Fleet, the Naval General Staff, and South Seas Force all had their own ideas about the nature of this future operation.[80]

Admiral Yamamoto always regarded the carriers of the Pacific Fleet as prime opponents to be neutralized or destroyed. On 1 February the American carriers began a series of raids on positions in Japan's outer defense perimeter which forced reactions by the Japanese far above their nuisance value. In early February, Yamamoto decided to detach the *Shokaku* and the *Zuikaku* of the 5th Carrier Division for defense patrols in the homeland area. This was in response to the 1 February raids on the Marshalls and the

Gilberts. The 5th Carrier Division headed north from Truk, while the rest of Nagumo's carriers completed the conquest of the Dutc East Indies. The 5th Carrier Division remained in homeland water until the middle of March, when it proceeded to Java to join Na gumo for the Indian Ocean raid. In the interval, Vice Admira Halsey had struck at Wake Island and Marcus Island, but in neithe case were the Japanese carriers in position to intercept him. Pacifi Fleet intelligence picked up the presence of the 5th Carrier Divi sion in the Bonins area, beginning in early March. Intelligenc could not believe that the Japanese were so concerned about ai attack on the homeland that they kept two carriers on patrol to protect against such a happenstance. The Americans were suspi cious of a carrier raid in the Central Pacific, but by 11 March CinCPac had deduced that the Japanese were actually only execut ing defensive measures to protect themselves against possible Amer ican carrier raids.[81]

In the middle of March, Combined Fleet staff formulated a strategic plan which took into consideration Admiral Yamamoto's desire to crush the Pacific Fleet in battle and end the incursions by the seemingly ubiquitous American carriers. Rear Admiral Ugaki, seconded by his able but eccentric plans officer, Captain Kuroshima Kameto, proposed the capture of Midway Island, the gateway to Hawaii. They felt the Americans would fight for Mid way, bringing about the chance for decisive battle. The operation proved to be attractive for a number of reasons. First of all, it required only limited Army participation and that was the only way to prevent the inevitable Army veto in Imperial General Head quarters. Second, if the Americans did offer decisive battle, then Combined Fleet would be sure to triumph and provide the basis for negotiated peace. If the Pacific Fleet did not choose to sortie, then the Imperial Navy would possess a useful outpost to help curb the troublesome American carrier raids through air searches linking up with those from Wake Island. Midway seemed to pro vide all that Yamamoto could wish for. Ugaki in mid-March pre sented an outline of the plan to the Naval General Staff. Yamamoto had examined the outline and forwarded his approval along with the plan.[82]

The stage was set for an epic collision of the two plans at the Naval General Staff. Admiral Nagano convened a special session of the Naval General Staff in Tokyo, beginning on 2 April.[83] Commander Watanabe Yasuji, an assistant plans officer in Com bined Fleet, presented the plans for the Midway Operation. Briefly stated, Combined Fleet proposed to attack Midway in early June

ith the full strength of their battleships and carriers. Watanabe
ggested that the Naval General Staff's South Pacific operations
e delayed until after the completion of the Midway Operation.
he Naval General Staff's plan called for the invasions of New
aledonia, Fiji, and Samoa to take place sometime after the com-
letion of the Port Moresby–Solomons operation.

Commander Miyo Tatsukichi, First Section Air Officer in the
aval General Staff, evaluated the strengths and weaknesses of the
vo plans during the first session. Miyo brought out the fact that
e Naval Aeronautical Department would not be able to finish
ormal re-equipping and refurbishing of the carrier air groups in
me for the Midway Operation, as few aircraft were available as
pares. He added that operations in the South Seas seemed more
asible because preparations for them at least had already begun.
Vith regard to the Midway plan itself, Miyo noted the distant
ocation of the objective, that Midway was beyond the limit of
apanese land-based air support, but within land-based air range
f Hawaii. This implied that the Americans could stage aircraft
rom Oahu to Midway. If Midway were taken, there would be
normous difficulty in supplying the Japanese garrison there. He
oubted that Japan could even retain Midway under those circum-
tances. As for Combined Fleet hopes that the possession of Mid-
vay would help curb the American carrier raids, Miyo pointed out
hat carriers could easily slip by the aircraft based on the island,
nd could actually attack the island at will. He thought that the
oss of Midway would not substantially lower American morale.
According to the Midway plan, the principal reason for attacking
was to draw the Pacific Fleet into decisive battle. Miyo wanted to
know what would prevent the Americans from "rolling with the
punch," regrouping and retaking the island at a later date after
the Japanese fleet had returned to the homeland.

Miyo then defended the idea of an advance to New Caledonia,
Fiji, and Samoa. He noted the Army's objection that they were
very far from Japan, but stressed they were also distant from the
American center of gravity at Hawaii and the West Coast. In a
highly prophetic statement, Miyo said that the attempt to sever
the supply line to Australia rather than the Midway Operation
would be more apt to draw the Pacific Fleet into decisive battle.
Political pressure from Australia and New Zealand as well as vital
strategic considerations would bring the Americans to the rescue
to save Australia as a militarily useful base. Conversely, the loss of
the islands would greatly affect Australian morale and possibly
shorten the war. Finally, Miyo stated that if there were no decisive

battle, at least Japan would be in possession of more strategical valuable positions in the South Pacific than Midway. Miyo's cogent arguments tightened for a time the resolve of the Naval General Staff to carry out the Fiji–New Caledonia–Samoa operations.

The next day, 3 April, experts on the Naval General Staff stated they could provide only 70 percent of the requirements materiel for the Midway plan. The fourth of April saw neither side give in, but on 5 April Watanabe played his trump card. During an impassioned discussion with the Deputy Chief of the Naval General Staff, Vice Admiral Ito Seiichi, and the head of the First (Operations) Section, Rear Admiral Fukudome Shigeru, Watanabe insisted that the admirals call upon Admiral Yamamoto to give his opinion. He telephoned Yamamoto on board his flagship, the battleship *Yamato*. Yamamoto offered his wholehearted agreement with the Midway plan, stressing that victory depended upon destroying the Pacific Fleet, especially its carriers. The best way to do this was through the Midway Operation, which, he insisted would bring the decisive encounter he desired. Once Combined Fleet won this battle, then there would be no way for the Americans to protect the supply line to Australia, and the islands would fall easily. If the Pacific Fleet refused to fight, then Japan would win Midway for the defensive perimeter at little cost. Yamamoto's prestige carried the day. Ito and Fukudome conceded the same afternoon. The Naval General Staff had two choices, agree with the Midway plan or relieve Yamamoto from command. The latter course of action they were not prepared to take. They still impressed upon Combined Fleet the need to postpone the Midway attack about three weeks to allow materiel requirements to be filled. However, Ugaki and the staff knew they would triumph in this as well. As will be shown, the 18 April Doolittle Raid on Tokyo compelled the Naval General Staff to follow Combined Fleet's lead in adopting the whole Midway plan.

Vice Admiral Inoue was not party to the planning sessions going on during the first days of April in Tokyo. The first he knew that something had changed was on 5 April, the day after he had announced that the Port Moresby–Solomons operation would take place in late May. Ugaki sent him an ominous message which greatly altered his concept of the operation. In preparation for the Second Operational Stage, the Imperial Navy was to undergo extensive reorganization to redeploy its forces for future operations.[84] This change was to occur on 10 April, but Ugaki on 5 April circulated an outline of the changes. The orders specified that the Port Moresby Operation, given the code designation "MO Operation,"

uld take place *early* in May, less than a month away, before the
idway Operation. Combined Fleet would attach to South Seas
rce for the period 20 April to 10 May the fleet carrier *Kaga*, two
iiser divisions totaling six heavy cruisers, and two destroyer divi-
ins. In addition, they authorized the use of the light carrier *Shoho*
combat, hitherto restricted to ferry operations. These forces were
addition to Fourth Fleet's own division of light cruisers, de-
oyer flotilla, submarines, and auxiliaries. Also from the order,
oue learned that his two air flotillas would come directly under
e Eleventh Air Fleet commander, Vice Admiral Tsukahara Ni-
izo. Previously Inoue had exercised direct control over his air
iits.

Undoubtedly the orders received on 5 April were a great blow
r Admiral Inoue and his staff. He had to hasten his preparations
r the MO Operation, and would not have a full carrier division
promised in March. Whatever Combined Fleet did lend to
ioue, they would want back as soon as possible and preferably
ndamaged so that the units could participate in the Midway
peration. Had the operation taken place late in May as Inoue
anted, he would have been able to secure the services of two or
iore fleet carriers. Inoue was a great opponent of the Midway
peration, particularly as it would be his responsibility as Com-
iander of South Seas Force to garrison and supply the wretched
lace after its capture. Inoue, a fiery officer, made no secret of his
istaste for the planners in Combined Fleet.[85] It was probably with
ime relish that Combined Fleet staff despatched the orders for
ie MO Operation the same day that their great victory in Tokyo
ccurred. There was nothing for Inoue and his staff to do but
egin detailed planning for the Port Moresby Operation, as time
wiftly slipped by.

7
American Strategic Planning for the South Pacific

To facilitate United States participation in the multinational meet
ings of the Combined Chiefs of Staff, the chiefs of staff of the tw
services organized themselves into the Joint Chiefs of Staff (JCS)
replacing the old Joint Board as the principal grand strategy plan
ning agency. On 9 February the Joint Chiefs inaugurated a regula
series of meetings to decide basic American strategy and to formu
late fundamental American positions for the sessions of the Com
bined Chiefs of Staff. As first organized, the Joint Chiefs comprised
Admirals King and Stark, General Marshall, and Lieutenant Gen
eral Henry H. Arnold, head of the Army Air Force. On 26 March
President Roosevelt relieved Admiral Stark of his post of Chief o
Naval Operations, combining both that office and the Commander
in-Chief, U.S. Fleet (ComInCh) in the person of Admiral King
Stark went abroad to take charge of U.S. Naval Forces in Europe.[8]

The meetings of the Joint Chiefs of Staff served as the main
forum where rival strategic plans from the Army and the Navy
appeared for discussion and decisions, subject to overall review
by the president. Regarding strategy in the Pacific, there developed
a basic Navy position which was in stark contrast to that held by
the War Department planners. After the isolation and virtual loss

the Philippines, evident by February, strategy in the South Pacific centered around two areas, actual defense of Australia and protection of the line of communications to Australia through the acquisition of island bases which, in turn, could serve as offensive bases for attacks against the Japanese. The major question under discussion was how much effort to expend in the Pacific in light of the primary policy decision, reaffirmed during the Arcadia Conference, of defeating Germany first.

From the beginning, Admiral King expressed his determination to fight the Japanese in the South Pacific by garrisoning island bases to extend American sea and air power into areas held by the Japanese. King saw the mission of the Pacific Fleet as checking the Japanese southward advance and rapidly changing over to the offensive to drive them back. The only way to do this was for the Navy to have a goodly amount of Army troops and aircraft to hold the island bases. To get them, King would have to buck General Marshall and the War Department planners who were convinced that as little effort as was feasible should go into the Pacific. In December 1941, King stressed the need for a fueling base in the South Pacific and secured the use of a small Army force to garrison Bora Bora for that purpose. By early January, the Army had promised to send garrisons to Canton and Christmas islands on the route to Samoa, and also valuable New Caledonia flanking the Coral Sea. The Army had bolstered the flanks of the line of communications to Australia, but the area in between was still very much exposed.

King's next proposal for an island base came on 5 February, when he recommended that Funafuti in the Ellice Islands be made an advance base to cover Fiji and Samoa. King was concerned about Japanese activity in the Gilberts and wanted to interpose an outpost between there and the valuable island groups to the south. King's request elicited a noncommittal response from the War Department planners, "Our island commitments should be limited to those necessary to secure our routes to critical areas." There was no definition as to the nature of these "island commitments."[87]

Undaunted by the Army's rebuff, on 18 February King informed the Joint Chiefs that the Navy thought it would be wise to garrison Efate in the New Hebrides and Tongatabu in the Tonga group. King wanted to build Tongatabu into the "principal operating naval base in the South Pacific." He also made it clear that he desired Efate to serve as a base from which a "step by step general advance could be made through the New Hebrides, Solomons and Bismarcks."[88] King already had formulated the basis for American strategy resulting in the Guadalcanal campaign later that year. The Army replied on 24 February, cautiously trying to gau the Navy's ideas for the South Pacific. General Marshall stated a memorandum for Admiral King that the Army was willing to "anything reasonable" to facilitate "offensive action by the fleet," but wanted a general statement of the Navy's strategic plans f operations in the Pacific. Basically Marshall hoped to learn wheth the Navy envisioned defensive operations or an offensive again the Japanese. He asked King rather facetiously whether the Nav had fully explored the possibility of using Marine units as garr sons instead of soldiers. Marshall stressed that American strateg in the Pacific must remain the strategic defensive because of mor important opportunities in the European theater.

In the latter part of January, planners of the Army's Wa Planning Division (WPD) began to develop the idea of dire American intervention in Northern Europe as the best course c action for the United States to follow in order to win the war. On of the chief proponents of the plan was Brigadier General Dwigh D. Eisenhower, appointed chief of the WPD on 16 February. O 28 February he submitted to Marshall an important statement ou lining WPD's ideas for the South Pacific.[90] In the memorandun Eisenhower stated three conditions which he considered "nece sary" to ensure the winning of the war. They were the maintenanc of the United Kingdom, the continued active participation of th Soviet Union in the war, and the security from Axis attack of th Middle East and India to prevent a junction of the Germans an Japanese. The basic premise for this was that the United State and Hawaii were safe from a major attack. In the category o "highly desirable," Eisenhower listed in order of importance th security of Alaska, the supply line to Australia, Burma, and finall Australia. The WPD proposed that the primary theater be Europ and the major action encompass the opening of a second front ir Northwest Europe, comprising air attacks and even a full-scale in vasion if it were feasible. This was to divert large numbers o German troops from the Russian front. He hoped to inaugurate an air offensive from England in early May and possibly by late summer have ground troops on the European continent.

As for the South Pacific, Eisenhower noted that the real need to fight in that area ended when the Japanese captured the oil-rich Dutch East Indies. Therefore he saw no advantage in expanding the fighting in that region; rather, the primary objectives were defensive. These objectives included the maintenance of the line of communication to Australia, the need to hold bases as forward s "possible" for an eventual counteroffensive, and the denial of ue Southeast Pacific to the enemy. However, he noted that these bjectives "are not immediately vital to the successful outcome of ue war." As for required forces in the Pacific, Eisenhower thought hat those already allocated were largely sufficient. Indeed, he en- isioned a withdrawal of Army troops from the Southwest Pacific nce the Australians had built up their forces with the return of ome Australian Imperial Force (AIF) divisions from the Middle ast. The idea was to organize a mobile reserve in the Hawaiian rea for use as needed in the South Pacific. The Pacific would have o subsist on the minimum forces available, because of "limitations n shipping, equipment and trained troops."[91] The 28 February tatement remained basic Army policy toward the Pacific for the ext several crucial months.

Meanwhile Admiral King followed on 2 March with a letter to he Joint Chiefs succinctly stating his intentions.[92] His strategy for he South Pacific encompassed not only the security of the line of ommunication to Australia but also the establishment of "strong oints" for the gradual advance to the Bismarck archipelago. This dvance would serve as a powerful diversion to draw the Japanese way from such important areas as India and Australia. Finally, King sought to impress upon the War Department that an offensive vas the best way to cover the string of bases in the South Pacific. He was willing to restrict his request for Army garrisons to Efate nd Tongatabu for the time being, but in no way was he content o remain idly on the defensive. King and Marshall readied their strategic proposals in early March to present to a higher power— President Roosevelt.

Watching the collapse of the ABDA Command with obvious horror, President Roosevelt became gravely concerned with the defense of Australia. On 15 February he told Harry Hopkins that the United States should assume responsibility for reinforcing Australia and New Zealand. Apparently the president exerted considerable pressure on the War Department, for the same day with unusual alacrity the Army planners completely reversed their previous policy toward Australia. Heretofore they had restricted American reinforcements to Australia to service troops, ostensibly for the major supply base to the beleaguered Philippines. Suddenly they ordered the 41st Division and attached troops, 27,000 men in all, to prepare for shipment to Australia. Previously the War Department had planned to send only two divisions in all of 1942 to the South Pacific. On 18 February Roosevelt told Prime Minister

Churchill that America would send troops to Australia and Ne
Zealand in an effort to persuade the two governments to retai
their own troops in the Middle East.[93]

Next Roosevelt informed Prime Minister Curtin on 20 Fel
ruary that the United States was in the best position to reinforc
Australia. He added that the U.S. Navy had already begun oper:
tions which would help to safeguard Australia and New Zealan
from outright invasion by the Japanese. Curtin tested the pres
dent's resolve on 4 March, when he requested that the Unite
States provide two more divisions to take the place of the on
Australian division and the one New Zealand division remainin
in the Middle East. Churchill, eager to keep the valuable Commor
wealth troops for British theaters, urged Roosevelt to help in th
matter. The president was not found wanting. Within a few day
the War Department reluctantly cut orders allocating the 32n
Division for Australia and the 37th Division for New Zealand
both units to sail in April.

It was in this mood of concern for Australia and the Southwes
Pacific that Roosevelt convened on 5 March a meeting with th
Joint Chiefs to discuss strategy in the Pacific. Admiral King pre
pared a memorandum for the president. Repeating the position
outlined on 2 March, King stressed that an offensive toward th
Bismarcks depended upon a secure line of communication leading
to Australia and the allocation of requisite forces. Security could
be achieved only by building up the "strong points," Samoa, Fiji,
New Caledonia, Tongatabu, Efate, and Funafuti. Referring to the
step-by-step advance to the Bismarcks, King concluded that:

> Such a line of operations will be offensive rather than passive—
> and will draw Japanese forces there to oppose it, thus relieving
> pressure elsewhere, whether in Hawaii, ABDA area, Alaska or
> even India.[94]

He summed up his strategic position thusly: "Hold Hawaii, Support Australasia. Drive northward from New Hebrides." General
Marshall and Secretary of War Henry Stimson pressed for the
strategy outlined in the 28 February Army memorandum. They
sought to gain approval for an early cross-channel attack from
England to the French coast. During the meeting, however, the
president made it clear that Australia would be held. He stated
that the Navy's strategy would be the one followed.[95]

While ComInCh in Washington fought his battles in the con-
fines of the Joint Chiefs' meetings, Admiral Nimitz and his staff

ook a serious look at the question of basing strong fleet units in he South Pacific. This was prompted by a communication received n 16 February from ComInCh. In it King suggested the establishent of a main fleet base at Auckland and an intermediate base at uva in the Fijis. The CinCPac staff considered the matter the next lay and concluded that they lacked the materiel and manpower t that time to organize the two bases. They were not sure whether t was wise to utilize such bases. "It is also not clear whether the trength of the fleet is to be employed defending ANZAC or Havaii," Plans Division noted on 17 February.[96] There was the nag-;ing fear that the redeployment of the fleet southward would ompromise the defense of Hawaii. On 21 February Nimitz replied vith a definite negative to a query from Admiral Stark as to vhether Lieutenant General Delos C. Emmons' Hawaiian Department was sufficient to defend the island chain in order to allow the fleet to be "footfree."[97] Regarding bases in the South Pacific, the staff felt it was risky to retain strong units of the fleet there for any length of time. There were no repair facilities there capable of dry-docking a battleship or carrier in the event of severe damage. Also there was the old problem of the vulnerability of the Central Pacific to Japanese offensives or raids should the majority of the fleet move south of the equator.

In the end, though, the CinCPac staff recognized the inevitability of large-scale commitment to the South Pacific. The hints were certainly strong in the directives from Washington. On 21 February the CinCPac *Greybook*, the war diary of Plans Division, stated:

> However that area [the South Pacific] is the one in which our forces
> will meet advancing enemy forces, and we may be forced to make
> the move due to political or "desperation strategical" consideration.[98]

Still there was the dilemma on just how much would be sent south. On 27 February Vice Admiral Pye returned from a trip to Washington with the comment that the planners there had not yet adopted an overall strategic scheme. The *Greybook* lamented, "We don't know how 'all-out' our help is to be to Australia."[99]

On 22 February Admiral King informed CinCPac that he planned to develop Tongatabu as the intermediate operating base instead of Suva or Samoa, which he considered too exposed. He followed on 3 March with definite orders to that effect. Admiral Nimitz opened discussion the next day on the suitability of Tongatabu as opposed to Nandi Roads in Fiji, which he seemed to prefer.

A prime consideration in his mind was the presence of a New Zealand division as the garrison of Fiji. The establishment of base at Tongatabu would require one of his Marine defense battalions, of which he had only a few. King hoped to obtain an Army garrison for Tongatabu, but until the soldiers arrived, the Marines would have to guard the base. Plans went ahead in mid-March for the occupation of Tongatabu according to the ComInCh directive CinCPac issued the orders on 13 March to send construction and supply forces to the island.[100]

The question of an intermediate fleet base in the South Pacific needed a fast answer, because on 12 March King ordered Nimitz to retain Fletcher's Task Force 17 with the *Yorktown* in the ANZAC Area. King kept Task Force 17 under direct ComInCh control and gave Fletcher command over Rear Admiral Crace's ANZAC Squadron as well. He ordered Fletcher to continue offensive action against Japanese forces in New Guinea and the Solomons area warning him of enemy designs on Port Moresby and the Solomons Fletcher received discretion to operate as he thought best.[101] Vice Admiral Brown received orders to transfer fuel and supplies to Task Force 17 before separating the two task forces in order for Task Force 11 to head for Pearl Harbor. Brown's Task Force 11 with the *Lexington* reached Oahu on 26 March. Vice Admiral Halsey with Task Force 16 had returned to Pearl Harbor on 10 March and remained in the Oahu area all the rest of the month. The need for a fleet base in the South Pacific made itself known acutely as early as 14 March. Rear Admiral Fletcher requested permission to move the fleet train vessels (oilers and stores ships) from Samoa to Suva or Noumea, where he could have access to them. On 16 March Admiral Nimitz felt constrained to reject this proposal because the forward bases were too exposed. Fletcher would have to draw supplies directly from Noumea.[102] However, Task Force 17 would have to curtail operations soon and properly reprovision with fleet materiel.

The War Department planners mustered their forces to counterattack after the setback of 5 March. Stimson noted in his diary on 6 March that Eisenhower was against "King's creeping movement through New Caledonia."[103] It became evident to the Army that the Navy would be the principal adversary for their European plans. Circumstances in early March aided the Army in its quest to win over the president. The Soviet Union began arguing vigorously for a second front in the summer of 1942. Their winter offensive had bogged down, and they feared the resumption of the German attack in the spring. Churchill acknowledged the need to

me to some agreement with the Soviets and consulted with Roose-
elt. On 8 March the president informed Churchill that he would
ome to the aid of the Russians by starting a second front. This
theme envisioned at least a massive air offensive against the Germans and possibly landings on the continent that summer. Roose-
elt began to take interest in the Army's plans.[104]

Simultaneously the Joint Chiefs compiled three broad outlines
or American grand strategy. The first was basically the Navy's
plan, envisioning the allocation of strong reinforcements to the
Pacific at the expense of an immediate major effort in Europe.
This plan would ensure security of Australia and the line of communication from the West Coast and offered the prospects of an
early counteroffensive to retake Rabaul. General Arnold's Army
Air Force planners sponsored the second proposal, which encompassed an all-out effort in Europe to defeat Germany in western
Europe. Under this scheme, reinforcements for the Pacific would
be cut almost completely, even accepting the loss of Australia and
he rest of the Southwest Pacific to Japan in order to secure the
speedy ruination of Germany. The third plan was a compromise
between the first two, and was favored by the War Department
planners. Only minimum forces were to be allocated to the Pacific,
enough to protect Hawaii and perhaps Australia, but none to be
used in an early counteroffensive. Forces would concentrate in
Britain to undertake the invasion of western Europe at the earliest
possible moment. The Joint Chiefs on 14 March began consideration of the three alternatives.[105]

During the next session of the Joint Chiefs, 16 March, King's
strategy for the Pacific suffered a major defeat. The Joint Chiefs,
"with little recorded discussion," decided to implement the War
Department's plan, calling for a rapid build-up of forces in Europe
and the restriction of reinforcements in the Pacific to "current
commitments."[106] They approved King's request for bases at Efate
and Tongatabu, but declined to give the Pacific any more troops.
The Army felt that three divisions in the Southwest Pacific were
sufficient. Regarding air strengths, the Joint Chiefs on the basis of
recommendations from the Joint Planning Staff approved the allocation of single AAF pursuit squadrons for Christmas Island, Canton, Tongatabu, and Efate. Fiji and New Caledonia were to have
more powerful air garrisons, splitting a medium bomb group of
about 57 medium bombers, two squadrons in each area. Fighter
strength for New Caledonia was to be 80 aircraft, and in the Fijis
55 aircraft, roughly the equivalent of one pursuit group with spare
aircraft included. Previously, on 20 January, the AAF had indi-

cated its desire to base only five pursuit squadrons and no bomber in the South Pacific.[107]

Under the circumstances, King was compelled to compromise and agree to the Army's plan. It became evident that the Navy could not obtain approval of its strategic goals in the face of still opposition from Marshall and Arnold both. King had to give in to Marshall or run the risk of not obtaining any reinforcements for the Pacific, as in Arnold's plan. But if the Army planners thought they had secured a clear field for Europe, they were mistaken. On 17 March King responded with a memorandum for Marshall noting both the recent Japanese invasion of New Guinea and the conquest of lower Burma. He wrote that he "assumed" the Army would allot first priority to reinforcements for Australia and the line of communication. Meanwhile he expedited the shipment of troops and engineers to build the bases already approved.[108] On 19 March, he informed Nimitz of the general reinforcement plan for the South Pacific. CinCPac would have to garrison Tongatabu and Efate with Marines until the arrival of the Army defense troops. King arranged for a provisional Marine brigade to augment the Samoan garrison now that it looked as if the Army was not going to spare any more troops for the South Pacific.[109] It was a needless dispersion of well-trained amphibious troops in garrison duty which could be performed by other units. The Marine brigade was to arrive at Samoa in early May. The forces already there (a reinforced Marine regiment) were to construct bases on several islands in the archipelago. The Army commander at New Caledonia dispatched a reinforced infantry company to occupy Efate on 18 March. King hoped to have the installation on Tongatabu partially functioning by the middle of April.

In a radio message sent on 18 March to General MacArthur newly arrived in Australia, Marshall detailed the War Department's plans for the Southwest Pacific Area.[110] The planners decided to begin bringing the AAF squadrons in Australia up to strength with replacements shipped or air-ferried from the West Coast. Marshall noted that the arrival of the 32nd Division, then preparing to move to Australia, was conditional on whether the Australians retained their own troops in the Middle East. The New Caledonia garrison was to consist of a reinforced division, most of which was already there, while Efate and Tongatabu would each receive a reinforced infantry regiment to arrive in the next few months. The AAF still only promised to deploy five pursuit squadrons in the South Pacific, despite the Joint Chiefs' directive. Marshall indicated the recent ormation of the Amphibious Corps and its eventual mission of attacks against island positions in the Pacific. There was no definite commitment for the Southwest Pacific Area to undertake any kind of offensive. That apparently was the task of the Amphibious Corps, two reinforced divisions, one Marine and the other Army, training largely on the West Coast.

Rear Admiral Richmond Kelly Turner, King's Director of War Plans, analyzed the Army's position for ComInCh in a memorandum dated 26 March. Turner concluded that there was no indication that the Army would change its mind and release troops and aircraft for the defense of the South Pacific, even given the conditions stated in the 17 March letter. Europe still remained the theater with the highest priority, particularly for the Army Air Force. Even worse, Turner said it looked as if General Arnold would not provide the aircraft strengths already approved by the Joint Chiefs. He finished on a gloomy note, stating that there was no way the Navy could launch a successful offensive into the Solomons, given the present conditions. King himself brought up the question of Army aircraft strengths and deployment in a letter to Marshall on 29 March. He noted the Army's idea of deploying heavy bombers on the extremities of the Hawaii-Australia ferry route with the intention of flying in B-17's to a critical point. He disagreed with this strategy because he felt the forces allocated were insufficient both to protect the extremities of Hawaii and Alaska and to support the central island bases of the South Pacific. Instead, he asked that a heavy bombardment group be furnished for the South Pacific and retained there. He agreed with the general concept of Europe first, but argued that the Pacific suituation was critical and depended upon quick action to restore it. Consequently, he recommended that the Army give first priority in aircraft allocation to the South Pacific over the other theaters.[111]

The months of February and March also saw the attempt by the Joint Chiefs to devise a workable command structure in the Pacific. In December 1941 the United States had four separate commands in the Pacific. Two of them, the Pacific and Asiatic Fleets, were Navy, and the other two, the Hawaiian Department and MacArthur's U.S. Army Forces in the Far East (USAFFE) were Army. There was no real coordination between the four in planning or operations.[112] General Wavell's jerry-built ABDA Command affected only the Asiatic Fleet. After the February collapse of ABDA, King suggested that Australia and the ANZAC Area be combined into one area under an American because the Pacific Fleet would be called upon to defend it. A few days later, King woul have reason to reconsider his proposal. On 22 February Roosevel ordered MacArthur to Australia.

By early March there developed a two-way fight over the natur of command in the Pacific. It was obvious that MacArthur woul hold supreme command in the Southwest Pacific. The only ques tion concerned the extent of his control over the line of communi cation to the east. On 8 March King told the Joint Chiefs tha Australia and New Zealand should be in separate areas, as th Navy had jurisdiction over the defense of the line of communica tion. King proposed that a naval officer command New Zealanc waters and the line of communication, while Australia and Nev Guinea comprise the Southwest Pacific Area. The Navy had nc confidence in MacArthur's ability to command air and sea forces On 19 March Turner wrote King, remarking that MacArthu would tend to misuse his forces "since he has shown clear unfamil iarity with proper naval and air functions."[113]

On 18 March, the Joint Chiefs agreed with the Navy's plan General MacArthur, who arrived in Australia on 17 March, wa to be Supreme Commander, Southwest Pacific Area (SWPA). Gen eral Sir Thomas Blamey of the Australian Army was appointed his ground force commander and Lieutenant General George Brett, U.S. Army, his air commander. Taking control of SWPA's naval forces was Vice Admiral Leary. The old ANZAC Area would disappear, its forces divided among other commands. The official Joint Chiefs directive, issued 30 March, listed MacArthur's tasks as the general defense of Australia and associated areas against Japanese attack and also the retention of bases which could be used for offensive operations. MacArthur was to ready his forces to take the offensive. He also received instructions to render support to the operations of the Pacific Ocean Areas under Admiral Nimitz. MacArthur was to receive his orders directly from General Marshall in his capacity of Chief of Staff of the Army.[114]

The sweeping reorganization of the Pacific also covered the Pacific Fleet. Admirals King and Nimitz had several times conferred as to the proper command structure in the Pacific. The current organization was inadequate. Under it King directly controlled the naval forces of the old ABDA Area (i.e., western Australia) and the ANZAC Area, while Nimitz handled the South, Central, and North Pacific. Direct control by ComInCh in the crucial ANZAC Area was cumbersome. As early as 6 March, Nimitz recommended to King that the area be put under his command.[115]

Rear Admiral Fletcher on board the *Yorktown* certainly wished that there was better liaison with ComInCh in distant Washington. On 21 March he informed Leary that he planned to make an offensive sweep into the Coral Sea toward the end of the month. On 29 March Leary radioed that there were 30 transports at Rabaul, undoubtedly presaging some sort of offensive movement to the south. The same day he also reported that an Army search plane had sighted Task Force 17 only 230 miles southeast of Rabaul. Both King and Nimitz were surprised that Fletcher had come so near to Rabaul, considering the excellent Japanese search network. Still if Fletcher was so close, they expected his Task Force 17 to attack small Japanese forces filtering south from Rabaul to land unopposed at Buka and Bougainville, and possibly raid Rabaul itself.[116]

On 30 March Fletcher reported his actual position, which was far south of the reported one. He said he was en route to Noumea to refuel there, but added, "If force reported heading south I will proceed at once to operate until further orders in vicinity 15° South, 160° East." King was furious and snapped off a reply, "Your 292346 [message] not understood if it means you are retiring from enemy vicinity in order to provision."[117] What had actually happened was that the Army aviators had both greatly overestimated the number of ships at Rabaul and had spotted a small Japanese force of gunboats and auxiliaries and mistakenly reported it as Task Force 17. Fletcher was not anywhere near Rabaul. He was following the situation closely, but could discover no concentration of shipping for him to attack. He thought of raiding Rabaul but realized that Japanese patrol planes would spot his force and warn the forces there to clear the harbor. He decided to wait until the Japanese came south and then hit them. Under such circumstances they would not be able to escape his strike planes. When Leary reported some ships at Shortland off the southern coast of Bougainville, Fletcher moved to attack them, but found on 6 April that the Japanese ships had departed before he could get within attack range of them.[118]

Fletcher remained in the South Pacific until the end of May and did not have an opportunity to explain in full what had happened. Admiral King, renowned for his hard-boiled attitude toward officers he suspected of incompetence or worse, wrongly held the 29 March incident against Fletcher. During a conference with Nimitz in April, King expressed his uneasiness over Fletcher's supposed lack of aggressiveness.[119] Only in May and June was Fletcher able to explain to Nimitz the true circumstances behind the incident. Despite the reports of enemy ships in the area, Fletcher wrote that there was "no definite information of any concentration of any enemy ships for me to attack under the directive contained in COMINCH 261630 of February until forces were reported which I attacked on May 4 at Tulagi."[120] The incident underscored the fact that King had little business trying to control fast carrier operations from his office in Washington, half the globe away.

On 30 March the Joint Chiefs issued their directive forming Admiral Nimitz's command into the Pacific Ocean Areas (POA). Henceforth, Nimitz's complete title was CinCPac-CinCPOA: Commander-in-Chief, Pacific Fleet and Commander-in-Chief, Pacific Ocean Areas. The directive divided the Pacific into three areas, the North Pacific, the Central Pacific, and the South Pacific. Nimitz retained direct control over the first two, but was to appoint a commander for the South Pacific Area. The boundary between the South Pacific Area (SoPac) and MacArthur's Southwest Pacific Area followed in part longitude 165°, or roughly through the center of the Solomons chain. Nimitz had as his basic task the defense of the island positions between the United States and Australia to secure the line of communication and offensive bases against the enemy. He was also to prepare for the execution of large-scale amphibious attacks initially to begin in the South and Southwest Pacific Areas. He was also to support the Southwest Pacific Area. He received his orders directly through Admiral King as ComInCh.[121]

PART I

THE
BATTLE
OF THE
CORAL SEA

8
Japanese Planning for the MO Operation

On 5 April, as related before, Combined Fleet provided the time-table which South Seas Force was to follow for the MO Operation, ordering that it be completed by 10 May. Vice Admiral Inoue and his staff were surprised and not pleased with the order for two reasons. First of all, an early starting time for the offensive did not give the land-based air units assembling at Rabaul time to subdue enemy air opposition in the area. Only four days previously the 25th Air Flotilla began organizing at Rabaul, but one of its major components would not be fully operational until around 20 April. Inoue was also dismayed to see that Combined Fleet gave him only one fleet carrier, the *Kaga*. Three weeks before, Captain Miwa had promised him a carrier division. Inoue asked Combined Fleet to reconsider the matter and specifically requested that the 2nd Carrier Division be attached in addition to the *Kaga*. The 2nd Carrier Division, comprising the carriers the *Soryu* and the *Hiryu*, was a crack unit renowned for proficiency in battle.

Combined Fleet reconsidered the question of carrier support for South Seas Force. Allowing Inoue to use the 2nd Carrier Division, however, was another matter. The staff wanted to reserve that division and the equally illustrious 1st Carrier Division for the

Midway Operation, allowing them to refit and train in Japan through the month of May. Instead, on 10 April, Admiral Yamamoto promulgated the official task organization for the Second Operational Stage. In place of the *Kaga*, which returned to the 1st Carrier Division, Yamamoto allocated to Inoue the use of the 5th Carrier Division under Rear Admiral Hara Chuichi. Composed of the new carriers *Shokaku* and *Zuikaku*, the 5th Carrier Division was the least experienced of the fleet carrier divisions in Striking Force. Combined Fleet wanted the aviators in the division to gain more combat experience in preparation for the Midway Operation, in which they were slated to join. The 5th Carrier Division had fought in almost all the battles of Striking Force and performed most creditably, but they were not considered the equal of the other two divisions. Ugaki cut orders on 12 April assigning the 5th Carrier Division, the 5th Cruiser Division under Rear Admiral Takagi Takeo, and two destroyer divisions to South Seas Force, effective 18 April.[1]

With the preliminaries behind, the staff of South Seas Force could concentrate on completing detailed planning for the Port Moresby invasion.[2] The problems were many, not the least of which was geography. The direct sea route between Rabaul and Port Moresby passed through a maze of reefs, fast currents, and narrow straits in the form of the D'Entrecasteaux and Louisiade archipelagos, jutting out far into the Coral Sea from the tip of eastern New Guinea. There were only three practical sea routes. The first was the shortest, directly through narrow China Straits close to New Guinea. It was only 670 miles, but passed through the worst hazards. Going entirely around the Louisiades was possible, but the route was 950 miles and exposed a convoy to air attack for too long to be safe. The only solution, and the one adopted by the planners, was through the center of the Louisiades, passing through the reefs at Jomard Pass. The Jomard route was 840 miles.

The Japanese planners had at their disposal the techniques for amphibious attack developed during the Sino-Japanese War and refined during the offensive against the Philippines and the East Indies. Basic to Japanese amphibious doctrine was the seizure of islands along the route to serve as seaplane bases to provide air support for the invasion convoy. In anticipation of operating in the South Seas, Japanese naval aviation developed a varied and extremely useful coterie of seaplanes from small float-fighters to large flying boats. The seaplane bases were easy to erect, given the large number of quiet lagoons and sheltered harbors dotting the egion. Within hours after a visit by a seaplane tender, a base would be functioning. South Seas Force decided to capture Tulagi during the opening phase of the operation and base flying boats there to conduct searches far to the south into the Coral Sea. This would help to secure the left flank of the invasion convoy. In addition, the staff wanted to set up similar bases in the Louisiades and on the south Papuan coast to give close air support to the convoy as it passed each point. To further this end, the 24th Air Flotilla began in March a series of reconnaissance flights over the projected route to determine the best sites for the bases. The new 25th Air Flotilla, superseding the old one, continued the work. Inoue ordered the 33rd Submarine Division at Truk to conduct an extensive reconnaissance of the area to check the accuracy of charts.[3]

General Horii and the South Seas Detachment did not sit idly. The Army was appalled at the damage inflicted on the Lae-Salamaua invasion force by the enemy air strike. They did not have full confidence in the Navy's ability to protect them in the event another such thunderbolt caught them at sea. Indeed, their own transportation was nothing to inspire confidence. In 1942 the Japanese Army maintained a fleet of transport and supply vessels reserved for its own use. Horii would have to travel on five old, decrepit ex-merchant vessels capable of only eight knots in convoy. On 20 March Horii contacted his superiors in the Army Section in Tokyo, asking for reinforcements and fast transports. He received no further communications from them. His staff tried to devise a safe way to get the South Seas Detachment to Port Moresby. They considered an overland advance across the Owen Stanleys, but had to reject that course because there were only native tracks across the forbidding mountainous jungle separating the two coasts of Papua. Horii settled on the use of landing barges, a tried Army amphibious technique and one very popular with the generals. The barges, known as *Daihatsu*, could carry 70 men or 10 tons of supplies about 100 miles. This would require relay points along the way. Horii tentatively planned to transport all of his troops by ship to Samarai Island on China Straits, and there transfer the troops to barges. The barges would use relay points along the New Guinea coast and finally land at Port Moresby. On 15 April he asked the Navy to provide topographical data on the south Papuan coast to determine the locales for relay points.[4]

Vice Admiral Inoue convened on 16 April a two-day meeting of the staff to test the plan and arrange for final orders. Apparently the meeting was a spirited one, with subordinates voicing their misgivings regarding the operation or certain phases of it. Lieutenant Colonel Tanaka Toyoshige attended as Horii's representative He brought up the concern of the South Seas Detachment regarding the long exposed sea route and noted the Army's desire to use barges instead of ships for the final leg. Inoue felt constrained to remind his subordinates why they were invading Port Moresby, that is, to facilitate deployment of naval air power in the Southwest Pacific. He emphasized that the MO Operation was to be accomplished "at all costs."[5] The Navy's planners strongly impressed upon Tanaka that assigned carrier forces would give ample protection against interference by Allied aircraft.

On 23 April Inoue issued "South Seas Force Order No. 13," the basic directive for the MO Operation.[6] The order provided for the formation of three groups, MO Striking Force, MO Invasion Force, and Tulagi Invasion Force. Cooperating with them would be units of the Base Air Force and submarines of the Advance Expeditionary Force. Briefly, the plans provided for the capture of Tulagi on 3 May, followed by the establishment of a seaplane base at Deboyne in the Louisiades. The invasion convoy was to sail on 4 May from Rabaul and land at Port Moresby six days later. After the capture of Port Moresby, elements of the MO forces were to participate in the capture of Ocean and Nauru on 15 May.

MO Striking Force had the task of providing security for the invasion forces, but through indirect support. Centered around the 5th Carrier Division, the force was to watch for the approach of powerful Allied naval forces and destroy them if they appeared. If they found no enemy carriers in the area, Inoue instructed MO Striking Force to swing around the Solomons, cross the Coral Sea, and launch air strikes on the Allied air bases at Townsville and Cooktown in Australia and Port Moresby, if the situation allowed. Its primary mission, however, was to protect South Seas Force from carrier attack. MO Invasion Force comprised the troop convoy and a close escort force of the light carrier *Shoho* and four heavy cruisers. Also attached were auxiliaries and tenders to construct the seaplane bases along the convoy route. Tulagi Invasion Force consisted of several auxiliaries, a large minelayer, and two destroyers, which would seize Tulagi and build a flying boat anchorage there, disbanding after they completed the mission. Part of the force would join MO Invasion Force, while the rest became the nucleus of the RY (Ocean-Nauru) Invasion Force. Inoue instructed the task force commanders to issue detailed orders for their groups.

It took most of April to assemble the scattered forces assigned to the MO Operation. On 12 April the 5th Carrier Division was at Singapore with the rest of Striking Force, having successfully raided Ceylon a few days before. Rear Admiral Hara radioed Inoue the next day that he planned to proceed to Formosa to refuel and refurbish, and then sail on to Truk on 28 April. This was not good enough. On 17 April Inoue ordered Hara to sail immediately for Truk after a brief stay at Formosa. Rear Admiral Takagi's 5th Cruiser Division was in the homeland, as were also six submarines of the 8th Submarine Squadron assigned to the operation. Inoue hoped to rendezvous his forces at Truk and Rabaul in the third week of April. The organization of Base Air Force proceeded slowly. After the 10 April reorganization, Vice Admiral Tsukahara commanded all of the land-based combat air units in the Navy, including the 25th Air Flotilla at Rabaul. The last air group of this flotilla reinforcing Rabaul would not arrive until 1 May.[7]

On 18 April there occurred an event which threatened to wreck Inoue's timetable. On that date, B-25 medium bombers launched from American carriers attacked Tokyo and other Japanese cities before disappearing over China. A Japanese picket boat reported sighting three enemy carriers about 650 miles off the coast of Japan. The entire Combined Fleet rose to meet this outrage. Vice Admiral Nagumo's carriers, en route to Japan, received orders to steam east at high speed to try to intercept the raiding force. Likewise units assigned to the MO Operation attempted to find the enemy. The 5th Carrier Division touched briefly at Bako in Formosa and then turned northeast to give chase in the Pacific. From Japan, the 5th Cruiser Division sortied with elements of Vice Admiral Kondo's Second Fleet. At the time of the raids, the six submarines of the 8th Submarine Squadron were plodding south toward Truk, escorted by Sixth Fleet flagship *Katori* and the seaplane carrier *Chiyoda*. The submarines received orders to pursue the raiders, while the two ships continued to Truk. By 20 April, it was evident that the Americans had escaped unscathed. Combined Fleet ordered the pursuit to be halted. The 5th Carrier Division arrived on 25 April at Truk, a day after the submarines, while Rear Admiral Takagi reached there on 27 April.[8]

Immediately upon arriving at Truk, Hara received a copy of "South Seas Force Order No. 13." He did not like the role chosen for his carriers, and protested the ordered air strikes on Australia. First of all, he thought it was extremely dangerous to penetrate so close to strong enemy air units which would surely detect his approach. Second, the presence of reefs and other maritime danger in the area would severely hamper the mobility of the carriers. Finally, Hara decried the fact that MO Striking Force had only one fleet oiler assigned to it, which would limit the operations of his destroyers. The slower tanker would not be able to accompany him on the dash across the Coral Sea.[9]

Takagi assumed command of MO Striking Force upon his arrival at Truk because he was senior to Hara. Takagi was a cruiser expert and acknowledged his lack of experience with air operations. He agreed with Hara that the commander of the 5th Carrier Division should handle air operations, subject to consultation with Takagi. On 28 April Takagi issued his operational orders. MO Striking Force consisted of two fleet carriers with 124 aircraft (111 operational), two heavy cruisers, six destroyers, and one oiler. Takagi included in his orders the attacks on Australia as instructed by Inoue. On 29 April, however, Inoue relented regarding the Townsville strike, leaving it to the discretion of Takagi. He was to cancel the strike if he thought it would not be a surprise. On the same day, Admiral Yamamoto settled the matter by ordering South Seas Force to suspend all attacks on the Australian mainland in order to use the carriers exclusively to watch for enemy carriers, leaving attacks on Australia to Base Air Force. Therefore, on 30 April Inoue canceled the strikes on Townsville, Cooktown, and Port Moresby. He also told MO Striking Force to transport nine Zero fighters for the 25th Air Flotilla from Truk to Rabaul, flying them off as they came within range of Rabaul, a seemingly unimportant addition, but one which would cause no end of trouble.[10]

Vice Admiral Inoue's problems with the Army continued. As of 18 April, Horii had still not received an answer from Tokyo regarding his 20 March query. On that date, he resubmitted his request for reinforcements and received a disquieting reply. The Army Section stressed that the Port Moresby invasion was vital to the course of operations they were considering, that is, the capture of New Caledonia, Fiji, and Samoa. Tokyo told Horii to "do as you think best."[11] At the same time they promised him a heavily armed Army antiaircraft ship, the *Asakasan Maru*, and added that the Navy's attachment of powerful carrier forces would compensate for the low speed of the convoy. Horii was not convinced and expressed his fears on 24 April to Rear Admiral Kanazawa Masao, commander of the Rabaul base detachment. Kanazawa immediately contacted Inoue, suggesting he send a representative to Rabaul to meet with Horii. General Horii and his staff on 25 and 26 April conferred with Captain Kawai Iwao of Fourth Fleet. Also attending were Hara's chief of staff, Commander Yamaoka Mineo, and the air officer of the Shoho, Lieutenant Commander Sugiyama Toshikazu. The subject was the arrangement for air protection of the convoy. Yamaoka and Sugiyama wanted to detach the Shoho from MO Invasion Force and include her in the 5th Carrier Division, adding 20 aircraft. Captain Kawai, at the insistence of the Army, firmly disagreed. The Army wanted the carrier close by. Sugiyama then requested that the Shoho be able to range around with her escorts, not being tied to the course of the convoy, but again Kawai said no. To mollify the Army it was necessary to keep the Shoho in direct escort of the convoy at all times. Horii and his staff were then satisfied with the air protection for the convoy and on 26 April signed the "Army-Navy Local Agreement" for the MO Operation. On 29 April Horii issued his operational orders, calling for the landing of two infantry battalions at Pari Mission west of Port Moresby and the other infantry battalion at Barute Mission. The units were to take Kila Kila airfield and then capture all of Port Moresby.[12]

The other commands also issued their detailed orders for the MO Operation.[13] Rear Admiral Goto Aritomo divided his MO Invasion Force into three task groups, MO Main Force, Port Moresby Invasion Force, and Support Force. MO Main Force consisted of the four heavy cruisers of Goto's own 6th Cruiser Division, accompanied by the Shoho and a destroyer. MO Main Force was to support the Tulagi landings on 3 May and then join the invasion convoy in direct escort. The Port Moresby Invasion Force under Rear Admiral Kajioka Sadamichi was the convoy force itself, nine transports, three oilers, and several auxiliaries escorted by one light cruiser, five destroyers, and a large minelayer. The convoy carried the South Seas Detachment of 4,500 men, elements of the Navy's Kure 3rd Special Naval Landing Force, and two Navy construction battalions. Support Force under Rear Admiral Marumo Kuninori comprised the group which would build the advance seaplane bases in the Solomons to support the Tulagi landing, as well as at Deboyne, Samarai, and along the south Papuan coast to cover the Port Moresby landings. It consisted of two light cruisers, one large seaplane tender with 20 floatplanes, three gunboats, and two minesweepers. Rear Admiral Shima Kiyohide led Tulagi Invasion Force of one large minelayer, two destroyers, two transports, and seven small auxiliaries. Shima had naval landing troops to occupy Tulagi on 3 May.

Land-based air support for the MO Operation came from the 25th Air Flotilla under Rear Admiral Yamada Sadayoshi, with head quarters at Rabaul. The command received the title "5th Air Attack Force" for operational purposes, and was under the overall command of Admiral Tsukahara's headquarters at Tinian. Yamada's task was to destroy Allied land-based air units operating out of Port Moresby and northern Australia. (Details of the preinvasion air strikes and the increasingly intense air combat over New Guinea will be discussed later—here it is sufficient to note the resources Yamada had at hand.) Base Air Force provided him with four air groups, one fighter, two bomber, and one reconnaissance, with an established strength of 45 fighters, 8 seaplane fighters, 81 medium bombers, and 18 flying boats—a total of 152 aircraft. As of 1 May, after all of Yamada's units had arrived, the 5th Air Attack Force had 24 fighters, 55 medium bombers, and 16 flying boats—a total of 95 aircraft. Only 73 of these were operational, including 18 fighters. The 5th Air Attack Force desperately needed the nine Zeroes to be air-ferried via MO Striking Force. The last of Yamada's reinforcements, 25 medium bombers, only arrived on 1 May.[14]

The last important points to consider regarding the planning for the MO Operation are the estimates of Allied strength made by South Seas Force and the other commands. The 23 April South Seas Force order specified that Tulagi had a small garrison, while Port Moresby had about 5,000 troops defending the place. Inoue rated the number of Allied aircraft in forward bases at about 200; this information he secured from American Army aviators captured on 18 April. He viewed the naval strength in the area at one battleship, two or three heavy cruisers, and light forces of the British Navy, while the Americans had "some ships in the area." He added, "Even though we are unable to determine the movements of the enemy carrier forces, it is not likely that powerful enemy forces are operating in this area."[15] Rear Admiral Goto's order, issued the same day, echoed these sentiments. It appears that these estimates were based on the assumption that the available American carriers were all committed to the Tokyo Raid, as the picket boat had identified three carriers. Only later when they had a chance to interrogate captured Army aviators, did the Japanese learn that only the *Enterprise* and the *Hornet* were on the raid, leaving the *Yorktown* and the *Saratoga* for use elsewhere. They erroneously believed that one of their submarines had sunk the *Lexington* in anuary 1942, not realizing that the *Saratoga* had sustained the amage and was still under repair.

Later in the month, certain commands entertained a different stimate of American strength in Australian waters. On 28 April Rear Admiral Takagi included in his operational orders that the British Navy had deployed one battleship, two heavy cruisers, four ight cruisers, ten or more destroyers, and several submarines in the region, while the U.S. Navy had one carrier, two or three heavy cruisers, and nine destroyers there, all apparently operating out of astern Australia or New Zealand. "It is not unlikely that the enemy might conduct their own operation against our South Seas Force operational area from the east or south,"[16] Elsewhere, intelligence reports stated the American carrier believed to be in the area was the *Saratoga*.[17]

The Japanese believed there was the possibility of encountering an enemy carrier force, but did not think it could be overwhelming considering the fact that two of the limited number of American carriers in the Pacific were already involved elsewhere and could not possibly arrive in time to interfere with the MO Operation. More importantly, Inoue and his planners counted on achieving surprise, forcing the Allies to react to the offensive and follow a series of preordained responses. Like the disastrous Midway Operation in June, success depended too much upon the enemy's closely following the Japanese script.

In launching the MO Operation, South Seas Force with the cooperation of Base Air Force, Advance Expeditionary Force, and the South Seas Detachment concentrated a total of three aircraft carriers, nine cruisers, fourteen destroyers, eight submarines, and 33 other ships, along with 282 aircraft of all types. The comprehensive plan envisioned the establishment of the Tulagi base before the convoy itself left Rabaul. Elements of the Tulagi Invasion Force and the Support Force were scheduled to leave Rabaul at the end of April and build seaplane bases at Shortland and Santa Isabell Islands in the Solomons. On 30 April, MO Main Force was to sail from Truk to cover the Tulagi landings, followed the next day by MO Striking Force. On 2 May, MO Striking Force would pass within 250 miles of Rabaul to ferry the nine Zeroes to the 5th Air Attack Force. Admiral Shima's naval infantry was to storm ashore at Tulagi during the predawn hours of 3 May, supported by aircraft from the *Shoho* and the seaplane bases. On 4 May flying boats would come down from Rabaul and begin operations from Tulagi. That same day, the Tulagi Attack Force was to disband.

With the capture of Tulagi, the MO Operation would enter second phase. MO Striking Force, proceeding down the easter flank of the Solomons, would provide air cover for the new Tulag base, while MO Main Force doubled back to the north to join th invasion convoy scheduled to sail that afternoon. The fifth of Ma was to see four submarines from the 8th Submarine Squadron a rive at their picket line across the direct route from Australia to th Coral Sea. Inoue hoped the submarines would spot Allied nava forces hurrying north from Brisbane and Sydney to counterattac the Tulagi landings. Two other submarines from the same uni were to conduct reconnaissance patrols, one off southern Australi and the other near Noumea. The same day, MO Striking Force wa to swing around the southern tip of the Solomons and enter th Coral Sea, making a wide sweep to the south to protect the seawar flank of the convoy. On 6 May Rear Admiral Marumo's Suppor Force was to rendezvous at Deboyne to construct a seaplane bas from which floatplanes would search to the south and cover the convoy as it traversed Jomard Passage the next day.

On 8 May Support Force was to build another seaplane base a Cape Rodney on the New Guinea coast to protect the convoy on its last leg to Port Moresby. On this day, MO Striking Force was to take station south of the Louisiades to be ready to destroy any attempt by the Allies to disrupt the invasion. They were to "prepare for the enemy," who would just be arriving according to Inoue's schedule. The tenth of May was to see the actual landings at Port Moresby, followed by the speedy capture of the place. Naval construction troops would repair the airfields and welcome the fighters of the 5th Air Attack Force, waiting at Lae for the signal to relocate at Port Moresby. On 12 May Support Force was to return to Samarai Island off the eastern tip of Papua and erect there a combination seaplane and supply base to protect the supply line to Port Moresby. Meanwhile the Ocean-Nauru (RY) Invasion Force under Shima would have sailed from Kavieng to seize those islands on 15 May. The RY Invasion Force would have the indirect support of MO Striking Force, streaking north after the capture of Port Moresby in order to reach Japan in time for the Midway Operation. On paper the MO Operation looked very easy, but there were factors of which the Japanese were unaware that would complicate matters greatly.

9
Opposition for the Port Moresby Operation

Someone was listening when Combined Fleet cut orders on 5 April assigning the carrier *Kaga* to Vice Admiral Inoue's South Seas Force for the MO Operation. This action meant that the *Kaga* would be a message addressee for communications concerning the MO Operation, messages passing between Combined Fleet and South Seas Force. Within a day or two, some of these messages were received at the 14th Naval District's radio intercept station at Wailupe in Hawaii. The station monitored Japanese fleet radio traffic and sent transcripts of some messages to the Combat Intelligence Unit, 14th Naval District at Pearl Harbor. Commanded by Lieutenant Commander Joseph J. Rochefort, the unit, whose title "Combat Intelligence Unit" was a misnomer, actually concentrated on analysis of Japanese naval radio traffic and naval coded messages. The unit, code name Hypo, soon noted a connection between the *Kaga* and South Seas Force. This was unusual because the *Kaga* was ordinarily part of Striking Force. They forwarded their traffic analysis and texts of deciphered messages to the Pacific Fleet staff, where it came to the attention of Lieutenant Commander Edwin T. Layton, Fleet Intelligence Officer. Layton noted on 9 April in the Pacific Fleet war diary that the *Kaga*, then believed to be at Sasebo

Naval Base in Japan, was expected to reach the New Britain area at the end of April.[18]

United States naval radio intelligence provided a tremendou advantage for the strategic planning of the Pacific Fleet.[19] In 194 there were three centers analyzing Japanese radio traffic, and the exchanged pertinent data to aid each other in traffic analysis, cal sign recoveries, and deciphering Japanese messages. In Washingtor Commander Laurence J. Safford ran Section G, "Communicatior Security Section" (code name Negat), within the Office of Nav; Communications under the Chief of Naval Operations (OpNav) In Hawaii, Rochefort's Hypo section provided intercepts for Pear Harbor, while another office, code name Belconnen, functioned ir Melbourne. Belconnen was the former station Cast which had transferred in early 1942 from Corregidor to Australia. All three sections worked on the basic Japanese fleet cryptographic system "JN-25" as the Americans called it. JN-25 was the most widely used system for high-level communications in the Imperial Navy about half of the messages sent utilized it.[20]

In the spring of 1942, the American naval cryptanalysts coulc not read all of a message sent with the JN-25 system, or even mos of the text. Nor could they even analyze more than a fraction o: the many thousands of communications transmitted by the Imperial Navy in any one day. What they were able to do mostly was rec ognize associations, realizing that one call sign represented a specific unit and tying that unit to another through the fact that they were mutual message addressees. Although they had deduced the meaning of some code groups, they could rarely read more than 10 to 15 percent of most messages. As April wore on, the cryptanalysts found they could decipher more and more of what they analyzed. The Japanese had used what the Americans called the "JN-25b" version for many months, giving the cryptanalysts more time than usual to work on it. The Japanese had scheduled a change in code for 1 April, but postponed it for a month. Had they gone over to the new variant, it would have left the cryptanalysts in the dark for many weeks. Even more unfortunate for the Japanese was that they decided to delay the 1 May scheduled change until 1 June, allowing the cryptanalysts to stay tuned into their coded messages.[21]

It is hard for one not intimately involved with the problem to fathom the difficulties under which the cryptanalysts and intelli gence officers worked to determine correctly the meaning of inter cepted messages. Even in May, the Americans copied only about 60 percent of Japanese naval transmissions, and of these only about 40 percent could be analyzed because of the lack of time and qualied personnel.[22] It is true that as knowledge of the meanings of individual code groups increased, more of the contents of decrypted messages or "decripts" became known. A message, however, which might have been as much as 80 percent complete in total words very often had blanks in places important with respect to grammar or subject, because the meaning of those code groups remained unknown. This problem made the correct analysis of the message contingent upon interpretation by skilled analysts.[23] Deciphering the Japanese naval cryptographic system and providing accurate and usable intelligence regarding enemy plans were far from the automatic and easy procedures depicted in some works.

The intelligence officers and cryptanalysts worked together to evaluate the texts of decrypted messages. From there, the intelligence officers of the various commands combined radio intelligence with combat intelligence information to produce a balanced estimate. Most important for the Pacific was CinCPac Fleet Intelligence under Lieutenant Commander Layton. Layton supplied information on enemy forces and possible intentions, for use by War Plans to compile their situation estimates. Each day, he composed a summary of pertinent intelligence data, entitled "CINCPAC Intelligence Bulletin," sent by radio to the commands involved.[24] These included ComInCh, OpNav, all CinCPac task force commanders, the Australian and New Zealand naval boards, Vice Admiral Leary's ComSoWesPacFor, the commander of the British Eastern Fleet based in the Indian Ocean, and the U.S. Special Liaison Officer stationed in London for cooperation with the Admiralty. Leary's ComSoWesPacFor also provided valuable intelligence summaries based on data from the Belconnen station and aircraft sightings. The Office of Naval Intelligence under OpNav broadcast general information on estimated Japanese fleet movements and forthcoming operations. Occasionally the urgent or special nature of intelligence information required that Nimitz's and Leary's intelligence officers send specific despatches to task force commanders for their immediate action. This occurred many times, as CinCPac and ComSoWesPacFor Intelligence provided information of great value to Rear Admiral Fletcher and later Vice Admiral Halsey in the South Pacific.

The knowledge that the *Kaga* was to sail at the end of April to the New Britain area provided the first concrete indication that the Japanese were planning offensive action in the South Pacific.

For over two months, Allied planners had been aware of Japane interest in the New Guinea–Solomons area. On 5 March, for e ample, the Australian staff noted the imminence of an offensi against Port Moresby, estimating that there were two or three ca riers plus an Army division in the Rabaul area ready for an oper tion.[25] Likewise, on 3 April the Pacific Fleet war diary deduce that, "The Japs are now in a position to strike Port Moresby an Tulagi simultaneously—a division is available for seaborne attack."[] Intercepted messages deciphered in part toward the end of Marc noted a build-up of air strength at Rabaul, no doubt catchin glimpses of the impending organization of the 25th Air Flotilla a Rabaul. Intelligence had determined from scattered decrypts an British combat intelligence that the majority of Japan's carrie forces, estimated correctly on 10 April as numbering six carriers had steamed into the Bay of Bengal to raid Ceylon. The staff de duced that it would be several weeks before any of them would b available for service with South Seas Force. On 10 April the *Grey book* noted that two carriers, the *Kaga* and the light carrie *Ryukaku*, could be used for offensive operations. The *Ryukakι* was an incorrect transliteration of the Japanese ideographs for th name *Shoho*. The Americans continued to mislabel the *Shoho* witl the name *Ryukaku* until after Midway.[27]

In early April, Admiral Nimitz had only one carrier task force at sea, Rear Admiral Fletcher's Task Force 17 with the *Yorktown* sailing in the eastern Coral Sea. Task Force 11 with the *Lexington* had arrived on 26 March at Pearl Harbor. The *Lexington* entered the yards for refit and would be docked until 15 April. On 3 April Rear Admiral Fitch relieved Vice Admiral Brown as commander of Task Force 11. Brown departed to San Diego to assume command of the Pacific Fleet's Amphibious Force. Vice Admiral Halsey's Task Force 16 with the *Enterprise* was at Pearl Harbor for the time being. Nimitz awaited reinforcements in the form of Captain Marc A. Mitscher's new carrier, the *Hornet*, organized with small screening force as Task Force 18. Mitscher was expected to sail in the first week of April from the West Coast. With regard to carrier deployment for April, Nimitz intended that Task Force 17 remain in the South Pacific. He anticipated obtaining direct control over Fletcher from ComInCh as specified in the reorganization of the Pacific Area. On 14 April Nimitz informed Fletcher that he had taken over command of the South Pacific Area and ordered Task Force 17 to sail to Tongatabu for refurbishment, expecting Fletcher to reach there about 19 or 20 April.[28] Fletcher was to depart Tongatabu on 27 April to head to the Coral Sea once more. On 2 April

78

he staff had deliberated about whether Task Force 11 should join letcher in the South Pacific or train with Task Force 1, the old attleships, south of Hawaii. Nimitz felt inclined to send the *Lexington* back down to the South Pacific, but decided to retain the carrier in the Hawaiian area for the time being. On 10 April he instructed Fitch to sail on 15 April from Pearl Harbor and exercise with the old battleships in the vicinity of Palmyra until 4 May, when the battleships would return to Pearl Harbor.[29]

CinCPac was not responsible for determining the activities of the *Enterprise* and the *Hornet* for the month of April. In January 942, Admiral King and his staff decided to "pull off a really spectacular diversionary raid on Japan."[30] In consultation with Lieutenant General Arnold, King decided to attack Tokyo and other Japanese cities with Army B-25 medium bombers flown off the deck of the carrier *Hornet*. The *Hornet* loaded sixteen B-25's of the 17th Bombardment Group (Medium) under the command of Lieutenant Colonel James H. Doolittle. The *Enterprise* with Vice Admiral Halsey would accompany in support of the raiding force. The two task forces met on 13 April in the North Pacific with Halsey incorporating the *Hornet* into Task Force 16. He planned to launch the bombers on the afternoon of 18 April at a distance of 450 miles from the target for a night attack on Japan. The bombers were to hit their objectives and proceed on to China. King and the president, who personally approved of the plan, conceived the Tokyo Raid as a diversion, but one which would greatly raise the morale of the American people. The Navy knew through radio and combat intelligence that almost all of the Japanese carriers were still far to the south of Japan and not likely to be a factor. As Nimitz would come to see, however, the raid tied up one-half of his carrier strength when it was badly needed elsewhere. It would be the last day of April before Task Force 16 would be able to clear Pearl Harbor and embark on a new operation.

On 15 April the Pacific Fleet learned that two more Japanese carriers were scheduled to participate in operations south of Truk. OP-20-G, Safford's Negat office in Washington, analyzed Hara's 13 April message to Inoue stating that 5th Carrier Division would proceed to Formosa on 18 April and depart ten days later for Truk. The American cryptanalysts recovered the message almost in full, but informed King and Nimitz that 5th Carrier Division would arrive at Truk on 28 April. The *Greybook* added that "an offensive in the Southwest Pacific is shaping up."[31] Throughout the early weeks of April, more deciphered intercepts indicated the continuing concentration of Japanese air power and shipping at Rabaul. On

11 April Vice Admiral Leary's headquarters estimated that th
Japanese offensive might begin as early as 21 April, this on th
basis of a decript detailing the assignment of nine auxiliary vesse
to Rabaul. The Pacific Fleet staff as well as King's planners i
Washington thought this was too early, based on the schedule c
known enemy carrier movements.[32]

Admiral Nimitz and his staff conferred on 17 April to examin
the situation in detail. A number of signs pointed without doub
to a Japanese offensive south of Rabaul to begin at the end o
April. First of all there was the wholesale withdrawal of Japanes
fleet units, including all of the carriers from the Bay of Bengal
freeing Striking Force for new operations. According to deciphere
enemy radio traffic, the Japanese apparently had allocated fou
carriers, the *Kaga,* the *Shoho,* the *Shokaku,* and the *Zuikaku* to th
crucial area, with a fifth, the converted carrier *Kasuga Maru,* t
become available on 23 April, according to one decript. Also, ai
operations in the area were slowly intensifying, with the Japanes
executing regular air strikes on Port Moresby. There was no definit
mention in the radio intelligence items of the ultimate Japanes
objective. There was little doubt, though, that the Japanese woul
center their offensive operations in the first stage at least aroun
the capture of Port Moresby.[33]

CinCPac quickly determined that he would oppose any Japa
nese attempt on Port Moresby, but it was a question of the avail
ability of forces. The fact that the operation might start at the end
of April worried Nimitz. "We are trying to get together a force to
oppose. Task Force 17 will be ready; Task Force 11 and Task Force
16 are otherwise committed."[34] It appears that Admiral Nimitz
deferred making the final decision on the movements of Task Force
11 until the completion of the Tokyo Raid. No matter what, Nimitz
was determined to stop the Japanese advance on Port Moresby.

By dawn on 18 April, Task Force 16 had reached a point almost
700 miles east of Tokyo, when a Japanese picket boat spotted them
and reported three enemy carriers. Halsey decided to launch im
mediately with Doolittle's concurrence. At mid-morning the sixteen
B-25 bombers headed toward Japan, while Task Force 16 began a
high-speed retreat. The Japanese were alerted, but expected that
the enemy carriers would close to about 200 miles from the coast,
normal carrier plane range, before launching strike planes. Con
sequently they were surprised in early afternoon to see the B-25's
streaking in at low level. Imperial General Headquarters, as related
before, ordered a large-scale pursuit of the raiders. From Japan
came elements of Vice Admiral Kondo's Second Fleet, while far

uth of Kyushu Vice Admiral Nagumo's Striking Force, returning
Japan, received orders to head east at high speed to overtake the
iders. Several units intended for the MO Operation became in-
olved in the pursuit as well. The Japanese called off their chase
vo days later when it became evident that their quarry was far
ut of range.

The day after the Tokyo Raid, Nimitz and the staff considered
ue situation once more. From the initial radio intercepts it was
vident that the Japanese were using powerful forces to try to de-
roy Task Force 16. Hopefully the raid would tie up important
nits and delay the Japanese offensive a few days. In a message
hich arrived that day, Admiral King warned of a Japanese offen-
ve against Port Moresby which would start during the first week
f May. Because of the delay to the Japanese caused by the raid,
Iimitz agreed with the schedule. He ordered Task Force 11 to
ead south, and the next day specifically told Fitch to prepare for
perations in the South Pacific.[35]

The greatest benefit of the Tokyo Raid would appear to be the
vealth of radio intelligence garnered from the many orders sent by
Tokyo to mass the pursuit forces. The intelligence personnel were
leased to see that the Japanese ships were just about where they
stimated them to be. Intelligence officers like Lieutenant Com-
nander Layton knew the value of radio intelligence and how ac-
urate their estimates were because of it, but others had to be per-
uaded. After the Tokyo Raid many facts regarding Japanese order
f battle began falling into place, particularly submarine deploy-
nent. Deciphered messages from Japan confirmed that the *Shoho*
ind the 5th Cruiser Division would arrive at Truk around 25
\pril. Intercepts also showed that the Eleventh Air Fleet/Base Air
Force headquarters was involved, which, according to the Pacific
Fleet war diary, "indicates thorough preparations for the Southeast
Area operations."[36]

Admiral Nimitz met with his staff on 20 April to plan for
operations in the South Pacific, and by 22 April produced a detailed
estimate of the situation.[37] The estimate noted that a Japanese
offensive in the New Guinea–New Britain–Solomons area would
begin about 3 May. The problem was "how to deal with the offensive and still carry out assigned tasks." Such tasks included as of
prime importance the security of Hawaii and the line of communication with the West Coast. "Only barely less important," however,
was the need to maintain communications between the United
States and Australia. ComInCh's increasing concern for the area
had finally made itself felt on CinCPac. Another mission assigned

to the Pacific Fleet was to support the Southwest Pacific Area, a that, the estimate emphasized, certainly applied in the current situ tion. As for the involvement of the Pacific Fleet, "It is inferred th ComInCh intends to employ large Pacific Fleet forces in the sol tion of this problem."[38]

The estimate indicated that ultimate Japanese strength to committed to South Pacific offensives was not yet known. As of April, the planners believed that at least five carriers, the *Shokak* the *Zuikaku*, the *Shoho*, the *Kasuga Maru*, and the *Kaga*, wou eventually be involved, with additional indications that Vice A miral Nagumo with his flagship *Akagi* might also participate late One battleship appeared to be allocated to the operation, wit another probably accompanying, as the planners remarked that th Japanese invariably operated their battleships in pairs. Five heav cruisers with the usual light forces, light cruisers and destroyer were thought to be en route to the area. As for ground forces in th Port Moresby attack, the estimate was rather vague. The Pacifi Fleet planners thought the Japanese would use enough to do th job, estimating that perhaps 20,000 men, a reinforced division would likely take part in the expedition.

Regarding Japanese intentions, the planners knew there was t be a concentration at Truk with operations to the south of there "Will it only be for Moresby or Moresby and the Solomons at thi time or will a direct advance to Noumea or Suva be attempted?"[3] The staff thought that in the light of previous Japanese amphibiou operations the enemy would settle for Port Moresby and points i the Solomons as the first wave of a probably widespread Soutl Pacific offensive, because the Japanese much preferred a step-by-step advance with each increment supported by their own land-based aircraft. This did not preclude carrier raids on New Caledonia o Fiji or perhaps more distant locales. The planners warned against possible Japanese attempts to interfere with the landings of Ameri- can troops at Efate, Tongatabu, and Samoa later in May. It was not certain how the Japanese would deploy their carrier strength, but the planners doubted that they would put them all in the first wave. Rather, they thought the Japanese would hold some in sup- port to intervene if the main thrusts were blunted.

In dealing with the Japanese offensive, the obvious solution was the commitment of the "full strength of the Pacific Fleet." There were a number of factors militating against this course of action. The heart of the attack power of the Pacific Fleet lay in four carriers and seven old battleships available at the end of April.

ere was no way the old battleships could be used in the South
cific. There were not sufficient bases there to support the opera-
ns of battleships, and the fleet oilers would not be able to pro-
le them with sufficient fuel. Nimitz was not sure they could be
eful, as they were slower than the carriers and would hinder their
erations if attached as a screen. The battleships in turn could not
erate alone under the threat of Japanese air power, as they re-
ired close fighter support. Even more elemental was the fact that
e Pacific Fleet did not possess enough destroyers to screen both
e battleships and the carriers in combat. There was a great dearth
destroyers which affected adversely many operations. Because of
el considerations, the lack of screening vessels, and their own vul-
erability to attack, Nimitz felt compelled to recommend that the
d battleships, sailing as Task Force 1 near Christmas Island, re-
rn to the West Coast. Pearl Harbor was still too exposed for their
fety, and fleet logistics could not provide the fuel oil from the
ocks on Oahu necessary to support them at sea. The strategic de-
loyment of the old battleships would probably have been the same
en if none of them had been damaged in the Pearl Harbor attack.
here was no way at present that they could be utilized in the
rucial area in the South Pacific.

Thus the carriers were the key means available to the Pacific
leet for repulsing the Japanese offensive in the South Pacific. At
he present time, Nimitz had one carrier in the Coral Sea area, the
orktown in Fletcher's Task Force 17. Fletcher had been at sea
ince the middle of February and his ships soon would require
pkeep and normal refitting at Pearl Harbor. Fitch's Task Force 11,
lready south of Pearl Harbor, could join Task Force 17 around 1
May northwest of New Caledonia. Because Fletcher would ordi-
arily have to return to Pearl Harbor before the end of May, this
would leave only the *Lexington* in the South Pacific after the middle of the month. The *Lexington* was clearly unable to deal with
the expected five or six Japanese carriers which would eventually
be committed to the South Pacific. Thus Nimitz would have to send
as reinforcements at least one carrier from Task Force 16 to join
Task Force 11 after the departure of Task Force 17. The planners
decided that leaving one of Halsey's carriers at Pearl Harbor would
be a waste of resources. It was not justified in terms of passive defense, given CinCPac's knowledge of Japanese intentions. Neither
could one carrier any longer comprise a striking force to make an
effective diversionary raid on Japanese island positions. Besides, in
the light of the decrypts indicating Japanese movements: "Nothing

appears to be making for Hawaii yet. Other demands do not appe
very strong, so we may find a force in the Southwest even larg
than listed."[40]

Nimitz and his planners decided to commit all four of the ava
able carriers, representing about 300 combat aircraft, in the Sou
Pacific to oppose the Japanese advance on Port Moresby and oth
strategic locations in the South Pacific. Task Force 11 could jo
Task Force 17 in early May in the Coral Sea and operate togeth
against the first impulse of the expected Japanese offensive, th
attempt to take Port Moresby. The planners expected Halsey
Task Force 16 to arrive at Pearl Harbor on 25 April and cle
harbor around the end of the month. Depending on what Halse
did on his trip south, Task Force 16 with the *Enterprise* and th
Hornet could rendezvous with Fletcher in the Coral Sea aroun
14 to 16 May. This would give Halsey as the senior commander
massive concentration of four fleet carriers to deal with five to si
Japanese carriers. According to tentative fuel schedules appende
to the situation estimate, CinCPac's seven fleet oilers could suppo
the four carriers and their screens in the South Pacific until aroun
1 June. Any longer time would force Nimitz to divert to Fiji an
Samoa chartered commercial tankers carrying fuel to Oahu fror
the West Coast. Because of stocks at Oahu, the fleet logistics office
thought that this plan was acceptable. Stores ships and supplie
loaded on the fleet tankers could reprovision the task forces. Barrin
sinkings of fleet oilers, CinCPac could keep the four task forces i
the South Pacific almost indefinitely, provided that he did no
operate the old battleships at sea or out of Pearl Harbor.

In the 22 April situation estimate, CinCPac set the basis for hi
forthcoming campaign in the South Pacific and operations else
where. The prime decision was to send three carriers south to rein
force Task Force 17 in the Coral Sea. Halsey's Task Force 16 wa
to proceed to the area as soon as possible, fight together with Tasl
Forces 17 and 11, and then relieve those forces in the area. Tc
support the operations of the carriers, Nimitz planned to double
the number of PBY flying boats at Noumea to 12 by flying down
the required aircraft from Hawaii. Leary's ComSoWesPacFor controlled submarine patrols in the Rabaul area, but Nimitz sought
to place by the middle of May about five submarines from the
Pacific Fleet in the Truk area. Regarding the old battleships,
Nimitz arranged to have Task Force 1 arrive at San Francisco
around 2 May. As a diversion and also to attack a valuable Japanese economic resource, a light cruiser from the Pacific Fleet was to
leave Pearl Harbor around 2 May, stop off at Midway, and proceed

the Japanese fishing grounds off Kamchatka to destroy fishing boats. The light cruiser would also conduct radio deception, possibly mimicking the presence of a carrier task force. The light cruiser *Nashville* was chosen for the raid. The ship proceeded to Midway, but ran aground there, damaging the hull, and had to return to Pearl Harbor. After that the idea of a raid on the Japanese Siberian fisheries was canceled.[41]

The 22 April situation estimate is remarkable for a number of reasons, but mainly because it represented the ultimate change in Pacific Fleet strategy regarding the protection of Australia. Admiral Nimitz proposed to use all of the carriers currently available to him to meet a Japanese offensive against Port Moresby, nearly 4,000 miles southwest of Oahu. This was in contrast to the previous procedure of retaining at least one-third of the Pacific Fleet's carrier strength in the Central Pacific. Nimitz expected that Port Moresby would be the first, but not the only Japanese target in the South Pacific. Clearly a major enemy effort in the region was imminent, and Nimitz wanted to deal with it to protect key locations in the area as outlined in his basic directive from ComInCh. Because of the magnitude of the estimated enemy strength, Nimitz felt he had to commit all of his carrier task forces in order to have enough to do the job.

It was not merely for defensive reasons that Nimitz sought to do battle with the Japanese in the South Pacific. The enemy would presumably commit most of his carrier forces to this offensive, and Nimitz was fully aware that the Combined Fleet would rise or fall on the fortunes of its carriers. He wanted to inflict attrition upon the enemy carriers through any reasonable fashion. Since January 1942, the Japanese had employed their carriers in the ABDA Area or in the Indian Ocean, not where the Pacific Fleet could get at them. Indeed, Nimitz could send his forces against a vital Japanese sector, and that would draw them out into battle. The subsequent engagement, however, would have taken place under circumstances favorable to the enemy, and that was not Nimitz's way. He wanted to engage the Japanese carriers under circumstances which would afford the Pacific Fleet some advantages, allowing him to use the principle of "calculated risk" in battle. In the Southwest Pacific the Japanese would for the first time encounter a fairly strong land-based air force operating in conjunction with powerful carrier forces. For the Japanese to attack Port Moresby and the Solomons or raid New Caledonia and Fiji, they would have to expose their carriers to some sort of counterattack, whether it be from carrier aircraft, land-based air units, warships, or submarines, whatever circumstances were open to an opportunistic commander. Considering that the enemy's objectives appeared to be so widespread, there w always the chance of finding an isolated Japanese force and d stroying it.

Nimitz saw there could easily be a disparity in actual numbe between his own four carriers and the Japanese carriers which coul eventually number five, six, or even more flattops. He knew, hov ever, that the Japanese usually carried fewer aircraft on their ca riers than did the Americans. Nimitz analyzed the strengths an weaknesses of both sides, taking due account of the proficiency (the Japanese in air operations, especially carrier operations. H felt though that committing his carrier forces to battle was we within the realm of calculated risk inherent even under the mos favorable circumstances. "Because of our superior personnel in r(sourcefulness and initiative, and the undoubted superiority of muc of our equipment, we should be able to accept odds in battle i necessary."[42] Nimitz's plans were not formulated in desperatior but rather in quiet confidence over the ability of his forces to de feat the Japanese despite being outnumbered. Thus his major ob jective was to use the South Pacific battles to sink or damage heavil the carriers of the Japanese Striking Force, thereby taking the ini tiative away from the Japanese. Admiral Nimitz and his Pacifi(Fleet were far more aggressive-minded and eager to come to grip with the Japanese carrier forces than they are generally believed t(have been.

Thus CinCPac had definite strategic reasons for sending all four carriers down to the South Pacific. It was not just to apply overwhelming strength against Japanese attempts to capture Por Moresby and the Solomons. Vice Admiral Halsey did not hurry down to the Coral Sea on the "very slim chance"[43] that he might make it in time to help Rear Admiral Fletcher deal with a weaker force of two Japanese fleet carriers and one light carrier. Nor did Nimitz intend the defense of Port Moresby as a quick prelude to countering the more deadly Japanese offensive against Midway, which some authors have indicated that he knew about on 1 May, one day after Task Force 16 sailed from Pearl Harbor:

> May Day 1942 was anything but cheerful for Admiral Nimitz. Coral
> Sea was on his hands and something nasty was cooking for the
> Central Pacific; but he figured that there was time to stop the enemy
> in the south before deploying to defend the Hawaiian chain.[44]

The above quote implies altogether too much knowledge to Nimitz of Japanese intentions. As will be shown, Nimitz did not learn of e impending Midway offensive until several days after the Battle the Coral Sea. Nimitz meant the Coral Sea to be so much more an merely a strategic check for one Japanese advance. It was, to m, an opportunity to begin to hit the Japanese so hard that he uld assume the initiative. It failed because the Japanese did not mmit the bulk of their carriers to the Coral Sea. However, imitz's expectations were fulfilled under the similar circumstances Midway in June, when the Japanese did come out in great rength and suffered defeat under what only could be described as nique circumstances.

During the period in which the staff compiled the 22 April stimate, Nimitz ordered Fitch's Task Force 11 to join Task Force 7 on 1 May near Noumea. On 24 April Nimitz informed Fletcher t Tongatabu of the forces that would be allocated to him for the oming operation. Under his direct command would be the old NZAC Squadron, now Task Force 44 under Rear Admiral Crace, oyal Navy. It comprised two heavy cruisers, one light cruiser, and wo destroyers. He also told Fletcher that the patrol planes at Joumea would soon be doubled to 12 and would soon come under is command. The next day, CinCPac told Fletcher of plans to uel his forces, adding that it was not definite but possible that Task orce 17 might leave for Pearl Harbor around 15 May. However, he message also indicated that CinCPac was diverting the chartered ankers to Samoa to establish there a fueling base, pointing to the act that Nimitz was preparing for possible extended operations by is carrier forces in the South Pacific.[45]

On 25 April Nimitz traveled to San Francisco to meet with Admiral King. They discussed CinCPac's general plan for concentrating in the South Pacific forces to number four carriers, nine heavy cruisers, and 21 destroyers from the Pacific Fleet. King certainly favored the idea of hitting the Japanese hard as soon as possible. Indeed, he brought to Nimitz's attention "the desirability of ridding Pearl Harbor of pessimists and defeatists."[46] In approving Nimitz's plans for the South Pacific, King went further, ordering him to retain in the South Pacific a force at least as strong as Task Force 16 until further notice. This meant two carriers with suitable escorts. King brought up the question of security for Midway and the Central Pacific, given the intention of CinCPac of concentrating his striking force in the South Pacific. He inquired about the strength of the Midway garrison and recommended that it be reinforced. The two talked of the command situation for the South Pacific. Nimitz nominated and King approved of Vice Admiral Robert L. Ghormley as the Commander, South Pacific Area (ComSoPac). Ghormley was in Washington and could not possibly arrive in time to exerci effective command during the current crisis. King directed Nimi to retain direct command of the South Pacific Area until the pre ent operation had concluded.

Other topics touched upon during the meeting included rad intelligence. King and Nimitz discussed the value of radio intell gence and the need to watch their own security in this regard. S far as they knew, their own cryptographic systems were safe for th time being, and they were correct. King outlined his plans to us Tongatabu as an advanced base in preference to Samoa, Fiji, an New Caledonia, all of which he considered too exposed. Regardin fleet organization, the two noted that by early June there would b five carriers in the Pacific Fleet, counting the *Saratoga*. They de cided the best way to handle the matter was to have a flag office for each carrier, that is, five carrier task forces, but to operate thei in pairs as the preferred stength. The meetings lasted until 2 April, when King returned to Washington, and Nimitz flew bac to Oahu. The ComInCh staff the next day sent messages to Pear Harbor outlining as orders what King approved during the meeting

With the return of Admiral Nimitz on 28 April, the Pacifi Fleet finally had full approval of the plan mapped out on 22 April The staff drew up CinCPac Operation Plan No. 23-42, dated 2! April.[47] The plan sketched the situation much as in the 22 Apri estimate, but there were a few new bits of radio intelligence gar nered from recent decrypts. The Hypo unit had secured some refer ences in Japanese messages to the Ocean and Nauru Operation indicating a possible change in direction from the south to the southeast. The *Greybook* on 28 April called this "wishful thinking," but it did serve to highlight Japanese interest in the Ocean-Nauru Gilberts area. Hypo also learned of the operational connection be tween Fourth Fleet and the 5th Carrier and 5th Cruiser Divisions, which led to the speculation that these units might comprise part of a combined task force. From the addressees in an intercepted message, Hypo noted the existence of the MO Fleet, MO Occupa tion Force, Support Force, and the "RZP Occupation Force." Hypo could not identify the location of "RZP," but it indicated an addi tional objective for the Japanese, probably in the Solomons. RZP was actually the Japanese code name for Tulagi.[48]

On the basis of the latest intelligence information, Operation Plan 23-42 described a Japanese offensive to start in the first days of May against Port Moresby, points in the Solomon Islands, and the Gilbert Islands, the latter to include Ocean and Nauru islands. In addition to this, CinCPac expected the Japanese to make strong raids on New Caledonia and Fiji. The basic premise upon which CinCPac's participation was based specified that Task Forces 17 and 11 would join for operations in the Coral Sea, to be followed by the arrival of Task Force 16 in the South Pacific. Depending on the situation, CinCPac would withdraw Task Force 17 about 15 May and Task Force 11 around 1 June to return to Hawaii. The order instructed Halsey as senior carrier commander to "check further advance of the enemy in the New Guinea–Solomon area by destroying enemy ships, shipping and aircraft."[49] Task Force 16 was to sail from Pearl Harbor on 30 April. The heavy cruiser *Pensacola* and a destroyer would follow as soon as they were ready to sail. On board the two carriers was a Marine fighter squadron which Halsey was to ferry to Efate. On the southern passage, Halsey had orders to conduct air reconnaissances of Howland and Baker islands because of recent Japanese interest in that area. He was also to prepare to attack Japanese shipping in the Gilberts-Ocean-Nauru area if an exceptionally favorable opportunity presented itself. The main force of Task Force 16 comprised two fleet carriers with about 155 combat aircraft, three heavy cruisers, seven destroyers, and two fleet tankers. Sailing in early May to join Halsey in addition to the *Pensacola* and her escorting destroyer were one light antiaircraft cruiser (the *Atlanta*), one destroyer, and two fleet tankers.

It would be useful to give a brief statement on the strength of the important island bases in the South Pacific as they were in early May.[50] New Caledonia (code name Poppy) had as its garrison a reinforced division of 22,000 men under Major General Alexander M. Patch. Patch's force was an ad hoc grouping of troops soon to be named the "Americal Division." The island had the AAF's 67th Pursuit Squadron with about 30 fighters. At Noumea there were six PBY flying boats served from the seaplane tender *Tangier*. It appears the Japanese were not aware of the American base on Efate in the lower New Hebrides. The extremely malarial island, code name euphemistically Roses, had as a ground garrison a Marine defense battalion and two Army infantry companies. Seabees worked on the island's airfield, but as Vice Admiral Halsey would discover, it could not yet handle aircraft. The Fijis (code name Fantan) had as its garrison the 3rd New Zealand Division of about 13,000 men, with an air contingent of 24 Royal New Zealand Air Force patrol planes. The only fighters based in the islands were 25 AAF aircraft of the 70th Pursuit Squadron.

New Caledonia, Efate, and Fiji were the most likely points for the Japanese to raid, but the two second line bases in SoPac were also in some danger. Tongatabu (code name Bleacher) in the Tonga group served as a convenient location for Task Force 17 to reprovision from supply ships. As of yet no American troops were ashore there, but a convoy carrying a reinforced infantry regiment was to arrive around 9 May, followed a week later by an AAF pursuit squadron from Australia. Samoa (code name Straw) was the major American base in the South Pacific and had as a garrison the 2nd Marine Brigade and two Marine defense battalions. Scheduled to reach the islands on 8 May was a convoy carrying the 3rd Marine Brigade. In contrast to the ground forces, the air defense of the islands was weak, only one Marine fighter squadron. Twelve obsolescent Marine dive bombers were to arrive with the 8 May convoy. As can be seen, the forward island bases in SoPac had nowhere the air strength to interfere seriously with a Japanese carrier raid. The defense of the South Pacific rested squarely on the carriers of the Pacific Fleet.

On 30 April and 1 May, more important radio intercepts were processed through Hypo. The American analysts discovered the Japanese planned to construct a base at Deboyne on X-5 day, while other bases were to appear at Samarai Island and Cape Rodney in eastern New Guinea.[51] That cinched Port Moresby as the ultimate objective. They also intercepted the order from Vice Admiral Inoue to Rear Admiral Takagi canceling air strikes on Townsville and Cooktown in Australia. Unfortunately Hypo could not fully decipher the code groups and thought Inoue was ordering rather than calling off the air attacks. In general, Hypo noted the imminence of active operations in the Rabaul area because of the many messages labeled "urgent" in Fourth Fleet radio traffic.[52]

Lieutenant Commander Rochefort on 1 May provided in response to an inquiry from Washington a comprehensive estimate entitled, "HYPO's Evaluation of the Picture in the Pacific."[53] The message went to OpNav, probably Commander Safford's Negat office. Rochefort noted the wholesale retirement of Japanese fleet units from the Bay of Bengal and the quieting down of activities in that area. He could see no indications of offensive movements from the Netherlands East Indies either, thus contradicting British fears of continued Japanese attacks in the Indian Ocean. Rochefort went on to sketch the development of the MO Operation, suggesting that MO stood for Moresby. Fourth Fleet commander was in charge of the operation, according to Hypo, using 5th Carrier Division, 5th Cruiser Division, other units, and the 5th Air Attack Force as well. He indicated his personal opinion that despite the Townsville message, the Japanese would not attack Australia at present.

The most interesting portion of Rochefort's analysis concerned his forecast for the second phase of the Japanese offensive. He thought Combined Fleet had the following forces available in Japan for immediate operations: 1st and 2nd Battleship Divisions, 4th and 6th Cruiser Divisions, and the carriers *Kaga* and *Soryu*. The other carriers were in the yards on a two or three days' sailing notice. Rochefort believed that all or most of the above named units "will cover MO Campaign with possible raids on Samoa and Suva areas."[54] From intercepted radio traffic, he knew that the Japanese were interested in the Palmyra, Samoa, Canton Island, and Hawaiian areas, with actual reconnaissances of Howland and Baker islands. He thought that the Aleutian Islands might come in for a raid sometime in the future. "Best indication of future operations is Tokyo office which assigns place name designators. Last January this office listed places in Aleutians, indicating they were areas of forthcoming operations." Rochefort listed the Aleutians as the second choice of objectives for the forces available in Japan. However, "This is considered unlikely at this time, but certainly probably at a later date."[55] Thus Rochefort placed his emphasis on Japanese operations squarely in the South Pacific, especially against the island bases guarding the line of communication to Australia. As of yet, there was no indication that the Japanese were planning a Central Pacific offensive.

Plans Division of the Pacific Fleet staff noted on 1 May in their *Greybook* the general scenario of attacks on Port Moresby and the Solomons, strikes on northeastern Australia, and possible raids on Efate, Noumea, Fiji, and Samoa. In addition, they felt there was at least a remote possibility for a raid in the North or Central Pacific. "All positions as far east as Pearl Harbor may possibly be recipients of a raid. However it appears that the general known location of Japanese forces today preclude anything which threaten our positions or general security." The diarist mused that a "small raid on Oahu, for example, might benefit our ultimate position more than it would Japan."[56] He thought the threat would help CinCPac squeeze more land-based aircraft out of the Army, noting that on 1 May there were only sixteen B-17 heavy bombers flyable in Hawaii. He later probably thought the Japanese were overdoing it a bit when he learned of their plans for the Midway Operation!

10
The Southwest Pacific Area Prepares for the Port Moresby Offensive

On 18 April, just as definite knowledge of Japanese intentions for a Port Moresby offensive emerged, General MacArthur assumed formal command of the Southwest Pacific Area. The Australian chiefs of staff long recognized the importance of Port Moresby, but apparently were not sure it could be held in the face of strong attack. The garrison received orders in February to hold out "as long as possible," in order to inflict as heavy casualties on the enemy as possible.[57] On 4 April an Australian staff study stressed that the crucial point of the defense of Australia lay in Port Moresby; if it fell, the whole eastern coast of Australia would be exposed.[58]

Despite its acknowledged importance, Port Moresby had for a garrison only the Australian 30th Brigade Group (Major General B. M. Morris) with three infantry battalions and several artillery batteries. In the middle of April, the Australian Army at home numbered two first-line divisions (Australian Imperial Forces or AIF), an armored division, and eight second-line militia divisions. The brigade at Port Moresby was also a militia unit. There were also two regiments of the U.S. Army's 41st Division in Australia.[59] It appears that the Australian chiefs of staff, in keeping only one brigade at a location they otherwise deemed vital to the defense of the continent, had no confidence in the ability of Allied air and naval forces to support the Port Moresby garrison. They wanted to retain their best troops for the defense of Australia itself.

In 1943 General MacArthur declared publicly that it had been his intention, from the time he assumed command of the Southwest Pacific Area, to defend Australian territory by holding New Guinea and especially Port Moresby. This, he noted, was in contrast to the more cautious policy of the Australian chiefs of staff in not committing troops outside of Australia proper. MacArthur's statement appears dubious in light of the fact that he also made no attempt to provide substantial reinforcements to Port Moresby before the Battle of the Coral Sea. The first reinforcements did not leave Australia until 14 May, after it became known that the enemy had retired from the area. At that time, MacArthur sent another militia brigade group to General Morris at Port Moresby. MacArthur had had at his disposal four veteran AIF brigades and most of one American division, but chose to send none of these troops. The Australian official history complained of the inability to reinforce Port Moresby:

> So hesitant had General MacArthur and General Blamey been to send reinforcements to New Guinea that on 10th May, the day on which the Japanese planned to land round Port Moresby, the defending garrison was not materially stronger than the one which General Sturdee had established there early in January.[60]

As for Australian troops in the Solomons, there was no thought of holding positions so close to the Japanese base at Rabaul and conversely so far from Allied air support. By the end of April, the Australians had in the Solomons only a 50-man garrison at Tulagi, where they maintained a seaplane base for four or so Catalina flying boats. The aircraft conducted a useful patrol of the Rabaul area and the waters east of New Britain–Bougainville. MacArthur and the Australian chiefs could see no reason to sacrifice this garrison and ordered them to evacuate if they found the Japanese were southbound from Rabaul. Warned by coast-watchers in the northern Solomons, the Tulagi garrison demolished on 2 May the installations of military value on the island and set sail for Efate.

Having discussed what MacArthur failed to do in the face of the offensive on Port Moresby, it is necessary to note how he did attempt to forestall the Japanese attack. On 24 April he requested carrier forces and reinforcements from General Marshall, but Marshall refused, saying there were not enough carriers available to go around. MacArthur then voiced his complaints to an especially receptive audience in the form of Prime Minister Curtin and his staff. On 26 April MacArthur told Curtin he would require a carrier from the Royal Navy's Eastern Fleet in the Indian Ocean, use of two British divisions then rounding the Cape of Good Hope for the Middle East, and increased shipping for the run between California and Australia. The next day Curtin forwarded the requests to Churchill, noting that they came from MacArthur. Curtin still had the lever of Commonwealth troops in the Middle East which he had previously threatened to pull out if the safety of Australia was not assured. On 29 April Churchill, highly irritated at MacArthur's move, told Roosevelt of the communication and asked whether it was official policy or was MacArthur now determining grand strategy? Roosevelt quickly told Marshall to inform MacArthur of his displeasure in the matter. On 3 May MacArthur counterattacked with a long message explaining the concern of Prime Minister Curtin and himself over the defense of Australia and stating that as Supreme Commander he had to take into account political pressure from the Australians. The interchange of the past several days catapulted MacArthur boldly into the Europe-first controversy, but helped in no way to solve the immediate problem of the Port Moresby offensive.[61]

Meanwhile, Admiral King became furious over a very serious security leak emanating from MacArthur's headquarters. On 27 April there appeared in several Washington, D.C., newspapers under the dateline "Allied Headquarters, Australia," the following release: "Japanese naval forces including ships, planes, supplies and men are concentrating in Marshall Islands apparently preparing for a new operation."[62] The next day, King sent Marshall a vigorous protest, causing the War Department on 30 April to warn MacArthur to tighten censorship. Such detailed statements on Japanese intentions could not possibly come from submarine scouting, the only actual way to determine what was going on in the Marshalls, and might have tipped the Japanese to the fact that their code was broken. Fortunately, it appears that Japanese agents were not reading such mundane items as the Washington papers.

Barring immediate shipment of ground reinforcements to Port Moresby, the only way the Southwest Pacific Area could contribute to the defeat of the Port Moresby offensive was through their naval and air forces. Vice Admiral Leary as Commander, Southwest Pacific Force (ComSoWesPacFor) controlled a submarine force of 11 old "S-boats," dating from the twenties. Because of operational limitations, Leary could place only four to six submarines at sea at one time, assigning them patrol areas around Rabaul and eastern New Guinea. He had already detached most of his surface forces, the ANZAC Squadron, to Rear Admiral Fletcher. In addition, Leary's headquarters performed a most valuable function. The staff forwarded intelligence data and sighting reports to Task Force 17 to keep Fletcher informed of current developments. Leary also served as liaison between Fletcher and Army land-based air units in Australia. Fletcher later praised the manner in which Leary provided necessary information to him.[63]

For Lieutenant General George Brett and the men of the Allied Air Forces, Southwest Pacific Area, the Battle of the Coral Sea started about three weeks early, as it was they who contended with the Japanese preinvasion air strikes.[64] Brett's command consisted of eight Army Air Force air groups: three pursuit, one light bombardment, two medium bombardment, and two heavy bombardment groups, along with the 13 operational squadrons of the Royal Australian Air Force. It was an impressive force on paper, but one of the medium bomb groups and also one of the heavy bomb groups had no aircraft. Brett's air units were a mixture of both new, inexperienced groups and others which had escaped the ABDA disaster and were in sore need of a rest and refit. A lack of spare parts and general logistical difficulties caused high operational losses. The reinforcement rate from the United States was very small, as the air ferry routes were still largely uncompleted. Short-range fighters had to be brought by ship. Most of the Royal Australian Air Force consisted of search planes, light bombers, and other marginally combat-effective aircraft.

In keeping with the premise that the air forces were the first line of defense for the region, Brett deployed most of his combat planes to meet the threat from the north. At Port Moresby were three Australian search squadrons, one Australian fighter squadron, and one squadron of American dive-bombers. Brett based his own bomber force on airfields in northern Australia, Townsville, Cooktown, and Charters Towers. By mid-April, he had most of one light bomb group, a medium bomb group, and a heavy bomb group deployed there, some 100 medium bombers and 48 heavy bombers, although fewer than half were operational. Protecting them were elements of two pursuit groups, about 90 fighters. Brett's tactics were to make small raids, usually under ten aircraft, against Rabaul whenever the weather permitted. Occasionally the forces at Port Moresby made fighter sweeps against the Japanese air bases at Lae and Salamaua, but that soon proved to be very costly. Brett depended more upon his fast medium bombers for surprise raids on those bases. The sorties of his aircraft represented but a fraction of the aircraft available, but Brett had to husband his forces through a long spring and summer with little relief and reinforcements from the United States. He also used a goodly proportion of his heavy and medium bombers for search missions to the Rabaul area and, after 27 April, over much of the Coral Sea as well.

The Japanese 5th Air Attack Force, organizing in early April at Rabaul, started the month with only 16 fighters and 17 bombers operational, clearly too weak to contest the Allies for air superiority over Port Moresby. Consequently, on 10 April Vice Admiral Tsukahara, commanding Base Air Force, arranged to reinforce Rabaul with one bomber group in addition to the new fighter group already assigned. By 17 April, the 5th Air Attack Force was strong enough to begin the preinvasion air strikes. The Japanese began almost daily raids on Port Moresby, while hitting Tulagi intermittently. Aided by the superiority of their pilots and aircraft, the Japanese largely beat down the opposition at Port Moresby, virtually destroying the Australian fighter squadron stationed there.[65]

By 30 April Rear Admiral Yamada, commanding the 5th Air Attack Force, thought he had bombed Port Moresby sufficiently and ordered raids on Horn Island in northern Australia. He wanted to hit the fields through which the American bombers staged on their raids against Rabaul. Brett wisely kept his bombers at Townsville out of range of actual attack. Because of the fighter losses at Port Moresby, he had to rush two squadrons from the 8th Pursuit Group, 37 fighters, to Port Moresby, but only 26 arrived, indicating high noncombat losses in general in the area. The American P-39 fighters made their presence known on 30 April when they raided the Japanese air base at Lae. The presence of American fighters in strength at Port Moresby compelled Yamada to resume his strikes against that important airfield complex. By 1 May it was evident that neither the Japanese nor the Allies had air superiority over eastern New Guinea, and Yamada was worried about the ability of his aircraft to support the Port Moresby landings. His doubts led to new cries in South Seas Force that MO Striking Force attempt some sort of raid against Allied land-based air power, at least at Port Moresby.

11
The Battle
of the Coral Sea

The Battle of the Coral Sea began on 28 April, when the Japanese auxiliary *Nikkai Maru* reached Shortland in the Solomons and began building a seaplane base there.[66] The same day five big four-engine flying boats flew there from Rabaul to begin long-range patrols the next day. During the last two days of April, ships from the Tulagi Invasion Force and Support Force left Rabaul for destinations in the Solomons. The heavy forces sailed a little later; MO Main Force with four heavy cruisers and the light carrier *Shoho* left Truk on 30 April, while MO Striking Force with the two big fleet carriers sailed from there the next day. Vice Admiral Inoue also departed from Truk on 1 May, in order to direct the MO Operation from Rabaul. He traveled in his flagship, the light cruiser *Kashima*.

Up until 2 May, the operation went completely according to plan. Allied search planes were active, spotting many of the movements of Support Force and Tulagi Invasion Force as they threaded through the Solomons chain. Still, there was no opposition. On 2 May elements of Support Force constructed a seaplane base at Santa Isabell Island, and on the same day three floatplanes from there bombed Tulagi. Rear Admiral Shima reached the Tulagi area after dark and began disembarking his landing force. MO Main Force passed through Bougainville Straits and steamed south to get into position to support the Tulagi landings the next day.

The only obstacle to the operational plan so far occurred on the morning of 2 May, when MO Striking Force reached a point 240 miles northeast of Rabaul. There Rear Admiral Hara despatched the nine Zeros destined for the 5th Air Attack Force. Unfortunately for him, the weather was so bad that the fighters had to return to the carriers. Rear Admiral Yamada urgently requested that the transfer still be made. Rear Admiral Takagi decided to try once more the next day. MO Striking Force thus loitered in the area northeast of Rabaul instead of heading south as scheduled. Even worse, it appears that the weather did not allow the force to refuel from its fleet oiler, the *Toho Maru*; so even more time would be wasted in the next day or two through fueling. The delay of MO Striking Force had the approval of Vice Admiral Inoue, who believed that the nine Zeros were vital to the seizure of air superiority over Port Moresby. Whether it would be wiser to delay the whole operation apparently was not considered by South Seas Force.

On 3 May Rear Admiral Shima accomplished the capture of Tulagi without opposition, as the Australians had evacuated the place. Air strikes from the *Shoho* assisted in the Tulagi attack, as MO Main Force steamed in the waters 120 miles west of there. Satisfied that all was going well at Tulagi, Rear Admiral Goto and MO Main Force turned north to fuel at Shortland and then rendezvous with the Port Moresby invasion convoy two days later to provide direct support. From Rabaul sailed two auxiliary vessels from Support Force with materials to build the seaplane base at Deboyne in the Louisiades. Also in Rabaul, the Port Moresby Invasion Force loaded troops and supplies in preparation for sailing the next day. The soldiers of the South Seas Detachment "embarked in high spirits on their grand and ambitious scheme," apparently confident of the air support provided by South Seas Force.[67]

Rear Admiral Takagi tried once more on the morning of 3 May to ferry the nine Zero fighters to Rabaul as ordered. Again the squally weather forced the fighters to return to the two carriers, this time with less sanguine results, as one of them had to ditch in the sea. Takagi then decided to make the transfer after MO Striking Force fueled the next day. This would mean changing the operational plan again and risked detection by Allied search planes known to be operating east of Rabaul. Despite this, the need to reinforce the 5th Air Attack Force was great. Thus the failure to fly nine fighters to Rabaul on two separate occasions had seriously compromised the effectiveness of the powerful MO Striking Force in the early stages of the operation. It also meant that MO Striking Force would not be in range until sometime on 5 May to support the Tulagi garrison.

With the evident increase of Allied air operations out of Port Moresby, there were two attempts to change the role of MO Striking Force regarding attacks on Allied land-based air units. On 2 and 3 May Rear Admiral Goto requested that MO Striking Force transfer three Zeros and pilots to the carrier *Shoho*. Goto was apprehensive over the ability of his twelve fighters to support the invasion convoy once they steamed within fighter range of Port Moresby. Vice Admiral Inoue denied the request, adding that Rear Admiral Takagi had complete instructions to support the invasion convoy, and therefore a transfer was not necessary. On the same day, 3 May, Rear Admiral Yano, Fourth Fleet chief of staff, informed Takagi and Hara that it had been agreed informally that MO Striking Force should, depending on the situation, arrive at a point southeast of Port Moresby on 7 May or the dawn of 8 May, and launch air strikes on the airfields there. What Hara's reactions to the orders were has not been recorded, but he could not have been happy. His two carriers had only 37 of the precious Zero fighters themselves, five under authorized strength, and he would have to pit them against the expected American carrier force as well.[68]

On 1 May Task Force 17 with the carrier *Yorktown*, 67 planes, three heavy cruisers, six destroyers, and two fleet oilers reached a point about 350 miles northwest of New Caledonia.[69] There Rear Admiral Fletcher made contact with Rear Admiral Fitch with Task Force 11 fresh from Hawaii. Fitch had the carrier *Lexington* with 69 planes, two heavy cruisers, and six destroyers. Fletcher as senior task force commander exercised command of both forces and the reinforcements from Vice Admiral Leary. There had been some disagreement regarding this arrangement by the Australians. Rear Admiral Crace was senior to Fletcher; but Admiral Nimitz, seconded by Admiral King, insisted that the senior Pacific Fleet carrier task force commander must exercise command over a combined force of carriers and surface warships. Upon meeting Task Force 11, Fletcher sent Fitch south to join with the heavy cruiser *Chicago*, a destroyer, and the fleet oiler *Tippecanoe*. Task Force 17 would continue fueling throughout 1 May from the tanker *Neosho* and rejoin Task Force 11 the next day.

Unlike the Japanese command structure which had in Vice Admiral Inoue an area commander on the spot, CinCPac delegated authority to conduct operations directly to Rear Admiral Fletcher as the senior task force commander. CinCPac and Com-SoWesPacFor provided Fletcher with intelligence data on enemy movements and broad directives, but Fletcher would have to decide himself how to deal with the enemy. Only when Vice Admiral Halsey arrived in the Coral Sea would he assume overall command over the four carriers. On 1 May, Fletcher issued his "Operation Order No. 2-42," which would go into effect upon his signal.[70] The order outlined the incorporation of Task Forces 11 and 44 into an enlarged Task Force 17 made up of task groups. Task Group 17.2, the "Attack Group" under Rear Admiral Thomas C. Kinkaid, comprised the five heavy cruisers from the old Task Forces 11 and 17, with five destroyers as screen. Kinkaid had the task of surface combat with enemy warships as well as the protection of the carriers. Task Group 17.3 was known as "Support Group" and consisted of Rear Admiral Crace's old Task Force 44 or ANZAC Squadron. Support Group comprised one Australian heavy cruiser and light cruiser, one American heavy cruiser, and two destroyers. Rear Admiral Fitch's Task Group 17.5 was the two carriers with four destroyers in escort. The two fleet tankers and two destroyers made up the "Fueling Group," Task Group 17.6. At Noumea were six PBY patrol planes (soon to be increased to twelve) and the seaplane tender *Tangier,* forming the "Search Group," Task Group 17.9. Total for Task Force 17 thus was two carriers with 136 aircraft, seven heavy cruisers, one light cruiser, 13 destroyers, two fleet tankers, and at Noumea one seaplane tender with 12 patrol planes.

In the order, Fletcher stated his task, which was to "destroy enemy ships, shipping and aircraft at favorable opportunities in order to assist in checking further advance by enemy in the NEW GUINEA–SOLOMON Area."[71] As to the composition of the enemy forces he expected to encounter, Fletcher was necessarily vague. He noted only those forces which Naval Intelligence had definitely located south of Truk and Palau, as opposed to ships which might be en route from the homeland. Principal opposition rested in the Japanese 5th Carrier Division with the *Shokaku* and the *Zuikaku* and the light carrier incorrectly identified as the *Ryukaku,* which really was the *Shoho.* Fletcher thought the three Japanese carriers mustered 189 aircraft among them. From intelligence reports, Fletcher also believed there were two or three battleships in the waters south of Truk, along with three heavy cruisers, two light cruisers, 16 destroyers, and a host of auxiliary vessels such as minesweepers, gunboats, and transports. As for his operation plan, he described it succinctly in his order:

> This force will operate generally about seven hundred miles south of Rabaul. Upon receiving intelligence of enemy surface forces advancing to the southward, this force will move into a favorable position for intercepting and destroying the enemy.[72]

In other words, Fletcher wanted to remain out of enemy search radius and allow the Japanese to make the first move before counterattacking with his forces. This had also been his basic policy in the activities in March and April of Task Force 17.

On 2 May Fletcher rejoined Task Force 11 and found to his dismay that Fitch did not expect to complete his refueling until 4 May. Fletcher was disappointed and believed he would have to separate from Task Force 11 in order to head northwest to meet the advancing enemy, in light of search reports emanating from Australia which revealed widespread Japanese ship movements south of Rabaul. That afternoon, planes from the *Yorktown* had sighted and attacked a surfaced Japanese submarine only 32 miles from the task force. From this Fletcher believed the enemy knew his approximate position. In fact, submarine I-21 did not report the incident, her skipper apparently thinking that he was bombed by aircraft based on New Caledonia. He continued south to reconnoiter Noumea.[73] Fletcher told Fitch to meet him on 4 May at the same rendezvous point planned for Crace's force coming from Australia. That evening Task Force 17 departed to the northwest. Fletcher also learned that Task Force 16 would arrive in his area about 12 May.[74]

During the course of 3 May, Fletcher headed slowly to the northwest, taking the opportunity to top off his destroyers with fuel oil. Fletcher's concern for his logistics was warranted. After Task Force 11 emptied the oiler *Tippecanoe*, presumably on 4 May, the whole of Task Force 17 would have only one fleet tanker, the *Neosho*, to depend on for fuel. The *Tippecanoe* was to proceed to Noumea and there on 11 May receive oil from a chartered tanker. She could not return to Task Force 17 with fuel for at least ten days. The fleet oiler *Platte* was scheduled to arrive in the New Caledonia area around 13 May, and Task Force 16 with two fleet tankers about the same time.[75] Thus, until about 13 May Fletcher would have to depend upon the *Neosho* for fuel. ComSoWesPacFor had deployed a tanker at Noumea and one north of

Brisbane, but Fletcher could take advantage of these sources of fuel only in an emergency. These tankers were auxiliary vessels and not equipped or trained for refueling underway at sea. Thus Fletcher took every opportunity to fuel his destroyers to keep a safe margin of fuel in those short-ranged vessels.

During the late afternoon of 3 May, Fletcher learned from ComSoWesPacFor sighting reports that aircraft had spotted Japanese vessels near Tulagi and that invasion of the island was likely. He was determined to attack the invasion force, noting, "This was the kind of report we had been waiting two months to receive."[76] He detached his fleet oiler and a destroyer to join Fitch and directed him to a new rendezvous to take place on 5 May. He upped speed to 27 knots to close the distance to Tulagi and Guadalcanal in order to launch an air strike early the next morning. Fletcher regretted that his whole force was not with him, but thought he had enough to do the job. He expected to execute a quick raid on Tulagi and return to the south. Shortly after dawn on 4 May, the *Yorktown* had reached a point about 100 miles south of Tulagi and launched an attack force of 40 bombers. The *Yorktown* flyers caught the Tulagi Invasion Force completely by surprise. Rear Admiral Shima had ten ships in the area, but virtually no air defense. Fletcher launched three attacks during the morning and afternoon. His pilots claimed the destruction of two destroyers and one large transport, with a light cruiser forced aground on the beach. The actual score was one destroyer and three small auxiliaries sunk, two other vessels lightly damaged. Shima's forces, however, had pulled out leaving a small garrison on Tulagi. American losses totaled only three aircraft.[77]

Fletcher launched several attacks on Tulagi because of the number of ships in the area. A weather front blanketed Task Force 17, making detection by Japanese search planes highly unlikely. In addition, Fletcher knew from monitored Japanese radio traffic that the enemy had not spotted him. Toward evening, he thought about despatching two heavy cruisers from Kinkaid's Attack Group to Tulagi to "clean up the cripples."[78] He wisely decided against such a dispersion of his forces. After dark, Task Force 17 hurried south to meet with Fitch and Crace, who had joined in the meantime. Pilots' reports indicated that the *Yorktown* had dealt a strong blow to the Japanese. During 4 May Fletcher had learned that air searches from Australia spotted one Japanese carrier, "probably *Kaga*-class," and two heavy cruisers or battleships south of Bougainville.[79] What the AAF bombers had sighted was the small carrier *Shoho* with a destroyer in attendance. Fletcher did not head in that direction, as he did not want to be sighted by land-based air, especially as he did not know the location of the two big Japanese carriers possibly in the area. He also learned from ComSoWesPacFor that radio intercepts indicated that two Japanese transports with escorts were to arrive on 5 May at Deboyne. This most likely heralded the advance of the invasion convoy.[80]

The American air strikes on Tulagi came as a shock to Vice Admiral Inoue. He learned about the trouble to Shima's force as he arrived at Rabaul that morning. Because of the delay in ferrying the nine Zeros to Rabaul, MO Striking Force was about 340 miles north of Tulagi, far out of supporting distance. According to the original plan, Takagi was to have been only 120 miles north of Tulagi at dawn on 4 May. It appears that South Seas Force had discounted the possibility of American carriers appearing so early in the MO Operation. There was little Inoue could do to deal with the situation. He ordered Takagi to pursue the Americans, but MO Striking Force was in the process of refueling. Takagi had to divide his forces into two groups, sending the carriers and cruisers south at once, while leaving most of the destroyers behind to continue fueling. Rear Admiral Goto and MO Main Force with the *Shoho* also turned south in an effort to overtake the American carrier force, but like Takagi could not catch Fletcher. Inoue recalled the pursuers late on 4 May.

Takagi received instructions to continue according to plan, taking any available opportunity to complete the transfer of fighters to Rabaul. He therefore decided to continue south around the southern tip of the Solomons into the Coral Sea and then head northwest along the western flank of the Solomons. Takagi had to rendezvous with his fleet tanker to resume fueling; because of the high-speed run to the south, his ships needed to fuel once more before beginning the attack on Port Moresby. Likewise Goto returned to the north to escort the Port Moresby Invasion Force which sailed that afternoon from Rabaul. Inoue cautioned for vigilance, but decided to continue according to plan.[81]

Fletcher on the morning of 5 May rejoined the rest of his forces far south of Tulagi. He spent the day replenishing his fuel oil bunkers from the *Neosho*. The *Yorktown* fighters shot down a Japanese flying boat from Tulagi, but the aircraft did not succeed in sending a message to 5th Air Attack Force headquarters. During the day, Fletcher received important intelligence information from CinCPac at Pearl Harbor. The first was a partial decript of orders sent by Inoue to Takagi.[82] The message noted that the Japanese carriers "will proceed north-northeast of Bougainville, thence southward," if it was determined by the Japanese that the American carrier force was in the Coral Sea. If it was not so determined, then the message indicated that MO Striking Force would go to Tulagi. Although Japanese records do not give the text of the message, it appears that Inoue did not know on which side of Tulagi the American attack originated, and he made allowances for either contingency. On the afternoon of 4 May and the morning of 5 May, MO Striking Force did launch search planes to check both flanks and ahead of its line of advance toward the tip of the Solomons.

The second message from CinCPac indicated that the Japanese carriers would attack Port Moresby on day X-3 or X-2.[83] CinCPac noted that there was one indication that X-day was 10 May. Hypo had not deciphered the code groups bearing the Japanese date ciphers, and would not do so until the end of May. Using a number of hints from various messages, they deduced that the Japanese would most likely attack Port Moresby on 10 May. In fact, Hypo had intercepted and accurately rendered the 3 May order from South Seas Force to MO Striking Force ordering air strikes on Port Moresby before the landings.

On the morning of 6 May, Fletcher put into effect "Operation Order No. 2-42," combining his forces into one large Task Force 17. During the day, Fletcher largely completed fueling and then turned northwest. He sent the *Neosho* and a destroyer to the southeast to wait in a safe, but accessible point. From his intelligence summaries and sighting reports, Fletcher deduced that the enemy would advance on Port Moresby via Jomard Passage, supported by a base at Deboyne. He believed that the Japanese invasion convoy, probably supported by a carrier, would pass through the Louisiades, traversing Jomard Passage on 7 or 8 May in order to arrive off Deboyne by 10 May. As for the Japanese 5th Carrier Division, Fletcher and Fitch thought that the two fleet carriers were in the Bougainville area.[84] In the light of the deciphered message ordering air strikes on 7 May or 8 May against Port Moresby, they must have assumed the Japanese carriers would soon close on the target from the southeast. Thus they thought the Japanese were to the northwest of Task Force 17, moving south from Bougainville to guard the left flank of the convoy, traverse the Louisiades, and hit Port Moresby that day or, more likely, the next day.

For Fletcher, 7 May appeared to bode decisive action in the Coral Sea. He decided to take a position just south of the Louisiades. Fitch was to launch an air search on the dawn of 7 May to cover the northwest sector in detail. He hoped to locate both the nemy carriers and the invasion convoy. Japanese carriers were he prime targets, and Fitch held back a large air striking group o attack them the instant that they were spotted. Once he knocked ut the enemy carriers, Fletcher could destroy the invasion convoy vith aircraft and warships. There was always the chance the two arrier forces might neutralize each other. After all, this day shaped up as the first carrier-to-carrier battle in history, and no one was ertain how such an engagement might turn out. Fletcher informed Crace that he was to take his Support Group to cover the southern erminus of Jomard Passage to prevent the exit of the convoy from he Louisiades. He evidently hoped that Crace would have a chance at the invasion convoy even if the rest of Task Force 17 became embroiled in a fight with the Japanese carrier force.[85]

Rear Admiral Fletcher did not know it, but MO Striking Force was actually northeast of his position. On the morning of 6 May, Takagi was fueling in the waters south of New Georgia and about 180 miles west of Tulagi. MO Striking Force was enjoying the opportunity to finish the fueling interrupted on the morning of 4 May by the American attack on Tulagi. Shortly after 1000 hours, a flying boat based at Tulagi spotted Task Force 17 about 420 miles southwest of Tulagi and shadowed the force for four hours before returning to base. Sighting reports placed the American carriers about 350 miles south of MO Striking Force. Takagi had to divide his force again because not all of his destroyers had completed fueling. At noon, Rear Admiral Hara departed to the south, screened by two destroyers. Several hours later, Takagi followed with the remainder of MO Striking Force. By midafternoon, however, both Takagi and Hara decided to call off the pursuit. The 5th Carrier Division had entered a band of extremely bad weather. Hara knew the approximate location of the American carriers, but did not launch an afternoon aircraft search to confirm it. Both he and Takagi felt that they could not overtake the American carriers before nightfall. As will be shown below, they were not especially interested in doing so on 6 May. Takagi with most of the destroyers turned back to complete refueling, while Hara arranged to rendezvous the next dawn, 7 May, with Takagi at Point "A" about 280 miles southwest of Tulagi.[86]

With the reappearance of enemy carriers in the Coral Sea, Vice Admiral Inoue and his senior commanders took the opportunity to re-evaluate the MO operational plan. Inoue, Goto, Kajioka, and the others believed that the operation should continue as planned; that is, the Port Moresby Invasion Force, covered by MO Main Force, should pass near Deboyne and enter Jomard Passage after dark on 7 May. Presumably MO Striking Force would attack an destroy the American carriers, although the commanders acknow edged there was considerable danger for the invasion convoy. Kaj oka expected the Americans to take position south of the Louisiade to strike the invasion convoy as it neared Jomard Passage. Failin; that, Kajioka definitely felt that the Americans would attack hi force on the morning of 8 May, after it had left Jomard Passage Inoue instructed his commanders to be alert, while Yamada ar ranged for an air strike of bombers from Rabaul should the Ameri can carriers appear on 7 May.[87]

Rear Admirals Takagi and Hara had their own ideas on how they should conduct operations on 7 May. With the appearance o: American carriers in the Coral Sea, there was no question of raid; on Port Moresby until MO Striking Force had dealt with them They had been reluctant to offer battle on 6 May because they did not feel they were prepared. Hara decided it would be much better to execute a comprehensive search on 7 May to locate the enemy and make the first strike while the Americans were preoccupied with the invasion convoy. The Japanese admirals knew that the Americans had not sighted MO Striking Force and assumed their presence in the Coral Sea would come as a big surprise to the American carrier commander. Hara thought the American carriers were probably near the Louisiades, waiting to pounce on the invasion convoy. He wanted, however, to search to the south as well as to the southwest toward the Louisiades in order to safeguard his flank before MO Striking Force made a high speed run to the west to close on the invasion convoy. Hara felt that the enemy might not yet know the final destination of the invasion force, which could still be New Caledonia. Hara's hunch about searching to the south would prove most unfortunate for the Japanese the next day.[88]

The dawn of 7 May saw the forces of both sides poised for battle. Rear Admiral Fletcher with the main body of Task Force 17 maneuvered just southeast of the Louisiades, preparing to launch an air search to the north to locate the Japanese carriers and the invasion convoy. Rear Admiral Crace's Support Group (Task Group 17.3) left Fletcher shortly after dawn to proceed west to cover the southern exit of Jomard Passage. Fletcher's fueling group, the fleet tanker *Neosho* and the destroyer *Sims*, were about 280 miles to the southeast, waiting in a supposedly safe location. Fletcher's two carriers numbered 133 aircraft, 123 of which were operational. South Seas Force was deployed in two groups. Plodding the waters just north of the Louisiades was Rear Admiral Goto's MO Invasion

Force, divided into MO Main Force with the light carrier *Shoho* 18 planes), Rear Admiral Kajioka's Port Moresby Invasion Force, and most of Rear Admiral Marumo's Support Force. Far to the east was MO Striking Force, only 280 miles southwest of Tulagi. Thus while Fletcher was in range of MO Invasion Force, Takagi lay unsuspected to his rear, only about 175 miles straight north of the *Neosho* and her escorting destroyer. MO Striking Force wielded a striking force of 121 aircraft, of which 108 were operational.

The Japanese blanketed the Louisiades with a network of seaplanes from Deboyne, ship-based floatplanes from MO Main Force, bombers from Rabaul, and a flying boat from Tulagi. MO Striking Force searched to the west and south, while Task Force 17 searched to the north. AAF bombers from Australia also covered the Louisiades area. With so many aircraft in the air, the various forces soon located each other, except for MO Striking Force, which remained unsighted by the Americans. In all but one case, the aviators either wrongly identified what they saw or erroneously coded the message. Hara's search planes erred in identifying the *Neosho* as a carrier, so he launched his full strike force of 78 planes against what proved to be the wrong target. Only a few minutes after his aircraft departed, Hara received a sighting report from Deboyne which correctly located Task Force 17. Hara decided to destroy the American force he believed was south of him before heading west to attack the warships operating south of the Louisiades. The Japanese attack planes soon sighted the *Neosho* and the *Sims*, recognized them as a tanker and a destroyer, and searched the area for two hours looking for the reported carrier. Finally as their fuel ran low, the strike leader settled for the *Neosho* and the *Sims*. They quickly sank the destroyer and left the tanker drifting without power for the loss of one bomber. The air group straggled back to MO Striking Force, and the last aircraft did not return until 1515.[89]

Fletcher's dawn search sighted the two old light cruisers and two gunboats of Marumo's Support Force north of the Louisiades. The pilot wrongly coded his sighting report, leading Fletcher to believe the target was two carriers and four heavy cruisers. Fletcher and Fitch believed the pilot had located the 5th Carrier Division, so they despatched a strike group of 93 aircraft against the target. Fletcher learned of his mistake when the search plane landed back on board the *Yorktown*. There was nothing to do but continue with the strike. The *Lexington* strike group spotted MO Main Force with the *Shoho* and attacked. One of the AAF bombers from Townsville had also sighted the *Shoho* and reported its location to Task Force 17.[90] Consequently the *Yorktown* air group receive orders to head for that target. Aircraft from both air groups a tacked the *Shoho* shortly after 1100 and sank the hapless carrie easily for the loss of three aircraft. Goto's MO Main Force di persed in terror, not even rescuing survivors from the sunke carrier. Task Force 17 recovered its aircraft and was ready to launc a second strike by 1450. Fletcher was reluctant to make a secon strike on the invasion convoy and its escort, because neither hi own search planes nor bombers from Australia had located th other Japanese carriers. He knew of the loss of the *Sims* and fata damage to the *Neosho*, but that did not help to pinpoint the loca tion of the 5th Carrier Division. Fletcher decided to hold his plane in reserve until land-based aircraft found the Japanese carriers Task Force 17 sailed in an area of bad weather which effectivel masked its movements. He depended upon Support Group to pre vent the enemy from coming through Jomard Passage.

Support Group proved to be a magnet for Japanese searcl planes. Rear Admiral Crace did not have the fortunate coincidenc of operating in low visibility. The Japanese lost track of Tasl Force 17 early that morning, but mistakenly assumed Suppor Group had carriers and was the main American force. Kajioka learned that Crace at 1100 was only about 100 miles to the soutl of him. He decided to turn north with the invasion convoy until MO Striking Force and MO Main Force had dealt with the enemy. Soon after came the news that the Americans had sunk the *Shoho*. Because of this, Inoue ordered all forces not directly involved in the destruction of the American carrier forces to withdraw temporarily to the north. Goto issued instructions to concentrate MO Main Force and most of the destroyers guarding the invasion convoy at a rendezvous near Rossel Island for a night attack on the Americans. Inoue expected Takagi and Hara to launch at least one attack on the American carriers before dark.[91]

During the early afternoon, Takagi and Hara frantically waited for their strike planes to return. They were mortified to learn of the loss of the *Shoho* and eager to attack the American carriers. According to search reports, the American task force lay just south of Jomard Passage, out of range of MO Striking Force. This was Crace's Support Force, as the Japanese had completely lost track of Fletcher. A Japanese strike force made up of 31 bombers and 11 fighters from the 5th Air Attack Force attacked Crace in midafternoon. The medium bombers dropped torpedoes and made level bombing attacks, claiming the destruction of one battleship and one cruiser. Actually none of Crace's ships sustained any damage.

AAF units in Australia made a total of ten sorties on Japanese shipping in the Louisiades, but hit nothing. Three American B-17's misidentified Crace's Support Group as five Japanese transports and dropped bombs, but fortunately missed all the warships. Crace was thoroughly irritated because he could muster no air support.[92]

Takagi and Hara, their aircraft finally recovered, headed west at high speed to close on the American carriers believed operating south of Jomard Passage. Hara determined to launch a long-range search-and-destroy mission with his best pilots for an attack at dusk. At 1600, Hara sent 27 bombers aloft with instructions to fly 280 miles to the west. Actually Task Force 17 was not over 170 miles away. The Japanese pilots encountered increasingly bad weather and passed close to Task Force 17. Fletcher's radar allowed his aviators to set up an ambush by the fighters. In the ensuing fight the Japanese lost nine aircraft shot down in return for two fighters missing. The strike leader called off the mission, ordering his pilots to jettison their bombs and torpedoes and return to the ships. In the increasing darkness and poor visibility, several Japanese bombers encountered Task Force 17 and went low to investigate. It appears American radio traffic interfered with the Japanese homing devices. The Japanese met gunfire from the American ships and fled into the night, although after obtaining the correct position and composition of the American force. Hara's flyers managed to land back on board their carriers after a harrowing flight through storms and the darkness. Hara turned on his searchlights and landed 18 aircraft, illuminating for three hours despite the fact he knew the Americans were only 100 miles away. This was two years before Vice Admiral Mitscher's celebrated night landings at the Battle of the Philippine Seas. Mitscher had much less to fear than Hara, who believed the American task force contained battleships which could overwhelm MO Striking Force if caught in a night battle.

As 7 May ended, both sides took stock of the situation. Fletcher knew the location of the invasion convoy and that the Japanese carriers were within striking distance, roughly 200 miles. He carefully considered the prospects for launching a night surface attack with his cruisers and destroyers, but decided against it for a number of reasons. He did not know the enemy position and did not have the time for an extended search. Because of the separation of Support Group, he determined that his best course of action was to keep the task force concentrated to protect the carriers. There was also the question of fuel, considering the loss of the *Neosho*. Fletcher did not have the oil to spare for high-speed operations in a night attack. Indeed, the loss of his tanker, Fletcher informed CinCPac, "will cripple my offensive action and may cause my withdrawal in a few days."[93] As for his course of action he added, "I am operating to attack carriers in the morning, must then fuel destroyers and will continue oppose enemy movement toward Moresby." Thus he decided to remain south of the Louisiades, on the flank of any continued Japanese thrust toward Port Moresby. He knew that he had to find and destroy the Japanese carriers at the first opportunity the next morning. He detached the destroyer *Monaghan* to look for survivors of the *Neosho* and the *Sims* and to transmit messages to CinCPac and ComSoWesPacFor.

Vice Admiral Inoue was highly distressed at the turn of events on 7 May, which had literally been a tragedy of errors for the Japanese. Search reports were incomplete and very confusing, not allowing a reasoned estimate of American strength in the area. At 2040 hours, he issued a directive canceling the proposed night battle because the position of the American carriers remained doubtful and the warships could not reach the suspected area until after dawn. He decided to postpone the Port Moresby landings two days to 12 May, allowing ample time for his forces to destroy the American carriers and scatter all other opposition. Goto received orders to transfer two heavy cruisers to Takagi. MO Striking Force prepared for a dawn search which would locate the American carriers and bring about the decisive encounter on 8 May. The Japanese were disappointed over the inability of MO Striking Force to bring the Americans into battle and believed all would be made right the next day.[94]

On the morning of 8 May, both Fletcher and Takagi found what they were looking for—each other.[95] Dawn searches sent out by each carrier task force located the other. Task Force 17 had a total of 126 aircraft, of which 118 were operational. Fletcher despatched an air strike group of 75 planes to attack the Japanese carriers. MO Striking Force had fewer aircraft, 109, of which only 95 were operational, but Hara managed to put 69 planes in his attack group. The strike groups attacked almost simultaneously, and the carrier duel was sharp and quick. This day MO Striking Force had the benefit of cloud cover in the squally weather. Fletcher's aviators could only find the *Shokaku*, while the *Zuikaku* remained concealed. They hit the *Shokaku* with three heavy bombs, damaging the flight deck so that the ship could not launch or receive aircraft. The groups from the *Yorktown* and the *Lexington* had attacked separately and thought they hit different carriers, but the *Shokaku* was their only target. The pilots thought they had eft one carrier in sinking condition and heavily damaged another. The Japanese attack group made a coordinated strike and hit both he *Lexington* and the *Yorktown*. The *Lexington* sustained two bomb hits and two torpedo hits, but could conduct flight operaions and steam at 24 knots. The *Yorktown* took only one bomb it, which did not impair operations to any great extent. On the urface it appeared that Task Force 17 came off well in the encouner. One Japanese carrier was definitely out of the fight, and the apanese had suffered heavier plane losses, 27 aircraft lost or rashed into the sea as opposed to 19 for Task Force 17. Events would soon redress the balance in favor of the Japanese.

Fletcher found that his one fully operational carrier, the *Yorkown*, had relatively few operational aircraft. The *Lexington*'s conlition grew worse during the afternoon. Fires began to spread uncontrollably throughout the enormous carrier. Fletcher decided to break off battle by heading south. He again considered a night attack by his cruisers and destroyers, but the question of fuel was even more important. A communication from CinCPac received that morning informed Fletcher there was no way to augment the fuel on hand except as scheduled.[96] The nearest source of fuel was an Australian auxiliary tanker north of Brisbane. Fletcher also had to consider Japanese air superiority. Deciphered radio traffic led him to believe that at least one carrier remained undamaged and that it was recovering the aircraft of the crippled flattop. Worst of all, Fitch indicated that he had reason to believe that a third Japanese carrier had joined up, giving the enemy two undamaged carriers to his one operational carrier.[97] CinCPac Intelligence had outlined all along the possibility of additional forces reinforcing the MO Operation.

Fletcher adopted as his course of action a temporary withdrawal. He arranged to transfer all of the *Lexington*'s aircraft to the *Yorktown* and then send her with suitable escort back to Pearl Harbor for repairs. He planned to renew battle on 9 May with a combined air group on board the *Yorktown* should the Japanese continue their advance on Port Moresby.[98] Even this plan suffered a blow when it became evident that the *Lexington* was unable to conduct flight operations and could not be saved. Shortly after dark, Fletcher ordered a destroyer to sink her with torpedoes after the crew had been rescued. Thus the Pacific Fleet lost one-fourth of its available carrier strength. The *Lexington* took 36 aircraft with her, leaving only 39 operational planes on board the *Yorktown*. There was no recourse, because he had only half an air group, but to continue his withdrawal. Fletcher had tried during

the day to arrange for air support from General Brett's air uni
in Australia and at Port Moresby, but nothing came of it. Bre
sent two small bomber forces against the invasion convoy, but or
failed to find the target and bombed Deboyne instead. The othe
element failed to hit any ships in the convoy.[99]

The Japanese were equally troubled with the course of even
on 8 May. Early that afternoon, Takagi decided to detach th
Shokaku to proceed immediately to Truk for repairs. This left hi
with the Zuikaku and, oddly enough, also only 39 operational ai
craft to continue the operation. Takagi and Hara informed Inou
that they would not be able to launch a second strike that afte:
noon, and probably not the next day either. There was the que:
tion of the low aircraft strength, pilot fatigue, and, most impo:
tantly, the lack of fuel in the screening ships. Because of repeate
interruptions on 4 and 6 May, MO Striking Force had never draw
its fill of fuel oil from its tanker. Some destroyers had only 2
percent of their fuel capacity and the rest were down to 40 percen
MO Striking Force would have to rejoin the fleet tanker waitin
safely in the Solomons far to the north. It also appears that Takag
and Hara could see little urgency in pursuing the remnants of th
American force. After all, the Japanese aviators had claimed th
sinking of one American carrier and heavy, if not fatal, damag
to the other. MO Striking Force would pursue or withdraw accord
ing to the wishes of South Seas Force, and they did not car
which.[100]

Late on the afternoon of 8 May, Inoue and his staff made ;
detailed estimate of the situation. Only one aircraft carrier wa
left to him, and that had only half strength in aircraft. He wa:
jubilant over the fact that his aviators had destroyed one and prob
ably a second American carrier, but there still remained the ques
tion of forcing his way to Port Moresby. He felt that one weakenec
carrier air group was incapable of supporting the invasion convoy
against Allied land-based aircraft in Australia. There was also the
delay before MO Striking Force would be ready to proceed after
regrouping and refueling. Inoue decided that he must postpone
the attack on Port Moresby indefinitely. That morning permission
had arrived from Combined Fleet authorizing him to change the
date of the Port Moresby landings, and he determined to exercise
that option. He ordered the invasion convoy, supported by MO
Main Force, to return to Rabaul. Takagi and Hara were to take
MO Striking Force, less the Shokaku, north to cover the descent
on Ocean and Nauru which would proceed according to schedule.
Inoue felt he had won the battle but temporarily lost the cam-

aign. He would hold Tulagi, but would have to evacuate Deboyne s being untenable for the time being.[101] Inoue's despatch to his commands arrived at Combined Fleet headquarters as "Information." There it met with disbelief and great anger. Combined Fleet Staff thought that South Seas Force was winning the battle, as Inoue had reported sinking two American carriers. Not knowing of low plane strengths and the fuel problem, they saw no reason why the operation should not continue. Yamamoto could do nothing about the postponement of the Port Moresby Operation. He had given Inoue the power to do this. However, letting elements of the Pacific Fleet escape further attrition by the victorious Japanese was another matter entirely. He ordered Inoue shortly before midnight to resume his pursuit and "annihilate the enemy."[102] Consequently, at 2330 hours Inoue ordered Takagi and Goto to resume their attacks on the fleeing Americans as soon as possible on 9 May.[103]

Despite Inoue's orders, by the early morning hours of 9 May the Battle of the Coral Sea was as good as over. Both sides had broken off battle, but anticipated the possibility of renewing action the next day. In strategic terms the United States had won the battle because Task Force 17 had blunted the Japanese drive on Port Moresby, sinking one light carrier, a destroyer, and several auxiliaries. Fletcher also heavily damaged the carrier *Shokaku* and caused heavy plane losses to the *Zuikaku's* air group so that ultimately neither carrier would be able to participate in the upcoming Midway Operation. On the debit side was the deeply felt loss of the *Lexington*, plus the valuable fleet oiler *Neosho* and the destroyer *Sims*. Late on 8 May, the congratulatory telegram sent by CinCPac praising Task Force 17's "glorious accomplishments" that were the "admiration of the entire Pacific Fleet" sounded a little hollow because the *Lexington* was not there to share it.[104] Officially reported plane and personnel casualties were 77 aircraft and 1,074 men for the Japanese and 66 planes and 543 men for the United States.[105] The Battle of the Coral Sea was the first occasion where the opposing surface ships never sighted each other and all of the fighting was done by aircraft. Rear Admiral Fletcher and the men of Task Force 17 had accomplished their mission; the only trouble was that they became bloodied in the process.

12
Withdrawal from the Coral Sea

Shaken by the loss of the *Lexington*, Task Force 17 continue south to regroup. On the morning of 9 May, a search plane from the *Yorktown* reported sighting a Japanese carrier task force 17! miles northwest of Task Force 17. Fletcher immediately prepared for a possible Japanese air strike. He resorted to flying one of his officers to Australia in order to arrange personally for an air strike on the target by AAF bombers. He also wanted to keep radio si lence in order not to alert the enemy to his presence. For once Brett responded quickly. He despatched 14 Army bombers which reached the target area about the same time as a small strike force from the *Yorktown*. The target turned out to be a reef which had fooled the crew of the search plane because of its resemblance to the wakes of warships.[106] That afternoon Fletcher received an im portant directive from CinCPac. Nimitz instructed him to return to Pearl Harbor or the West Coast with the *Yorktown*, the *Lexing ton*, and screening ships of the old Task Force 17. Kinkaid's forces were to join Halsey when he arrived in the vicinity. As of yet, Nimitz did not know of the loss of the *Lexington*.[107] The same day, Fletcher detached Crace from his command, bringing Task Force

114

4 back into existence. Crace had waited southeast of Port Moresby ntil he was sure that the Japanese were not coming, then retired) Brisbane to refuel.[108] On 10 May Fletcher radioed his intention) stop at Tongatabu on the trip back and return to Pearl Harbor. t 1600 on 11 May, Fletcher detached Kinkaid with two heavy ruisers and three destroyers to proceed to Noumea. One heavy ruiser from Task Force 17 accompanied with orders to rejoin at ongatabu.[109]

Admiral Nimitz informed Admiral King of the reasons behind is decision to withdraw Task Force 17 from the Coral Sea. He ited the fact that the *Yorktown* had sustained damage and could e more easily crippled or sunk in a future battle; besides her air roup had only a small number of operational aircraft. He wanted he *Lexington* and the *Yorktown* to go directly to the West Coast f the ships needed extensive repairs which Pearl Harbor was not quipped to service.[110] Unaware of the sinking of the *Lexington* when he made his decision, Nimitz learned of it during the late ours of 8 May (Hawaiian time). On 9 May CinCPac staff reviewed he previous day's decision and concurred with it. Although it night have appeared desirable to retain the *Yorktown* in the Coral iea to serve with Halsey's Task Force 16 for one operation, Nimitz decided against this. By this time he realized that the Japanese had postponed the MO Operation and had only a fleet carrier, the Zuikaku, and supposedly the converted carrier *Kasuga Maru* in the Rabaul area. He knew that Task Force 16 could handle them easily. In addition, Nimitz wanted to have the *Yorktown* repaired as quickly as possible because of possible enemy intentions in the Central or North Pacific Areas. Nimitz requested in a subsequent letter to King that Fletcher be promoted to Vice Admiral and receive the Distinguished Service Medal for his fine service in the Coral Sea.[111] The responsibility for operations in the South Pacific had passed from Fletcher to Halsey.

Vice Admiral Inoue did not have the option of halting operations in the Coral Sea. His orders specified that MO Striking Force resume the pursuit on 9 May, while MO Main Force joined with Takagi later that day. He postponed the evacuation of Deboyne to retain it as a seaplane base despite increasing American air attacks. Thus Takagi, Hara, and Goto were to hunt down the American battleships and cruisers which Combined Fleet believed were still in the area. Despite Inoue's orders, both MO Striking Force and MO Main Force spent most of 9 May fueling. Only late that day did Japanese forces turn southwest into the Coral Sea to

look for American warships. The invasion convoy returned to R
baul that day, while preparations for the Ocean-Nauru Operatio
continued apace.

On the morning of 10 May, MO Striking Force launched
small search mission, but located only the oiler *Neosho* driftin
without power. The Japanese could hear radio transmissions be
tween Townsville and aircraft, as well as with what they though
was a carrier task force. I-24, part of Inoue's submarine picket line
reported being bombed by carrier-type aircraft 500 miles east c
Townsville. Thus Takagi believed there was still one America
carrier in the area. However, events moved swiftly to end Japanes
participation in the Battle of the Coral Sea. That afternoon, Yama
moto told Inoue to postpone the Port Moresby attack until tha
summer. Takagi was to head north to support the RY Operatio
if his aircraft spotted nothing that day. Inoue told Takagi to pas
around the eastern tip of the Solomons, essentially retracing hi
steps, in order to move into support distance of the RY convoy
Goto's MO Main Force was on alert to prevent any thrust b
American surface ships toward Rabaul and the Solomons. Th
Japanese evacuated Deboyne on the morning of 12 May. Onl
Tulagi in the Solomons remained as evidence of the MO Opera
tion.[112]

PART III

STRATEGIC AFTERMATH OF THE CORAL SEA BATTLE

13
Japanese Strategic Planning Resolved

As related previously, Imperial General Headquarters had before the Battle of the Coral Sea two rival strategic plans. They were the New Caledonia–Fiji–Samoa invasions proposed by members of the Naval General Staff and Combined Fleet's Midway Operation. Faced with the unremitting pressure of Admiral Yamamoto for the adoption of his Midway plan, the Naval General Staff reluctantly agreed that the Midway Operation should take place before other operations in the South Pacific. They ordered that the Port Moresby–Solomons operation be speeded up to occur in early May. Because of Naval General Staff concern over American airpower in the Aleutians, Combined Fleet added to the Midway plan provisions for a raid on Dutch Harbor and landings in the western Aleutians. There was still the question of the timing of the Midway attack. The Naval General Staff hoped to postpone the operation several weeks to allow time for refitting the carriers and meeting in full the many requirements for materiel. Yamamoto's planners wanted to undertake the attack in early June. The Doolittle Raid on 18 April aptly demonstrated to the Naval General Staff the need to crush American carrier strength. As a result, they agreed to Combined Fleet's schedule determining that the operation occur in early June.

With the Midway plan itself, there was no great opposition from the Army over the approval and allocation of troops. Indeed the Army planners were surprised when the Navy suggested the capture of Midway Island and points in the western Aleutians because of the Naval General Staff''s manifest interest in the South Pacific. In mid-April, the Army General Staff readily assented to the Navy's proposal, mainly because it was to be nearly an all-naval affair. The only Army troops required were a regiment to help take Midway and a reinforced battalion to garrison Attu in the Aleutians. On 5 May Imperial General Headquarters issued Naval Section Order Number 18 calling for the "occupation of Midway" and key points in the western Aleutians."[1] According to the "Central Army-Navy Agreement" promulgated at the same time, the Army would furnish for the Midway attack the "Ichiki Detachment," an elite assault unit, and for the Aleutians a reinforced battalion known as the "North Seas Detachment." Imperial General Headquarters gave the plan the code name "MI Operation,' and called for it to take place in early June.

By early May, Combined Fleet had completed much of the detailed planning for the MI Operation, assigning to it nearly all of the mobile resources of the fleet.[2] There were seven separate surface forces whose operations would be coordinated intricately according to a general plan. They would sortie from Japan and Saipan between 26 and 29 May, bound for Midway and the Aleutians. N-day, when landings would occur on Midway, the planners set as 6 June, local time. The operations in the Aleutians would open the attack, to be undertaken by the Northern Force of cruisers, destroyers, and transports supported by the 2nd Carrier Striking Force of two light carriers. On 3 June or N-3, these carriers would raid Dutch Harbor in the Aleutians, and on N-1 day the Japanese were to land troops at Kiska and on Adak. The Adak attack was merely a raid and the landing force was to re-embark for Attu. Two forces were to converge on Midway, Vice Admiral Nagumo's 1st Carrier Striking Force with six fleet carriers from the northwest and from the southwest Vice Admiral Kondo's Second Fleet with the invasion force and escorts. On N-2 day, 4 June, Nagumo was to close to within 250 miles of Midway and launch an air strike to destroy the aircraft based on Midway. The next day, part of Kondo's force was to occupy Kure Island about 60 miles southwest of Midway, then close on Midway to disembark troops at dawn on 6 June. The Midway attack would take place with the close support of the battleships and cruisers of the Second Fleet.

Midway, however, was only to be a prelude to an expected large encounter with the Pacific Fleet, which Yamamoto believed would sortie from Pearl Harbor to try to retake Midway. He decided to place lines of submarines along the likeliest routes of advance out of Pearl Harbor to warn the Japanese of the oncoming American forces. Yamamoto would wait seven days in the vicinity of Midway after its capture. Backing up the first line forces were two groups of battleships, the first under his direct command and the second under Vice Admiral Takasu Shiro. He planned to deploy his forces in a large rectangular configuration northwest of Midway to be able to strike the Americans no matter from what direction they appeared. Yamamoto's force was to take station 600 miles northwest of Midway, with Nagumo's carriers 300 miles east of them. Takasu would move into position 500 miles north of Yamamoto, with the carriers of Rear Admiral Kakuta Kakuji's 2nd Carrier Striking Force also 300 miles east of him. The tactical plan was for the submarines and carrier aircraft to attack the American fleet first, with the battleships then closing in for the kill. Kakuta and Takasu with the submarines of the 1st Submarine Squadron were to handle the Americans if they appeared north of latitude 40° north, while Nagumo, Yamamoto, and the boats of the 3rd and 5th Submarine Squadrons would attack them south of 40° north. If the Pacific Fleet came out in full strength from the south, Yamamoto arranged to join his forces with Takasu and Kakuta with Nagumo for an all-out battle. The whole plan was predicated on the belief that the Americans would not be prepared to meet the Japanese until after the capture of Midway.

Securing Army permission for the Midway Operation had been easy. The Naval General Staff's plan for subsequent attacks on New Caledonia, Fiji, and Samoa was another matter. After a month of debate, on 28 April the Army General Staff agreed to the compromise proposal, pleased that the invasion of Australia was no longer considered. The plans for the isolation of Australia from the United States were approved. The capture of key South Pacific islands to be built into air and submarine bases would prevent the flow of men and materiel to Australia. This at the very least would retard the development of the continent into a major offensive base. Some officers thought that isolation alone might force Australia to sue for a separate peace without a Japanese invasion. Detailed planning would proceed after the MO Operation, to which the Navy had looked confidently for a big victory.[3]

On 9 May Vice Admiral Inoue informed Combined Fleet of the failure of the Port Moresby invasion, somewhat complicating plans for renewed operations in the South Pacific. He advised that the second attempt on Port Moresby be postponed until July, unless he could be reinforced with additional carrier support, fast transports, and more flying boats for search duties. Members of the Combined Fleet staff conferred with the Naval General Staff in Tokyo and agreed that it would be impossible to meet the demand of South Seas Force in terms of materiel. Consequently the planners decided it would be necessary to defer the Port Moresby operation indefinitely until after the MI Operation and possibly after the New Caledonia–Fiji–Samoa invasions as well. The Army General Staff concurred, issuing orders for General Horii to stand down at Rabaul until his South Seas Detachment came under the jurisdiction of Seventeenth Army headquarters under Lieutenant General Hyakutake Harukoshi, already ordered into existence on 2 May. Hyakutake was to carry out the Port Moresby attack in early July, in addition to supervising attacks southeastward into the South Pacific. Combined Fleet cut orders on 10 May specifying the formal postponement of the MO Operation.[4]

Imperial General Headquarters spent the first weeks of May busily planning for post-Midway operations in the South Pacific. On 18 May they issued Naval Section Order Number 19 and Army Section Order Number 633, identical in text, which instructed Combined Fleet and Seventeenth Army to cooperate in operations in the South Seas, specifically the capture of Port Moresby, New Caledonia, Fiji, and Samoa.[5] They were to destroy enemy bases in those areas and establish operational bases at Port Moresby, Noumea on New Caledonia, and Suva in the Fijis. This would enable the Japanese to secure control of the waters east of Australia and cut the line of communication between there and the United States. Army forces earmarked for the operations included the 12 infantry battalions of Seventeenth Army and support troops. Combined Fleet provided the Second Fleet under Vice Admiral Kondo to control the invasion forces of New Caledonia, Fiji, and Samoa, supported by Vice Admiral Nagumo's Striking Force carriers. Fourth Fleet would again conduct the Port Moresby Operation. Also involved would be the land-based aircraft of Base Air Force. In addition, Combined Fleet planned to activate Eighth Fleet headquarters based at Rabaul to control the newly conquered areas.

The general plan called for most of the naval forces involved in the Midway Operation, less the 1st and 2nd Battleship Divisions under the direct control of Admiral Yamamoto, to proceed to Truk after the completion of that mission. They were to arrive there sometime between 15 June and 20 June. From there the naval planners would decide best how to divide the Second Fleet and Striking Force to conduct and support the invasions in early July of New Caledonia, Fiji, and Samoa. Presumably this would be no great problem, as Combined Fleet would already have destroyed the carriers of the Pacific Fleet at Midway. This could be the only logical reason behind such a gross dispersion of forces in attempting the three major operations almost simultaneously. Combined Fleet must have expected little opposition against any of the planned efforts. Vice Admiral Inoue's Fourth Fleet was to conduct the invasion of Port Moresby, using the forces at hand. Then his control in the area would be supplanted by Eighth Fleet based at Rabaul.[6]

The Army General Staff conferred with General Hyakutake and began detailed planning in late May. The general premise of the invasions was that the Allies had greatly strengthened Australia and New Zealand proper, but maintained only very weak outposts at Port Moresby, New Caledonia, Fiji, and Samoa. Major General Horii's South Seas Force built around the 144th Infantry Regiment would comprise the New Caledonia Invasion Force. He waited at Rabaul. Opposition at New Caledonia was thought to be about 3,000 U.S. Army and Free French soldiers with only ten combat planes. The Fiji and Samoa invasion forces were to gather at Truk. Against Fiji, General Hyakutake decided to use Major General Kawaguchi Kiyotake's 35th Brigade with the 124th Infantry Regiment as its main force. Two battalions of the 41st Infantry Regiment would be attached to the 35th Brigade, giving Kawaguchi five infantry battalions. Imperial General Headquarters thought there were 7,500 American and British troops at Fiji with 20 combat planes in support. The Samoa Invasion Force under Colonel Yazawa Kiyomi was to consist of only one reinforced battalion of the 41st Infantry Regiment. Imperial General Headquarters believed there were only 750 American marines and sailors based at Samoa with 20 combat planes. For the second Port Moresby attack, Seventeenth Army would commit a force about equal in strength to South Seas Detachment on the first attempt. It was the Aoba Detachment, based around the 4th Infantry Regiment. The Army completed its planning in the first days of June, and on 4 June in Tokyo, it was approved by the Army Section of Imperial General Headquarters.[7]

14
President Roosevelt Decides the Strategy for the Pacific

April 1942 for the United States was also a month of debate and indecision regarding American strategy for the Pacific. Both the Army and the Navy articulated their strategic plans and submitted them to the president for his decision. Roosevelt was anxious to have a general scheme of operations, but found that he had to choose between two seemingly contradictory objectives, security in the Pacific and rapid American intervention on the European continent. On 2 April he informed the Pacific War Council that he intended to review in detail the strategy for the South Pacific. The council had reconvened on 1 April in Washington and consisted of the president, Harry Hopkins, and political representatives from the countries concerned with the Pacific: Britain, Australia, New Zealand, the Netherlands, China, and Canada. Roosevelt used the organization to help keep him abreast of the political desires of the Allies regarding the course of the war in the Pacific. Needless to say, the Joint Chiefs of Staff were not sanguine toward such an "extraordinary" body.[8]

General Marshall was able on 1 April to offer to the president and the Joint Chiefs a statement of the War Department's basic position regarding intervention in Europe. Known as the "Marshall

Memorandum," the document outlined a plan of three phases to bring the war directly to Germany.[9] The first step entailed a massive build-up of forces in Britain. It was the keystone of the entire strategy because subsequent operations depended upon having the requisite troops and aircraft available in Britain. Consequently the first phase, later named Bolero, would require the maximum allotment of troops, aircraft, and shipping to achieve the quickest possible concentration of American forces in the United Kingdom. Thus Bolero became the principal obstacle to further reinforcement of the Pacific, because of the need to draw upon the vast majority of resources available to the War Department for use in Europe.

The whole object of the Germany-first strategy was to prevent the defeat of the Soviet Union and the crippling of Britain before the United States could unite with those two powers to destroy the Third Reich. By the spring of 1942, it became evident that the Soviet winter counteroffensive had petered out, and the Eastern Front awaited only good weather to see the resumption of the German attacks. Marshall expected the Soviets to be in grave danger in the summer of 1942. Consequently he proposed that there be a contingency plan for an emergency, limited-scale invasion of the continent, perhaps in early September 1942. This received the code name Sledgehammer. When he met the British war leaders in early April, Marshall stated that the American contribution to Sledgehammer would be one armored division, two and a half infantry divisions, 400 fighter planes, and 300 bombers, all to be ready for commitment by mid-September. The president took particular interest in the concept of Sledgehammer, as it offered a means to help the Soviets and show American good faith. The third step of the plan involved the actual major invasion of the continent, known as Roundup. This was very tentatively scheduled for April 1943.

To achieve approval from the president for his strategic plans, Marshall required the agreement of the British chiefs of staff. He traveled to Britain in early April and presented his proposals to Prime Minister Churchill and General Alan Brooke, Chief of the Imperial General Staff. The British were very skeptical about the prospects of Sledgehammer, but agreed in principle to the build-up for the eventual attack on the continent. Besides, Churchill had other ideas for the use of American troops sent to Europe, namely the invasion of North Africa. He felt that Sledgehammer was totally unrealistic, but in Washington his opposite number began to put more faith in it. Marshall on 14 April received British approval for his plan. This was extremely important for his fight with the

Navy over the allocation of resources. Strangely enough, the British did tell Marshall of their worries over the Japanese advances, but in the Indian Ocean, not the Pacific. Marshall went so far as to query King and Arnold in mid-April to determine whether they could spare forces to defend India. He received a rather curt negative from both.[10]

Admiral King and his planners also devised their basic strategic plans in April. On 16 April Rear Admiral Turner submitted a memorandum to King detailing a series of offensive campaigns in the Pacific leading to the defeat of Japan. There were to be four stages. The first was devoted to the concentration of strength and retention of strategic points in the Pacific as start points for the upcoming offensives. Attacks during this period were to be restricted to minor stabs against forward enemy positions. It was necessary to organize and ready the amphibious forces to be used in subsequent stages. The second stage was to see a coordinated Allied offensive through the Solomons and eastern New Guinea with Rabaul as the ultimate objective. During this time, there were to be "heavy attrition attacks against the Carolines and Marshalls."[11] The third stage would be the capture of the Carolines and Marshalls, while the fourth was to see an advance either into the Dutch East Indies or the Philippines, depending on the situation at the time. King was impressed with the plan and saw to its incorporation in the latest edition of WPL-46, the Navy's basic war plan.

By the end of April, planning by the Joint Staff Plans Committee under the auspices of the Joint Chiefs reached a crucial point. The Army and Navy planners had together drawn up a comprehensive memorandum outlining their views on the defense of the South Pacific. They submitted this important document, JCS 48, to the Joint Chiefs on 2 May.[12] As ways of defending the island bases on the line of communication to Australia, the Joint Staff planners listed a number of procedures, which included the direct escort by naval and air units of shipping en route to Australia and the ground and air defense of the bases used either for defense, refueling, or staging purposes. These were mostly static measures. Of a more active nature were covering operations by the Navy and also air bombardment to keep the enemy off balance and to meet his raiding forces. This document well described the course of the Pacific Fleet's operations in the first several months of the war. Positive measures recommended in the memo included the maintenance of air and sea forces with amphibious troops to prevent the enemy from capturing key positions and for dislodging them in case they did succeed in doing so. This was basically the Army's osition. The naval planners put in the estimate the statement that he best way to safeguard the South Pacific was to capture strategic points which would threaten the Japanese line of communication, in other words, seize the initiative.

Because of the nature of operations in the South Pacific, air power rather than large amounts of ground troops was more immediately important to the defense of the line of communication to Australia. Consequently General Arnold's Army Air Force planners played an important part in articulating the Army's strategy for the South Pacific. Arnold set the basic premise for his planners that there were to be no air reinforcements to the Pacific other than those previously allocated by the Joint Chiefs. He preferred to use his air units in the planned operations in Europe. Given the paucity of air base resources in the open spaces of the Pacific, the AAF planners decided to concentrate the heavy bombers in Hawaii and Australia, the extremities of the line of communication. There were to be no heavy bombers based in the South Pacific. This was the policy which Admiral King had opposed at the end of March. According to the AAF planners, the air units in the South Pacific should comprise 40 medium bombers and 162 fighters, to be reinforced ultimately to 193 fighters with no additional medium bombers, but with 20 new light bombers. This plan was in line with the recommendations approved by the Joint Chiefs on 16 March.

In practice, the AAF's air defense plan for the South Pacific consisted of flying in heavy bombers from Hawaii and Australia to areas endangered in the South Pacific. The idea was not to meet carrier raids on vital South Pacific positions, but to concentrate an air striking force to oppose landings against major bases. Direct defense of the air bases would depend upon the pursuit squadrons based there and the actions of naval carrier striking forces. The AAF planners hoped to increase the capacity of fields on New Caledonia and the Fijis to accommodate squadrons of heavy bombers flying in from Hawaii and Australia. For example, they estimated that Fiji could accommodate 12 bomb squadrons, two of which could stage in from New Caledonia. That would mean bringing in ten bomb squadrons from Hawaii and Australia, if the threat warranted such a concentration of air power. This plan would reduce the bomber strength in those areas by nearly 40 percent, but the Army planners felt such a depletion of strength would not be dangerous. Optimistic estimates on the part of the Army aviators indicated they could concentrate heavy bombers from Hawaii and Australia at a central point in the island chain in the time span of one day. This was contingent on having the airfields on the islands in proper condition. The AAF planners felt that the presence of medium bombers based at New Caledonia would ensure airfields capable of taking heavy bombers. Both types of bombers required essentially the same facilities.

The naval planners disagreed vigorously with the AAF's concept of air mobility for heavy bombers. They attacked the idea on two counts. First of all, they emphasized that the Army's estimates for the time needed to fly in bombers to the South Pacific were too sanguine, that the AAF did not realize the difficulties entailed in handling and maintaining aircraft in the South Pacific. It might take several days to assemble bombers in strengths capable of dealing with Japanese threats. The question was whether the enemy would give them the time to do this. The second and most important objection noted that the Army had allocated insufficient forces to defend the whole Pacific area, from Alaska to Australia. The defense of Hawaii and Australia could not afford even the temporary detachment of bombers to the South Pacific. Basic Pacific Fleet strategy depended upon the security of Hawaii from strong attack; such security allowed the fleet to be mobile. If the Army did not provide an adequate defense for Hawaii, the Pacific Fleet would have to do so. Instead of the AAF's plan, the naval planners called for an increase of aircraft strength in the South Pacific beyond the Army figures, in the South Pacific an additional 31 medium bombers, 35 heavy bombers, and 55 fighters. Under the Navy's conception, each of the key island air bases would have light bombers or fighter-bombers as well as fighters, while the South Pacific would also have one group of medium bombers and one of heavy bombers as well. The Navy's analysts added that the Army should turn over bombers from new production to be manned by naval flight crews in the South Pacific, if the Army felt they could not meet the Navy's requirements for air support.

The time for debate and indecision in the Pacific was rapidly drawing to a close, because the Japanese had begun to move once more toward Australia and the South Pacific. On 24 April General MacArthur began his requests for reinforcements, followed a few days later by his devious appeals through Prime Minister Curtin for British assistance. Both the War Department and the Navy for their own purposes called for a decision as well. By the end of April, planners on King's staff became aware of the possible wide-scale Japanese offensive in the South Pacific and increasingly frustrated at the Army's intransigence over sending the required reinforcements. One staff member wrote that this indecision at the end of April, "put the planners on COMINCH staff, who were particularly concerned with the SOPAC area, in the jumping up and down stage."[13] The War Department wanted to get along with the Bolero plan and submerge Navy interference with it.

President Roosevelt fired the first shot on 29 April, when he informed the Pacific War Council that he intended to reinforce the Australia garrison to 100,000 troops and 1,000 aircraft. Three days later, the Joint Staff Plans Committee submitted JCS 48 to the Joint Chiefs in prelude to a major decision on the defense of the South Pacific. General Marshall quickly replied to the president's desire to send additional troops and aircraft to Australia.[14] In a memorandum dated 4 May, the chief of staff threatened that such a redirection of shipping and resources to Australia would "virtually eliminate the United States from ground participation in a 1942 offensive on the continent."[15] He stressed that the tie-up of shipping alone because of the long turn-around time in voyages to Australia would reduce the American commitment to Sledgehammer by three divisions. He stated he would rather see reinforcements go to Hawaii and Alaska than to Australia and the South Pacific, as this would better serve American interests. He noted the threat in the Pacific but added, "I have preferred to accept that hazard in order to stage an early offensive on the continent of Europe."[16]

The meeting of the Joint Chiefs on 4 May was a spirited one, as the principals debated the conflicting positions stated in JCS 48. The encounter between Marshall and King resulted in two memoranda dated 5 May. The first was from King to the Joint Chiefs restating the reasons why he thought the Pacific should take top priority for the present.[17] He warned that it was far from certain that the Allies could hold their present positions in the Pacific. There was the distinct possibility that the Japanese could repeat their highly successful strategy used in the Netherlands East Indies of bringing overwhelming superiority in strength to bear at a crucial point. King warned that the Allies were spread "too thin" in the Pacific, allowing the Japanese to retain the initiative. The enemy was in position to attack Australia, the South Pacific, Hawaii, or even Alaska. "Even now they are massing strong land, sea and air forces in the Mandates area beyond our range of observation." King added that these attacks would occur "very soon," necessitating a change of priority from Bolero to the Pacific. "The disastrous consequences which would result if we are unable to hold the present position in the Pacific Area are self-evident." It was no longer 'a question of mounting an offensive, but rather of actual survival in the Pacific. He stressed that it was more important to face the threat in the Pacific than implement offensive action in another theater.

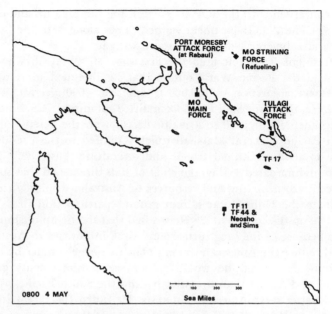

The Situation at 0800, 4 May

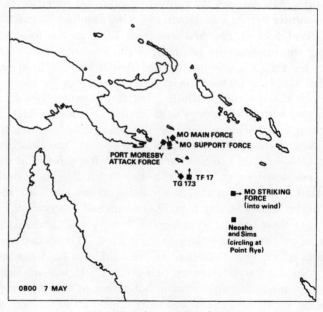

The Situation at 0800, 7 May

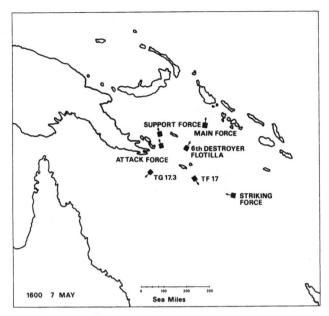

The Situation at 1600, 7 May

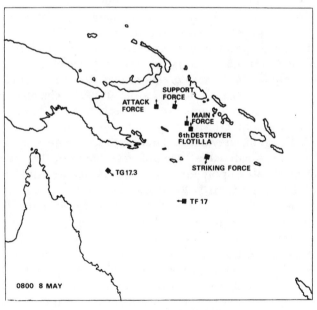

The Situation at 0800, 8 May

Speed was the most important factor, as the Japanese were not going to wait until the War Department got around to making the Pacific secure from their attack. He concluded with the statement that basic strategy for the Pacific must be "to hold what we have against any attack that the Japanese are capable of launching against us."[18]

The second memorandum went from General Marshall to the president. On 5 May Marshall restated his position regarding the feasibility of Bolero in the face of possible reinforcements for the Pacific.[19] If the Navy were to receive the aircraft they desired for the South Pacific, it would delay the opening of the planned air offensive against Germany for two months. Ground troops for the Southwest Pacific Area would likewise prevent the participation of American troops in the opening stages of active operations against the continent. Roosevelt well knew there was little chance that the British would ever implement Sledgehammer without the presence of American troops. Unless Bolero received the shipping and resources as planned, Marshall recommended that the operation be abandoned, in essence a revocation by the United States of the agreement achieved in London the previous month. He knew the president would react strongly to this point, with its implications for the Second Front. The Pacific was important and should be held if possible, Marshall acknowledged, but not at the expense of Bolero. He felt the forces already there were sufficient to do the job. As for King's plan to strengthen the island bases, Marshall observed, "It is impossible to make every point in the island chain impregnable to any attack the Japanese are capable of launching."[20] He clearly implied in the memorandum that Roosevelt would have to choose between security in the Pacific and Sledgehammer.

President Roosevelt announced his decision on 6 May. Bolero was to continue top priority despite the situation in the Pacific. He now believed his previous declaration to send reinforcements to Australia to be "inadvisable." He did state, however, that the War Department should supply aircraft to the Pacific as called for in previous directives. Clearly Roosevelt wanted to remain on the defensive in the Pacific; besides he had confidence in the Navy's power to break up a Japanese advance, noting, "The success of raiding operations seem to be such that a large scale Japanese offensive against Australia or New Zealand can be prevented."[21] Unfortunately Roosevelt did not realize that the Pacific Fleet had not yet grappled with the real strength of the Combined Fleet and that the early raids were made on the premise that there would be no strong opposition. He did not fathom the deep concern of King and Nimitz over the depth of the impending Japanese offensives. Raids would provide the Pacific Fleet little benefit. The Japanese were coming out in strength to challenge Allied control over objectives of great value to the strategic designs of both powers. There would be battles of great significance, not raids. Two days later, Washington learned of the loss of the *Lexington* and damage to the *Yorktown* during the Battle of the Coral Sea. In one action, the Pacific Fleet had seemingly lost one-half of its operational carrier strength.

With the president's firm approval for Bolero, the War Department began to make specific allocations based on JCS 48 for the Pacific. It is fortunate that the president mentioned aircraft strengths for the South Pacific, directing that the units promised by the Joint Chiefs be provided. General Arnold's AAF planners were attempting to lower the aircraft strengths for the South Pacific, pleading the inability to supply them and still meet Bolero requirements. On 4 May they informed Arnold that to date they had only been able to furnish about a third of the fighters and none of the bombers specified for the South Pacific in the March Joint Chiefs directive. They proposed that the Army equip the Royal New Zealand Air Force with planes for one medium bomb group and one fighter group in New Zealand and two fighter squadrons and one medium bomb squadron for Fiji. Presumably this would ease the requirements for AAF units in the South Pacific. As for the Navy's idea of turning heavy bombers over to them to be manned by naval flight crews, the AAF staff protested that they did not have sufficient aircraft of this type for their own groups.[22]

General Eisenhower and the planners in the War Department observed that Arnold was not even attempting to meet the allocations for aircraft specified by the Joint Chiefs for the South Pacific. On 8 May Eisenhower sent Arnold a memorandum directing him to speed reinforcements already allocated to the Pacific. Arnold and his staff on 9 May worked out a deployment schedule which still did not attain the levels as ordered by the Joint Chiefs. Arnold provided most of the fighters, but was very reluctant to supply the medium bomb group for New Caledonia. As for heavy bombers, Arnold indicated that 160 were to be stationed in the Pacific, specifically in Australia and Hawaii, while JCS 48 called for 206. Arnold replied on 12 May to Eisenhower's memorandum, stating that the AAF would despatch the necessary aircraft to the Pacific, but only if this would not seriously affect the build-up of air power in Britain according to Bolero.[23] The Navy's fears that the Army would not provide the aircraft already approved for the Pacific were coming true. Bolero had become the excuse to cut all rein forcements to the Pacific.

The War Department on 13 May completed a general study c Army strength in the Pacific according to JCS 48.[24] Regarding ai craft, it stated as an "immediate objective," strengths to be reache in the main on 31 August 1942. The final goals were set for some time in 1943. Total AAF aircraft in the Pacific were to reach 1,57 in the first category and 1,622 in 1943, an increase of only 51. Th South Pacific was to have 162 fighters and 40 medium bombers a the "immediate objective" with the addition of 20 light bomber and 29 fighters by sometime in 1943. The Central Pacific and the Southwest Pacific areas were to stay about at the same level. There were to be no major additions in ground troops for the Pacific other than for forces already en route to Australia, Fiji, Tongatabu and Efate. Such additional troops as would arrive later in 1942 were only replacements and fillers to bring the units already there to ful strength. General Marshall on 4 May had suggested re-routing the 37th Division en route for New Zealand to Fiji to obviate the neces sity of reinforcing that place. This suggestion was not in the spirit of prior agreements with the Commonwealth nations in the Pa cific, but the New Zealand government had little choice but to agree. Clearly the War Department was using the power given to them by the president to shut down the release of any more troops and aircraft for the Pacific. The question became one of whether the resources they so carefully husbanded for commitment in Europe could be better used elsewhere.

15
New Evidence
on Japanese
Intentions
after the Battle
of the Coral Sea

At the beginning of May, Pacific Fleet planners as well as analysts in Hypo thought the Japanese would probably expand their Port Moresby offensive into a general attack on Allied positions in the South Pacific. On 3 May the *Greybook* indicated that the Japanese were expected to use six carriers and two battleships in their South Pacific drives. Pacific Fleet would oppose with four carriers. On the next day, the *Greybook* summarized in detail the enemy forces that War Plans Division supposed were en route to the South Pacific. They noted a total of seven carriers and two to four battleships, with three carriers and one or two battleships already south of Truk.[25] This, of course, was the basic premise upon which Admiral Nimitz and the staff proposed to concentrate all four available carriers to meet the enemy in the South Pacific.

Radio intercepts garnered by Hypo in early May tended to confirm this assumption. On 2 and 3 May Hypo deciphered fragments of a number of messages sent by Vice Admiral Nagumo's First Air Fleet/Striking Force headquarters to his carriers, and also messages in which the 3rd Battleship Division (the four *Kongo*-class fast battleships) was an originator or addressee. At least one section of two battleships from that division of the First Fleet

always operated with Nagumo's carriers. Hypo noted that one orig
nator, believed to be a battleship of the 3rd Battleship Division i
the Marshalls, sent high-priority messages to Fourth Fleet and Fir:
Air Fleet. This indicated the possibility that the carriers and ba'
tleships might operate together in the Mandates or Rabaul area.[2]
Even more ominous was a message from Nagumo to the carrier
Kaga and *Hiryu* and three battleships from the 3rd Battleship Div
sion, assigning anchorages at Truk to them. The *Kirishima*, th
remaining battleship of the 3rd Division, replied with a message t
Nagumo stating, "will be unable to accompany you in the cam
paign."[27] Hypo knew the ship was to stay docked in the yards. The
thought on 3 May that the ship was supposed to have left for Tru!
on 3 May, and they added that they had no idea what the forth
coming "campaign" might be.

On 4 May, however, some of the staff at Pearl Harbor began to
have second thoughts. Hypo discovered that the ship they though!
was a battleship in the Marshalls was more likely a submarine uni!
or a flagship instead.[28] It was apparently the light cruiser *Katori*
flagship of the Sixth Fleet, submarines, under Vice Admiral Komatsu
Teruhisa. Komatsu communicated with Fourth Fleet regarding the
participation of six of his submarines in the MO Operation, four
directly and two on reconnaissance patrols. Hypo's discovery of the
identification error on call signs broke an important suspected link
between Nagumo's carriers, the 3rd Battleship Division, and Fourth
Fleet. In the next several days, Lieutenant Commander Layton and
others began to suspect that the South Pacific might not be the only
Japanese target, that they might be interested in advancing to the
east. Midway came easily to mind because Admiral Nimitz had just
returned from an inspection trip there in the wake of his April
meeting with ComInCh. He recommended that reinforcements be
sent to the island. On 6 May the *Greybook* stated, "While the Japanese offensive in SOPAC continues, it is noted they now have sufficient forces in the Central Pacific to raid in the Central and North
Pacific Areas."[29]

Hypo continued to monitor Japanese fleet radio traffic, but with
increasing unsureness as to Japanese intentions in the South Pacific.
On 6 May Lieutenant Commander Rochefort radioed that Hypo
was not sure that major Japanese fleet units were now heading for
Truk to berth there.[30] Two days later, Hypo provided a long summary of intercepts, indicating that "signs of renewed activity in
other areas were seen." Rochefort added that "efforts to locate any
additional fleet units to reinforce Jap fleet in that area [Coral Sea]
have failed to disclose any major units headed that way."[31] Hypo

laced only three carriers in the Coral Sea area with another, a onverted carrier, en route. However, there was a message from Nagumo on board the *Kaga* sent in his capacity as commander of Striking Force to the 2nd Carrier Division, the carrier *Akagi,* 8th Cruiser Division, and two units of the 3rd Battleship Division, with information addressees being Combined Fleet, First Fleet, and Second Fleet commanders. "This may be a striking force," was Rochefort's assessment.[32] On the same day, Hypo seemingly provided a confirmation of their suspicions. One message, a First Air Fleet operations order, assigned escorts to two carriers and three battleships to a destination the code groups for which Hypo had not before seen. Another intercept noted departures for this force from home waters on 15 May and 21 May.[33] Finally, Rochefort reported on 9 May that messages deciphered to date, "indicate commencement of operations involving carriers and Batdiv 3 will be about 21st."[34]

Clearly something was in the wind. If the Japanese were planning to support or follow up their Coral Sea offensive, then the forces involved should have been en route to or arriving in that area by this time. On the contrary, it appeared the Japanese were retaining the majority of their effective forces, including four fleet carriers and all the battleships, in homeland waters for a time. Indicated also was the fact that an operation involving Nagumo's Striking Force would begin on 21 May. The *Greybook* stated on 3 May, "There is a good indication that the attack on Port Moresby has been postponed and that the direction of the SWPAC offensive has shifted east."[35] Radio intercepts deciphered by Hypo had detected Japanese preparations for the seizure of Ocean and Nauru islands, showing that operation would occur next. As will be shown, CinCPac Intelligence obtained nearly complete information as to Japanese plans for the Ocean-Nauru Operation and knew the full extent of that offensive. By 9 May though, the Pacific Fleet staff was aware that the Japanese had something else planned, and not necessarily only for the South Pacific. Officers like Layton and Rochefort began to wonder whether the Japanese might have in mind Midway or even Oahu itself as their goal for a massive raid or an offensive. The next eight days would see Admiral Nimitz come to appreciate the depth of the threat against the Central Pacific and his own Pacific Fleet, as the cryptanalysts and intelligence officers provided information from deciphered Japanese messages. The Japanese operation turned into the type of offensive most feared in the early days just after the Pearl Harbor attack. Nimitz had two tasks immediately before him. They were to con-

clude operations in the South Pacific by his carriers speedily an
without further losses and to prepare for the Japanese attack i
the Central and North Pacific. Ironically, he would find ComInC
an obstacle to this and the Ocean-Nauru Operation a possibl
threat to the speedy return of Vice Admiral Halsey's Task Force 1
to the Hawaiian area.

16
The Ocean and Nauru Operation

South Seas Force originally planned the Ocean-Nauru or RY Operation as an independent venture, but Vice Admiral Inoue decided
in April to use part of the Tulagi Invasion Force, reinforced with
other ships, to seize the two islands.[36] According to plans issued on
25 April, Rear Admiral Shima was to head back to Rabaul with
most of his ships after capturing Tulagi. Then he was to assemble
his forces at Kavieng on New Ireland and depart there on 11 May
to land on the two islands four days later. Several other transports
and auxiliaries would sail south from Kusaie in the Carolines to
cooperate with the landings. Rear Admiral Fletcher's 4 May air
attack on Tulagi damaged several of the ships destined for the RY
Operation, compelling Shima to return to Rabaul for emergency
repairs. On the afternoon of 8 May, Inoue ordered the RY Operation to commence despite setbacks to the MO Operation. He instructed Shima to assemble his forces at Rabaul and depart from
there on 10 May. In place of the destroyer *Kikuzuki* beached at
Tulagi during Fletcher's raid, Inoue provided the destroyer *Uzuki*
from the Port Moresby Invasion Force. Shima's RY Invasion Force
comprised the minelayer *Okinoshima*, two destroyers, and two large
transports with naval landing troops on board.

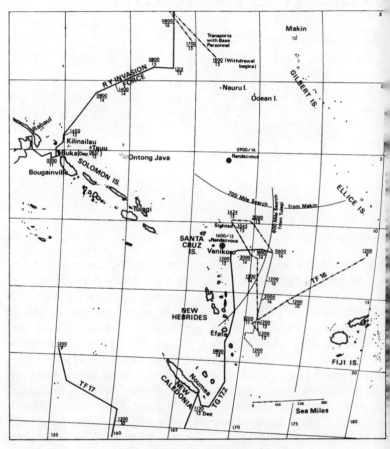

The Ocean-Nauru Operation

On 10 May Rear Admiral Shima completed his arrangements for the RY Operation and left Rabaul shortly after dark bound for Queen Carola anchorage on the western coast of Buka. The next morning, he suffered a major setback when the American submarine S-42 of Vice Admiral Leary's Southwest Pacific Force pumped two torpedoes into the Okinoshima's port side in a position about 32 miles northwest of Queen Carola inlet. The explosions tore into the minelayer's firerooms, cutting all power. Shima decided to tow the flagship to Buka and there salvage her, beaching the ship if necessary. He would take the remaining ships and sortie the next day for Ocean and Nauru. In the wake of the final postponement of the MO Operation, Inoue put his full attention to the completion of the RY Operation to salvage something other than the Tulagi base in the lower Solomons. At noon on 11 May, he issued a general order to South Seas Force, setting the date for the capture of Ocean and Nauru as 17 May. He added the minelayer Tsugaru and the light cruiser Tatsuta to the RY Invasion Force, ordering Shima to await their arrival. To save the Okinoshima, he organized a salvage force under Rear Admiral Marumo. The 5th Carrier Division received final orders to ferry Zeros to Rabaul and return to Japan forthwith. Before South Seas Force completed its reorganization, it suffered two additional losses. The Okinoshima on the morning of 12 May appeared to be in good condition with fires abated, but a gust of wind through open minelaying ports in her stern reignited the blaze with renewed fury. There was nothing for Shima to do but abandon ship. The Okinoshima capsized that morning. Another one of Leary's submarines that day sank the repair ship Shoei Maru as the vessel was returning to Rabaul after a vain effort to reach the Okinoshima before she sank.

Vice Admiral Inoue on 13 May presented specific plans for the final attempt to take Ocean and Nauru. He dissolved MO Invasion Force, withdrawing most of its forces to Truk and Rabaul. RY Invasion Force supported by Rear Admiral Takagi's MO Striking Force was to execute the attack on Ocean and Nauru. Inoue had received permission from Combined Fleet to retain Takagi's 5th Cruiser Division and escorts. Rear Admiral Shima's new RY Invasion Force, comprising one minelayer, one light cruiser, two destroyers, and two transports, sailed from Queen Carola on the morning of 13 May. MO Striking Force passed northeast of Bougainville and at noon launched eight Zeros from the Zuikaku to Rabaul. This time the ferry mission, which had caused so much trouble to the entire MO Operation, went without a hitch. That afternoon, Rear Admiral Hara with the Zuikaku and a destroyer escort turned

north for Truk and the homeland. Takagi with his two hea~
cruisers and several destroyers steamed to take station 200 mil
ahead of and on the northern flank of the RY Invasion Force.
appears that if Inoue expected any opposition at all, he thought
would come from the Central Pacific and encounter Takagi firs
rather than from the south. Otherwise the placement of Takagi
support force is unexplainable. Inoue had hopes that the R
Operation at least would take place without further incident. I
this he was also to be disappointed.

Vice Admiral Halsey's Task Force 16 made a fast trip fro
Hawaii to the South Pacific.[37] He did not detour to the west t
attack the Gilberts because CinCPac Intelligence had not place
any significant enemy forces in the region. On the afternoon whic
saw Task Force 17 lose the *Lexington,* Halsey was still over 1,00
miles away. Thus as events transpired, Task Force 16 would be to
late to fight in the Battle of the Coral Sea, but Halsey still mar
aged to make his presence count for something with Inoue, soon t
be bereft of carrier support of his own. CinCPac Intelligence kep
Halsey fully abreast of Japanese intentions through the daily intel
ligence bulletin and special communications. On 7 May Halse
learned of Japanese plans to take Ocean and Nauru islands. Tw
days later there came from Pearl Harbor word that the Japanes
had postponed the Port Moresby attack, but would continue witl
the invasions of Ocean and Nauru. CinCPac believed the actual RY
expeditionary force was rather weak, but added that there wer
indications that the Moresby Striking Force with the *Zuikaku* an
two heavy cruisers would refuel in the Bougainville area and ac
as a covering force on the convoy's southern flank. Two heavy
cruisers from the 6th Cruiser Division might join the covering
forces according to information received in Hawaii. CinCPac also
warned Halsey that Japanese air searches in the triangle Makin
Ellice-Solomons extended 700 miles from the Japanese base a
Makin.[38] From Tulagi the Japanese searched 600 miles.

Halsey was also party to CinCPac's messages regarding the
withdrawal of Fletcher's Task Force 17 from the Coral Sea. With
the breakoff of battle, there was no reason for Task Force 16 tc
rush into the Coral Sea. The evening of 10 May found Halsey
nearing the New Hebrides from the northeast. His first order o
business was to reach Efate and deliver the Marine fighter squadron
by air to the airfield at Vila. On the morning of 11 May, he sent
two aircraft to Efate to check the condition of the field. They reported that it was not suitable for operations, so Halsey despatched
the Marine fighters to Noumea. He forwarded with them a number

f messages for transmission at Noumea, as he wished to maintain
adio silence so as not to alert the Japanese of his presence. In the
messages, Halsey ordered Rear Admiral Kinkaid's Task Group 17.2
> join him as soon as possible. He also sketched his logistical situa-
ion, proposing to fuel his forces from one tanker, return that ves-
el to Pearl Harbor when it was emptied, and maintain the other
eet oiler in the Noumea area as a floating reserve.[39]

Like Fletcher before him, Halsey had to deal with an excellent
apanese air search network which covered most of the areas he
roposed to operate within. He had to wait to the south until the
apanese had committed themselves so that he could strike swiftly
efore the enemy could retreat to his own air cover. Halsey espe-
ially wanted a crack at the *Zuikaku*. Under these circumstances
e had to be patient until he received definite information as to
apanese plans and movements. That was the job of CinCPac In-
elligence. Meanwhile he attended to his deliveries and arranged
or his forces to refuel. On 12 May he steamed in the waters east
f the New Hebrides and New Caledonia. Around midday he re-
eived a CinCPac intelligence bulletin describing Japanese activi-
ies leading to the attack on Ocean and Nauru.[40] Part of the RY
nvasion forces was to have left Rabaul around 10 May with 14 May
as the likely date for the actual landings. Halsey responded to the
message by sending two dive bombers to Noumea that afternoon to
transmit messages. The communications requested Vice Admiral
Leary to arrange for air reconnaissance of Ontong Java, Tauu
Island, and the Kilinailau Group. These islands were east and
northeast of Bougainville. Halsey's intentions were plain, as his
message outlined the possibility of "offensive operations in that
area."[41] Task Force 16 clearly was preparing to go north to interfere with the Ocean and Nauru landings and attack the covering
forces in accordance with the directive from CinCPac.

Late that same day, Halsey received a second message from
Pearl Harbor which caused him to change his mind about going
north. CinCPac Intelligence had learned of Vice Admiral Inoue's
new orders postponing the Ocean-Nauru landings to 17 May. There
were new indications that the Japanese 5th and 6th Cruiser Divisions would comprise the covering force. Unfortunately it appeared
that the *Zuikaku* probably would break off operations and return
to Japan.[42] There was nothing for Halsey to do but remain south
of Efate. If he went north prematurely before the Japanese neared
Ocean and Nauru, he would have to pursue the invasion forces
into the Japanese land-based air umbrella surrounding Rabaul.
This would entail needless risks for his carriers. The Japanese had

to come out far enough so that Task Force 16 could pounce c them swiftly. Kinkaid with the two heavy cruisers and three destro ers of his Task Group 17.2 arrived on 12 May at Noumea. He i formed Halsey that he intended to sail the next day and wou: reach the waters about 200 miles south of Efate on the afternoc of 14 May.[43] This was the area in which Task Force 16 had saile during the last few days. Kinkaid told Halsey that if Task Fore 16 were not there, he would continue steaming north at 18 knot Halsey spent 13 May east of Efate marking time. The hea cruiser *Pensacola* and a destroyer which had departed from Pea Harbor on 5 May joined with Task Force 16 shortly after daw Halsey provided fuel for the two vessels, then transferred fuel o from one tanker to the other and sent the empty *Sabine* back t Pearl Harbor. The other tanker, the *Cimarron*, proceeded south t Noumea to act as a floating oil reserve. That morning as usual h despatched two dive bombers to Noumea to carry messages. In th way he instructed Kinkaid to join him on the afternoon of 15 Ma at a point about 50 miles southeast of Vanikoro in the Santa Cru Islands. If Task Force 16 was not there, Kinkaid was to stay in tha area to await further orders.[44] Halsey could not be more specifi because his movements depended on what the Japanese would dc As was his custom, Halsey that afternoon launched a midday searci of dive bombers to the north as a precautionary measure. Two SBI bombers failed to return from the mission. Halsey knew he ha time to look for the missing crews before going after the RY Inva sion Force, so he steamed north. At dawn the next day, he reache the vicinity in which one of the aircraft might have ditched. So fa everything was proceeding according to plan. Halsey had receivec no new information from CinCPac which would compel him t modify his plans to attack the Ocean-Nauru invasion forces abou 16 or 17 May.

On the morning of 14 May, Task Force 16 launched the norma dawn search of dive bombers and also a special flight to look fo the downed aviators. Neither mission netted any positive sightings Halsey continued his gradual advance to the north. He learned from ComSoWesPacFor that AAF search planes had not reached Ontong Java, but that there was another mission scheduled for the next day.[45] During the course of the day, it appears that his final plan for the descent on Ocean and Nauru matured. From his CinCPac intelligence bulletins, he possessed considerable information re garding Japanese strength and deployment. The invasion convoy, presumably with the covering force somewhere nearby, was to land troops on the two islands beginning on 17 May. It is quite likely that Halsey expected the Japanese to approach Ocean and Nauru on roughly a direct line from the Rabaul area, that is, from the southwest. Unbeknownst to him the Japanese took a roundabout course and descended upon Ocean and Nauru from the northwest. That would explain why he wanted Brett's aircraft to check Ontong Java, Tauu, and Kilinailau for evidence of Japanese seaplane bases and anchored tenders. The Japanese covering force supposedly comprised four heavy cruisers of the 5th and 6th Cruiser Divisions plus screening destroyers. There was certainly nothing that the *Enterprise* and the *Hornet* could not handle easily.

Halsey's major obstacle was Japanese air power. CinCPac Intelligence informed him that the 5th Air Attack Force had received heavy reinforcements of medium bombers capable of carrying torpedoes. Their attack radius was about 600 miles, marking the limit that Task Force 16 could safely approach Rabaul. Rabaul was about 1,000 miles southwest of Nauru, the western island of the pair. Japanese air bases in the Marshalls, likewise equipped with medium bombers, lay from 450 to 700 miles north of Ocean and Nauru. This put the two islands just within their reach. Thus the carriers were secure from attack if they operated in the waters south of the islands. The Japanese land attack planes were a potential threat, but the greater nuisance was the Japanese patrol plane network operating out of Tulagi and Makin. The disclosure of Task Force 16's position before Halsey was ready to strike would allow the Japanese to escape. The Japanese flying boats daily searched to a distance of 600 or 700 miles from their bases, and this Halsey knew. The search patterns fanning out of Tulagi and Makin overlapped in the area through which Task Force 16 would have to pass, but fortunately for Halsey they only converged at their outer limits. The Japanese flying boat search missions usually lasted from 12 to 14 hours. The aircraft took off at dawn or a little later, cruised at about 100 knots an hour, and returned to base around nightfall. This meant that the aircraft reached the end of their search radii late in the morning or very early in the afternoon, made a short dog leg to the left or right, and turned for home. Thus, by proper timing, it would be possible to pass undetected through the Japanese search zones after the aircraft had left their return points. The 5th Air Attack Force did not have enough aircraft for a two-phase search which would prevent such transits.

Regarding the details of Halsey's plan, much must remain supposition for reasons to be shown later. There does exist one positive indication as to his intentions. On the afternoon of 14 May, Halsey arranged for a new rendezvous between Task Force 16 and Kin-

kaid's Task Group 17.2.[46] The two groups were to meet at 090[0?]
16 May at a point south of and roughly between Ocean and Naur[u]
at a distance of about 300 miles southwest of the former and 3[5?]
miles southeast of the latter island. The rendezvous lay about 5[5?]
miles northwest of Task Force 16's noon position on 14 May, b[ut]
the direct course there would pass through the center of the Tula[gi]
search sectors, making it quite likely that the Japanese would sig[ht]
Task Force 16. However, Halsey had 45 hours, starting at noon, i[n]
which to reach the rendezvous, giving him time to maneuver t[o]
escape being spotted. According to previous orders, Kinkaid was t[o]
arrive at 1600 on 15 May at a point about 50 miles southeast [of]
Vanikoro. This was about 375 miles straight south of the ordere[d]
16 May meeting place, which would compel Kinkaid to steam 1[7?]
hours at 22 knots in order to join Halsey on time.

Given the spare nature of the information available, it is po[s-]
sible only to estimate what Halsey's plan of operation might hav[e]
entailed. It appears probable that Halsey intended to avoid the 1[5]
May search by remaining far to the east of longitude 170° east. B[y]
steaming northeast during the night of 14 May and the morning o[f]
15 May, Task Force 16 could have remained beyond the 600-mil[e]
search radius from Tulagi. In the afternoon after the flying boat[s]
had begun their return flights, Halsey could then have set a direc[t]
northwesterly course to reach the morning rendezvous without [a]
chance of being spotted. By the time the carriers had traversed th[e]
Makin search zone, the Makin-based flying boats would have long
since started their return legs. Thus by shaping the proper northeasterly course to the region of latitude 10° south, longitude 172°
east, Halsey could avoid both the Tulagi and Makin searches and
still turn northwest to reach his rendezvous in time without steaming at excessive speeds the whole time. Because of the limitations
of time, Kinkaid's ships, several hundred miles south of Task Force
16, could not afford to take any detours. It was possible that the
Japanese might sight Task Group 17.2 on the morning of 15 May
as it steamed north toward Vanikoro. However, the impact of Kinkaid's sighting, because he had only two heavy cruisers and three
destroyers, would have alarmed the Japanese infinitely less than
spotting two American fleet carriers. Indeed, Halsey thought that
the Japanese covering force far outnumbered Task Group 17.2, and
possibly he felt the Japanese would not consider Kinkaid much of
a threat. The rest of Kinkaid's passage north would have been
shielded by darkness.

It is possible to deduce from the point chosen by Halsey for the
16 May rendezvous what his attack plans may have encompassed.

The morning of 16 May would have found Task Force 16 and Task Group 17.2 seemingly on the flank of and fairly close to the Japanese invasion convoy and covering forces. This would have been true if the Japanese had taken the direct route from Rabaul to Ocean and Nauru. Utilizing his search planes to a radius of 250 miles, Halsey probably would have expected to find the Japanese ships sometime that day, hopefully early enough to have launched one or more air strikes against them before nightfall. There would also have been the possibility of utilizing some of his heavy cruisers and destroyers for surface attacks. That would be one explanation of why Halsey ordered Kinkaid to hurry north to join up with him. The sudden appearance of enemy carriers confronting the RY Invasion Force only one day from the objectives would certainly have been expected to cause extremely favorable tactical situations for the Americans.

In the late afternoon of 14 May, Task Force 16 steamed slowly northward in the waters just east of the 170th meridian. At 1700, Halsey detached the destroyer *Benham* to head northwest toward Vanikoro to rendezvous with Kinkaid at 1600 the next day to pass on new instructions. It seems rather unlikely that Halsey would have detached the *Benham* at that point, unless he soon intended to sail on a considerably different heading away from Vanikoro. It is quite possible that at this point Task Force 16 had begun the northeasterly detour to avoid the Tulagi searches the next day. It was at this juncture, probably around 1800 on 14 May, that Halsey received two communications from CinCPac which greatly altered his mission. To understand the full importance of the new directives, it is necessary to discuss developments between Admirals King and Nimitz and their respective analyses of the situation in the Pacific.

17
CinCPac Redeploys His Forces for the Midway Operation

While Vice Admiral Halsey awaited the opportunity to strike CinCPac began assembling definite intelligence regarding Japanese intentions. In a message to his task forces commanders on 9 May, Admiral Nimitz noted that the Japanese were forming a striking group of carriers in homeland waters destined for an operation.[47] The same day, the *Greybook* warned of indications that the enemy would execute a second raid on Oahu by large flying boats, as occurred on the night of 3 and 4 March. This raid was thought to be going to occur sometime between 15 and 20 May.[48] As of yet there was no definite indication as to where the enemy would strike, but the analysts worked hard to cull such information from the deciphered messages. As early as 11 May, the Belconnen station at Melbourne picked up indications that Japanese ships were to rendezvous at Saipan late in May. The idea of Saipan as a collection point led to the belief that the Central Pacific might be the target.[49] Truk was far more likely if the force were headed for the South Pacific. Intercepted messages used the code letters AF for one of the objectives. Lieutenant Commanders Layton and Rochefort believed AF stood for Midway, but they were not certain. Around 10 May, they secured CinCPac permission for a bit of radio deception.

Midway sent a plain language message saying the base was low on fresh water. In a few days, Hypo deciphered a Japanese message noting that AF had fresh water problems. Through such clever devices and much hard work, the intelligence officers and cryptanalysts began working out in detail Japanese designs for the Central Pacific.[50]

Admiral Nimitz on 10 May provided Admiral King with a summary of battle lessons and analysis based on the fragmentary reports from the Coral Sea.[51] So far the losses were nearly equal. The Pacific Fleet sustained the loss of the *Lexington* and damage to the *Yorktown* in return for destroying one Japanese carrier and inflicting heavy damage to another. Nimitz stressed that the United States could not afford to take losses equal to those of the enemy, because the Japanese had more carriers. He believed that Japanese success in the South Pacific lay in "decisive air superiority" and interlocking island air bases. In contrast, the Allies possessed bases too far apart for mutual defense and each too weakly defended to withstand a major blow. The only course of action was to build up air power in the Pacific, particularly by using carrier-type aircraft in defense of bases and long-range heavy bombers for search and attack missions. "Importance Pacific Area to our national interest requires resurvey of distribution of American plane output with larger allocation planes to Pacific Areas." Strengthening the island bases with aircraft would offer the possibility of inflicting heavy losses on the Japanese should they attack.

On 12 May the *Greybook* outlined what the planners thought were Japanese objectives. They expected the enemy to attack Port Moresby once again after receiving reinforcements in the Rabaul area, occupy Ocean and Nauru, and begin an operation on 21 May with a force numbering two to four carriers and about three battleships, target possibly Oahu. Plans Division outlined a procedure to meet the enemy. "In general we must make our Pacific positions dangerous to attack, secure and provide for an adequate striking force."[52] The latter was difficult since the loss of the *Lexington* and bomb damage to the *Yorktown*. Estimates as to the time needed to repair the *Yorktown* ran as high as three months. There was hope at Pearl Harbor that the *Yorktown* could be made battle-ready quickly, but without her only the *Enterprise* and the *Hornet* would be available to oppose the Japanese. The *Saratoga* was to depart in the first week of June from the West Coast, but it was doubtful that she could reach Pearl Harbor before the Japanese struck. Admiral King was able to offer the good news that he was assigning the carrier *Wasp* from the Atlantic to the Pacific Fleets, but it would take until late June before the ship reached Hawaii.

ComInCh was very concerned over the apparent threat in th Pacific, one he described on 12 May to the Joint Chiefs that coul emerge anywhere along the line Alaska-Hawaii-Australia by 1 June Early on 13 May, King sent a very important policy statement t Nimitz.[53] He was as worried about attrition in carrier strength a CinCPac, so much so that he recommended several measures to pre serve carrier strength. To spare Task Force 16 any useless risk, h told Nimitz he thought it was "inadvisable" for Halsey to operat beyond the support of Allied land-based air or within reach o Japanese shore-based aircraft. Of course, Halsey could respond t a major enemy attack or take advantage of exceptionally favorabl opportunities to inflict heavy damage on the enemy. King nex observed, "Our plans should remain fluid and adaptable to chang based on best information of latest developments," something in which Nimitz fully concurred.[54] King's own idea of enemy inten tions tended to emphasize the danger to the South Pacific bases which he thought the enemy might try to seize, perhaps after mak ing another attempt against Port Moresby.

King's next suggestion could not have pleased Nimitz at all "In order to preserve our carriers during such attack on islands i may be better to operate one or more carrier air groups from shore."[55] These would be combined with bomber and patrol plane reinforcements flown in from Hawaii and Australia. King stated that the Army was to build up service units at New Caledonia, Efate, Fiji, and Tongatabu. He suggested to Nimitz that he provide service units for airfields at New Caledonia and Fiji sufficient to operate one carrier air group at each place. The next logical step was for him to recommend that the Yorktown and the Lexington air groups remain in the South Pacific to help defend those two areas. Obviously King despaired of obtaining adequate air strength from the Army to defend islands he thought were absolutely vital. Consequently he resorted to the expediency of placing in static positions aviators and aircraft uniquely adapted for ultimate mobility on carrier decks. Although he mentioned only the two air groups made supernumerary by damage or loss of their flight decks, there was the implication of the possibility of using the other groups if need be.

Late on the same day, Nimitz replied to King with a general policy statement of his own, outlining the situation as he saw it along with his suggestions on how to deal with it.[56] He told ComInCh that the enemy was planning several operations: namely, a renewed attack on Port Moresby, the capture of Ocean and Nauru, and possibly raids by cruisers and destroyers on the bases between Hawaii and Samoa. The Japanese had also expressed interest in the Central Pacific, planning a flying boat raid on Pearl Harbor. Of the greatest importance, Nimitz stressed, were indications that the Japanese were forming a striking force possibly loaded with poison gas for an attack against a populated area, Oahu most likely but perhaps even the West Coast. Nimitz knew what he had to do to meet these attacks. First it was necessary to make Oahu impregnable from attack to avoid tying the fleet directly to its defense. Then one could provide reinforcements to the island chains in the South Pacific so that they would inflict maximum attrition on the Japanese if they attacked there. Finally, Nimitz stressed the need to form a powerful striking force which, using maximum mobility, could help blunt an enemy advance or counterattack against a weak point. That the carriers, including the air groups, should not be employed in a static role was the tenor of CinCPac's recommendations. To buttress the defense of the South Pacific, Nimitz once again suggested additional land-based aircraft be sent there. He stipulated that the planes should not be stripped from Hawaii or Australia as the Army would try to do. Those areas required all the air power they possessed to repulse imminent Japanese offensives.

Nimitz then turned specifically to the carriers, He did not agree with the detachment of the *Lexington* and the *Yorktown* groups to defend points in the South Pacific. He needed the planes and pilots to fill out the *Yorktown* group to enable that carrier to participate in the striking force he hoped to create. Tactfully Nimitz stated that he was in favor of stationing supernumerary carrier air groups on island bases, but recommended that this be accomplished when air base facilities were better developed in the South Pacific. Regarding Task Force 16, Nimitz acknowledged his agreement with King's suggestion that Halsey remain out of range of enemy attack planes, but he specified fighters, torpedo bombers, and dive bombers. He observed that if Halsey headed north from the New Hebrides, then Japanese long-range patrol aircraft were almost certain to sight him. This, he cautioned, "would reduce but perhaps not prevent his prospects of obtaining marked success if the enemy moves to Nauru and Ocean. Halsey has ample latitude."[57]

Nimitz was worried about his own latitude in controlling his carrier task forces. He requested that, because of the shortage of carriers until the arrival of the *Saratoga* and the *Wasp*, ComInCh review his April directive ordering CinCPac to keep two carriers in the South Pacific. The enemy's strength and threats to other areas in the Pacific had changed the situation. He interpreted King's comment about preserving carrier strength to mean that "they should not be risked against superior forces in defense of bases which can defend themselves," and this he agreed with.[58] It was a much more positive statement than that made by King. As a part of this, he inquired as to King's thoughts regarding the nature of Pacific Fleet support to aid MacArthur in meeting an almost certain second attack on Port Moresby. It was important to know whether King intended to commit Halsey to the defense of Port Moresby or other locations in the South Pacific, particularly in the light of the growing threat to the Central Pacific. MacArthur had the right to know whether he could count on carrier support to make his deployments accordingly. As for his own actions, Nimitz stated that he would take measures to prevent a second flying boat raid on Oahu and would also give consideration to moving Halsey to the Central Pacific, "if enemy drive to southeast is not indicated." He warned, "Time and distance involved require a definite decision in the near future."[59]

Unbeknownst to Admiral King, Admiral Nimitz took steps to ensure that the Japanese would not drive toward the southeast, thereby giving him the pretext to withdraw Task Force 16 to the Central Pacific. On the evening of 14 May, Halsey began moving north to attack the Ocean-Nauru invasion force. Sometime before 2000 hours, he received a message from Admiral Nimitz passing on the text of King's message:

> I consider operations of Task Force 16 inadvisable in forward areas beyond own shore-based air cover and within range enemy shore-based air until necessity requires such operations to oppose major enemy offensive or unless especially favorable results are to be expected.[60]

Nimitz tacked on his own interpretation that ComInCh's order applied only to combat planes, ruling out search planes by implication. As will be shown, this was an important change. Halsey was extremely irritated at the receipt of this order, which he noted, "greatly restricts the operations of this force at present."[61] His own air cover out of New Caledonia consisted of some shore-based fighters with attack radii of 200 miles or less and a few PBY Catalina flying boats.

Nimitz sent a second message to Halsey privately, which he apparently received the same time as the first.[62] ComInCh was not a message addressee in contrast to most of the other CinCPac communications. The orders directed Halsey to arrange deliberately for the Japanese to sight Task Force 16 the next day. After being observed at a safe distance from the Japanese, Halsey was to withdraw to the south so as not to expose his carriers to any form of counterattack. Nimitz had closed the previous ComInCh message with the statement that he felt complete confidence in Halsey's discretion. This applied as much to the second message as the first. No doubt realizing the implications of the order to have the enemy sight Task Force 16, Halsey did not note it in his war diary. Nor do the CinCPac message files contain the text of the communication. Evidently the original was destroyed. Halsey's actions, however, conclusively demonstrate its existence. This applies both to what he did on 15 May, and to what he wrote in his memoirs to disguise its effects.

Not long after 1800, Halsey changed course to the northwest with a heading of 327° True, speed 15 knots. This course put him on a direct line toward the center of the Tulagi search zone. That evening he crossed the 170th meridian and continued to close the distance between Tulagi and his carriers. There was no real necessity for recalling the *Benham* with new orders for Kinkaid. After he had disclosed his position to the Japanese, he would no longer have to maintain radio silence. At dawn, the *Enterprise* launched a search mission to the north to a radius of 200 miles. The SBD's spotted no enemy ships. By 0800 on 15 May, Task Force 16 had reached a point 475 miles east of Tulagi, well within the known Japanese search zone.

The expected contact with Japanese patrol planes occurred at 1015, as Halsey had cut the distance to Tulagi down to 450 miles. The *Enterprise*'s radar detected the presence of a snooper 70 miles away. The weather in the immediate vicinity of Task Force 16 was unusually clear, and the Japanese search crew was able to spot and correctly report the position, composition, and course of Task Force 16 without having to approach closer than about 60 miles. Halsey scrambled his fighters for an interception, but in no case could they overtake the wily Japanese pilots who sheered off and ran when the fighters headed toward them. So skillful were the Japanese in shadowing the force, that Halsey believed erroneously that they used a form of airborne radar. From his own radio analysts and messages from other Allied commands, Halsey quickly learned that the Japanese had seen what he wanted them to see and were broadcasting a general alarm within South Seas Force.

His mission essentially completed, at 1045 Halsey changed course to the north to make at least a token effort to head toward the 16 May rendezvous. The turn north was probably more for appearance' sake than anything else. At the time of his turn, the rendezvous point was due north, distance 270 miles. Flight operations with an unusual plague of operational accidents greatly slowed Task Force 16's rate of advance. A second air search to 250 miles that afternoon spotted nothing. Finally at 1424, Halsey decided to end the charade and turned to a new heading of 090° True. Task Force 16 upped its speed to 20 knots. The Japanese shadowers remained in the area until 1500 and evidently departed with the satisfaction that the American carriers had turned away. Halsey logged the official reason for his change of course and obvious abandonment of any attempt to attack the Ocean-Nauru invasion force. His war diary noted that Halsey had decided to abort the operation "due to being sighted by enemy air and subsequent position disclosed."[63] By radio he changed the rendezvous with Kinkaid to a new point and time: 0600 on 16 May, 260 miles southeast of Vanikoro.[64]

There were a number of reasons for which Nimitz had taken this extraordinary course of action, all based on his reliance on the quality of radio and combat intelligence furnished him by Layton and Rochefort. Largely because of its performance in determining the direction and extent of the Port Moresby offensive, Nimitz rapidly acquired complete confidence in radio intelligence information as analyzed by his experts. On the basis of this information, he thought that the appearance of Task Force 16 off Tulagi would bring about a number of desirable actions on the part of the Japanese. First of all, he expected South Seas Force to cancel the Ocean and Nauru invasions in the face of American carrier superiority in the area. If the Midway Operation developed as forecast, efforts by Halsey to repulse the Ocean and Nauru attack forces would not be worth the time lost or the risk of possible damage to the carriers. Just letting the Japanese spot the *Enterprise* and the *Hornet* would more than likely accomplish the same result.

Aside from its effect on the Ocean and Nauru Operation, knowledge of Halsey's presence in strength in the South Pacific would shift Japanese attention to that area. There was much less of a chance that the Japanese would go ahead with raids by cruisers and destroyers against the island bases south of Hawaii. Nimitz thought that the sighting would deter the Japanese from starting other operations in the South Pacific with local forces, while he prepared to meet Nagumo in the Central Pacific. As will be shown later, CinCPac later in May prepared an elaborate plan of radio deception in the South Pacific to lead the Japanese to believe that a carrier task force had remained in the South Pacific when in fact

Nimitz had returned all three carriers to Hawaii. This would aid him in defending Midway and help him spring a surprise on the Japanese Striking Force. The sighting would also have its effect on the Allied governments of Australia and New Zealand, offering the assurance because of the expected cancellation of local Japanese operations in the region that the Pacific Fleet was ready to offer its assistance in the event of renewed Japanese attacks in the area. Nimitz needed no political interference of the nature which MacArthur had tried to initiate through Prime Minister Curtin to tie down his forces. Thus the sighting was CinCPac's way to free himself temporarily of possible obligations in the South Pacific to allow him to concentrate on meeting the Japanese offensive in the Central Pacific. That Nimitz had to go to such extremes highlights King's deepening concern for the security of the South Pacific.

In retrospect, Halsey's actions are virtually inexplicable without knowledge of the secret order from Nimitz. Halsey's memoirs contain an interestingly obfuscated short account of the incident.[65] He avoided all mention of the Ocean-Nauru Operation or the secret order. Instead he stated that his mission was to prevent the Japanese from achieving "a break through between the New Hebrides and Fijis, as I would have done in their place."[66] He described his irritation at receiving the ComInCh order not to expose his carriers to Japanese shore-based air. He chose to characterize his decision to move northwest as an attempt to "scout a potential breakthrough area."[67] He took full responsibility for the decision, stating that it was on his own initiative. Thus he characterized the 15 May incident as resulting from his efforts to obtain "a better view," even though he knew it was a contravention of King's wishes. Halsey further added that the fact that his search planes (whose missions extended only 250 miles) failed to sight any Japanese warships "made me certain that a breakthrough was not imminent."[68]

Halsey's postwar version of his operations between 10 May and 16 May simply will not wash. Taken at face value with the intelligence messages and directives available today, Halsey's memoirs would sketch the operations of a rank incompetent who ruined a chance to strike a powerful blow against the Japanese. Nowhere in the CinCPac and ComSoWesPacFor bulletins is there any indication that the Japanese planned any immediate offensive operations in the South Pacific other than the capture of Ocean and Nauru. Halsey was far too competent a commander to jeopardize an entire operation by showing himself prematurely and needlessly. Certainly King, who had shown himself extremely sensitive to supposed timidness in Fletcher's operations in the Coral Sea, would not have tolerated such a missed opportunity to strike a significant blow at the enemy once Halsey had committed himself to the attack. The RY Invasion Force and its covering force were certainly worthy targets for Halsey's attention. As it was, King's directive not to enter enemy-controlled waters unless there was an especially worthwhile target served as a convenient excuse to break off the operation once the Japanese had sighted Task Force 16. One senses that Halsey's protests over the restrictions placed on his movements by the ComInCh order were deliberately exaggerated and designed to draw attention away from what really happened. Because Halsey operated under radio silence, King could not follow his movements at all. The Ocean-Nauru Operation quickly became forgotten by all (and virtually unmentioned by succeeding historians)[69] because of the dramatic Midway battle which followed so soon after. There can be little doubt that Nimitz's secret order existed and that it curtailed Halsey's expected attack on the Ocean-Nauru invasion forces. Thus Halsey handled Task Force 16 in full accordance with Nimitz's desires.

The effect of Halsey's disclosure of his position east of Tulagi had the impact on Vice Admiral Inoue that Nimitz wished.[70] The Tulagi-based flying boats reported sighting two enemy carriers and four heavy cruisers in a position bearing 090° and 445 miles from Tulagi. They tracked the carriers until 1500. The news electrified South Seas Force. Rear Admiral Yamada readied a strike group from his 5th Air Attack Force to hit the task force should it come within 700 miles of Rabaul. Local base commanders in the Solomons warned their men to prepare for an enemy strike. The situation required a change in plan for the Ocean-Nauru Operation. The enemy carriers as reported by Tulagi were about 700 miles south of the RY Invasion Force, which itself was 210 miles north of Nauru. Takagi's MO Striking Force was 380 miles northwest of the invasion convoy. At 1350, Inoue ordered the RY Invasion Force to suspend operations and retire to Truk.

For positive measures, Inoue ordered his surface forces to rendezvous in the hopes of launching a night attack on the American force if it continued on a westerly course. Takagi was to proceed southwest to join with two heavy cruisers of the 6th Cruiser Division, one light cruiser, and two destroyers at a point about 300 miles north of Rabaul. Inoue planned to bring the cruisers together on the night of 16 May and operate in the Rabaul area. Inoue believed that this carrier force was different from the one he had fought in the Coral Sea. Japanese radio intelligence had correctly detected the departure of carriers around 1 May from Hawaii, and he deduced it was this force that his aircraft had located. Inoue estimated that Allied naval strength in the area amounted to two carriers, seven to eight cruisers, and 16 destroyers, counting units known to be remaining from the Allied force originally encountered in the Coral Sea.

The 5th Air Attack Force lost contact with the American carriers after 1500 on 15 May. Throughout the night of 15 May and the morning of 16 May, Inoue concentrated his forces north of Rabaul to oppose the enemy. Fighters staged to Rabaul from Lae. By early afternoon, however, it appeared that the American force had retired, as the dawn search from Tulagi had failed to sight it. Inoue decided to postpone indefinitely the invasion of Ocean and Nauru, as the American carriers could disrupt the operation at will. He no longer possessed the forces to prevent them from doing so. He formally announced the suspension of the RY Operation during the afternoon of 16 May. With his action, the MO Operation as a whole came to a close, not having succeeded in any of its objectives except the seizure of Tulagi. On 17 May Combined Fleet removed the 5th Cruiser Division from South Seas Force, thus dissolving MO Striking Force. Inoue called off his alert the same day, as the American carriers did not appear that day either.

On 15 May King replied to Nimitz's messages.[71] His analysts had a different idea as to what the Japanese were planning. They agreed about the departure of the Japanese Striking Force from the homeland at the end of May, but thought that Truk was the destination. From there the Japanese were to initiate an offensive toward such locales as Port Moresby, northeastern Australia, New Caledonia, and Fiji. ComInCh Intelligence expected the enemy to commit four battleships and five to seven carriers as the main striking force. No definite objective had yet appeared in the radio decripts according to ComInCh planners. As for proposed Japanese operations in the Central Pacific, King acknowledged Midway as the probable goal, but downgraded CinCPac's estimate of the nature of the attack. He thought the enemy would depart from Saipan about 25 May but only with weak forces including the light carriers of their 3rd Carrier Division. He believed the Japanese desired the Midway Operation to serve as a diversion to distract the Pacific Fleet from the South Pacific where the real offensive would take place. He added that the Japanese might also be interested in eliminating Midway as an advanced submarine base. Alaska was involved in the Japanese plans, but King did not yet know to what extent. He warned that Howland and Baker islands might be targets as well, perhaps instead of Ocean and Nauru.

The analysts on ComInCh staff, like their boss heavily concerned with the South Pacific, fastened onto the intercepts outlining the arrangements the Japanese were making for a post-Midway general offensive in the South Pacific below Truk. Messages from Nagumo and other commanders assigning berths at Truk after the return of Striking Force from Midway had meant instead to ComInCh staff a concentration first at Truk for operations to the south. They unintentionally played down references to a large-scale Japanese attack in the Central Pacific. It was not enough merely to possess the fragmentary decrypts; rather, it was more vital how one pieced them together.

King's continued reliance on his own intelligence estimates which placed the Japanese main thrust in the South Pacific fully justified Nimitz's undercover efforts to return Task Force 16 to the Central Pacific. Late on 15 May, Nimitz sent another message to ComInCh clarifying his ideas regarding Japanese plans.[72] He envisioned three separate, perhaps simultaneous Japanese offensives. One had the western Aleutians as its objective and comprised carriers and cruisers. Port Moresby was the goal of the second enemy offensive, utilizing the forces already in the area with perhaps some reinforcements. The third Japanese attack would come against the Midway-Oahu line and was by far the most serious. It would involve the main Japanese striking force, most likely aiming to capture Midway. Nimitz was not certain about the timing of the three offensives, but figured they would fall between 25 May and 15 June. He noted that the sighting of Task Force 16 the previous day near Tulagi might cause the Japanese to expedite their attacks in the Central and North Pacific, that is, if the three operations were coordinated. This was a good reason for withdrawing Halsey to the Hawaiian area. In the face of the impending Japanese drive across the Central Pacific, he saw no recourse but to bring Halsey back to Pearl Harbor. There were not sufficient forces to defend all of the bases adequately, and Hawaii was more important than the rest. Nimitz also told King he would try to bring the *Saratoga* into the action, but feared the large carrier would not reach the battle area in time. He also outlined plans to deploy the old battleships in the Hawaiian area.

Indeed the very hour that he communicated with ComInCh, Nimitz sent orders to Halsey to return to Pearl Harbor. Halsey received the news from CinCPac on the afternoon of 16 May as he steamed southeast toward the New Hebrides. Nimitz informed him that the Japanese had canceled the Ocean-Nauru Operation and added, "Desire you proceed to the Hawaiian area."[73] Halsey spent two more days in the Efate area arranging for his support vessels and fleet train to rendezvous with him in the light of the change in plans. This would have taken much longer had Halsey continued north to engage the Ocean-Nauru Invasion Force. On 17 May CinCPac instructed him not to attack enemy positions on the trip back and emphasized, "Consider it important that you not be sighted by the enemy."[74] On 18 May, with Halsey still dallying in the South Pacific gathering his scattered forces, Nimitz prodded him with a sharp despatch, "Expedite return." Halsey wrote in his memoirs, "That could mean only one thing; trouble was brewing somewhere else in the Pacific."[75] Rear Admiral Fletcher arrived at Tongatabu on 16 May and began refueling and reprovisioning his ships. While there he received orders from CinCPac to return to Pearl Harbor at his best practical speed. Nimitz had learned from his experts that the Yorktown could be repaired at Pearl Harbor, but there still was no estimate as to how long this would take. On 19 May Halsey finally shaped his course to the northeast, and Fletcher at Tongatabu did the same. It marked the first time since early February that the Pacific Fleet did not have at least one carrier on patrol in the South Pacific. This was the culmination of Nimitz's efforts to concentrate his available carrier strength in the Central Pacific to help deal with the expected heavy attack on Midway.

The sixteenth of May at Pearl Harbor saw no response from King to Nimitz's situation estimate and orders to Task Force 16 to return to the Central Pacific. Consequently Nimitz sent a follow-up communication late that evening to Washington. He specified "considerable differences in estimates probably on the same data."[76] According to his analysts, there was no confirmation of a future Japanese concentration of warships at Truk; rather, they believed the enemy might exploit a Midway victory with an invasion of Hawaii to achieve strategic position with possible decisive results before American war production affected the balance of power in the Pacific. Nimitz had to tread lightly on the removal of Task Force 16 from the South Pacific because of the heavy political implications with General MacArthur and the Commonwealth governments, not to mention King himself. His efforts to that end had been conducted with skill and tact. He concluded the message, "Will watch situation closely and return Halsey to Southward if imminent concentration that area is indicated."[77]

King replied on 17 May, stating that he was now in general agreement with CinCPac's estimate, except for a few key points.[78] ComInCh Intelligence believed that the Midway-Aleutian attacks would begin about 30 May or soon after, rather than in early June as Nimitz thought. King reiterated strongly that the Japanese were planning a large-scale offensive in the South Pacific, either against Port Moresby and northeastern Australia or New Caledonia and Fiji. These attacks were scheduled to start in mid- or late June. Regarding strategy to cope with the Midway offensive, King likewise concurred that CinCPac should concentrate the bulk of his forces in Hawaiian waters. He thought the Japanese might precede their landing at Midway with a carrier raid on Oahu. Correctly he divined the overall purpose of the Japanese plan, that is, to destroy a large part of the Pacific Fleet. He outlined the proper procedure to meet this form of attack:

> Chiefly to employ strong attrition tactics and not repeat NOT allow our forces to accept such decisive action as would be likely to incur heavy losses in our carriers and cruisers.[79]

He also proposed the creation of a North Pacific Force to help in the defense of Alaska.

King's change of mind regarding the scope of the Japanese offensive in the Central Pacific represented the triumph of Nimitz's efforts to reconcentrate his forces in the Hawaiian area. Naturally the Pacific Fleet analysts were more concerned with the signs of an offensive building in their area; they always had been, as it was the deadliest threat. Consequently they looked for and emphasized those references in the decrypts which indicated Japanese designs on the Central Pacific, to the detriment of hints relating to the post-Midway general offensive in the South Pacific. After the ComInCh staff received the CinCPac estimates and re-evaluated the evidence, there must have been some consternation among them as their boss did not like to receive incomplete information. He relied as heavily on his experts as Nimitz relied on his. However, ComInCh analysts had correctly noted the plans for Japanese operations planned after Midway and provided an excellent balance for CinCPac estimates of the Midway-Alaskan offensives. One experienced intelligence officer subsequently highlighted the point by citing an old Hindu proverb: "The snake under your table is given more careful attention."[80] The vital fact remains that the intelligence officers and cryptanalysts did correctly divine the scope of the next Japanese operation and provided this incredibly valuable knowledge to leaders willing to heed their advice. At first there was disagreement between the two staffs, but Nimitz succeeded in engineering the necessary redeployment of carrier strength so that no harm was caused. Given the enormous difficulties in cryptanalysis and evaluation, the differences are entirely understandable considering the nature of the intelligence information. The two staffs did combine in the next several days to provide an amazingly accurate appraisal of the Midway Operation, and this proved to be one of the major reasons for victory at Midway.

In accordance with a joint directive sent by Marshall and King to all Pacific commands, Nimitz sought to coordinate his activities with MacArthur and to inform him of developments. On 16 May he sent a message via Leary to MacArthur informing him that he was withdrawing Task Force 16 to the Hawaiian area. To reinforce Crace's cruiser squadron, Nimitz instructed Halsey to detach one heavy cruiser and a destroyer to Leary. This, Nimitz noted, would make Crace's squadron for the time being stronger than the Japanese forces remaining in the New Britain–Solomons area. He outlined War Department plans to station 16 heavy and 26 medium bombers in New Caledonia and Fiji. CinCPac also told MacArthur that he would receive the gist of operational plans for carrier operations taking place in the Southwest Pacific Area prior to the time the warships reached waters under his jurisdiction. He thanked MacArthur for rendering cooperation to Fletcher during the Coral Sea battle and specifically asked for increased efforts at coordination of land-based aircraft and ships. Most important, Nimitz requested MacArthur's statement on whether he could provide aircraft from the Southwest Pacific Area to reinforce bases in the South Pacific Area in accordance with AAF policy. He referred to ComInCh's estimate of a large Japanese offensive in the South Pacific to begin in mid-June.[81] MacArthur's answer reached Pearl Harbor on 18 May. He alluded to efforts to increase air and surface coordination, but declined to offer any aircraft reinforcements to the South Pacific. His own responsibilities forced him to retain all his bombers in Australia; he could spare none for the South Pacific. Ironically he did end the message: "Call upon me freely. You can count on my most complete and active cooperation."[82]

The overriding importance of countering the attack on Midway submerged the question of the South Pacific to a large extent, but CinCPac proceeded with the scheduled reinforcements and construction of additional facilities on the SoPac island bases. There was the feeling on Oahu that the Pacific Fleet would have to redeploy its strength to the south after the Midway Operation.

Consequently Nimitz pressed for airfield construction with which to base bombers which the War Department hopefully would provide. Nimitz retained direct command of SoPac while Vice Admiral Ghormley inspected and acquainted himself with the command. He did not take over as ComSoPac until mid-June. During May, troops ordered to the South Pacific months before finally reached their destinations. Australia received the last detachment of the 41st Division and all of the 32nd Division, giving SWPA two full American infantry divisions. Likewise Efate and Tongatabu in May each received an Army regimental combat team assigned by the Joint Chiefs in March. In addition, an Army fighter squadron arrived on Tongatabu to serve as an air defense force. The 37th Division, originally intended for New Zealand, was rerouted to Fiji in early May and was en route to the island group, although part of the unit had to transship after arriving in Australia and New Zealand. During May, the 3rd Marine Brigade, based around the 7th Marines, and the 8th Defense Battalion reached Samoa. The only new occupation of note in SoPac took place on 28 May, when two Army infantry companies landed at Espiritu Santo, between Guadalcanal and New Caledonia. Brigadier General Harry D. Chamberlain, the Army commander on Efate, and Rear Admiral John S. McCain recommended the move on 20 May. King, Nimitz, and Ghormley agreed to garrison Espiritu Santo as an outpost for Efate. In one respect, that of ground forces, SoPac was much better off than in April, but no one knew whether the combined air, sea, and land forces would be sufficient to withstand the major Japanese offensive expected in mid-June.[83]

18
Strategy
in the Pacific
after the
Coral Sea Battle

In two sessions of the Joint Chiefs on 11 and 12 May, Admiral King reported the results of the Battle of the Coral Sea and questioned basic Army strategy for the South Pacific. On 11 May he called for a practical demonstration of the Army's procedures to concentrate heavy bombers from Hawaii and Australia in the South Pacific. The next day he explained the reason for his concern. The Battle of the Coral Sea had dealt a temporary strategic check to the Japanese advance, but at the cost of the *Lexington* sunk and the *Yorktown* crippled. This left only two carriers, the *Enterprise* and the *Hornet*, in fully operational condition. According to the latest estimates, the Japanese had two carriers in the South Pacific and six to eight in home waters, hardly favorable odds for the Pacific Fleet. From Naval Intelligence, King had learned that the Japanese were planning an offensive operation in which a powerful striking force was to sortie on 21 May from Japan. It could appear by early June anywhere along the line Alaska-Hawaii-Australia, and its destination was unknown. King's personal guess was that the Japanese would make a second try at capturing Port Moresby, because they had not achieved their objective in the MO Operation. There was the chance that the enemy would shift his emphasis eastward to attack New Caledonia or Fiji. Because of the great disparity in strength between the two carrier forces, King stated that it would be disastrous for CinCPac to engage the enemy except with strong land-based air support. Because of the uncertainty of the enemy's objectives, King requested that aircraft, troops, and antiaircraft units be sent to New Caledonia, Efate, Fiji, Tongatabu, and Samoa.[84]

The same day the Joint Chiefs discussed the measures needed to meet the possible Japanese threat. Generals Marshall and Arnold were reluctant to commit themselves until they knew more of the enemy's intentions. Arnold recommended that bombers en route from Hawaii to Australia be halted in the South Pacific to comprise a temporary defense for New Caledonia, Fiji, Tongatabu, and Efate, the last two islands not yet possessing operational airfields. Specifically, sixteen B-17's intended as replacements for the Southwest Pacific Area were involved. Orders went out to Lieutenant General Emmons, commander of the Army's Hawaiian Department, to prepare airfields in the Fijis for 70 bombers and to Major General Patch on New Caledonia to ready fields on that island to take 70 bombers. This was to pave the way for a massive staging of bombers from Hawaii and Australia. The next day, War Department planners suggested that two medium bomb squadrons destined for the Southwest Pacific Area also be detained in the South Pacific, adding 26 medium bombers.[85] There was no thought of allocating additional aircraft from the United States, aircraft in readiness to fly to England under the Bolero scheme. The Pacific would have to get along with the forces already provided. The Joint Chiefs knew General MacArthur would not be pleased with the proposed arrangement, as it cut deeply into his own strength. Given the low number of aircraft in commission in the Southwest Pacific Area, the 16 heavy bombers represented about the same number of heavy bombers that General Brett could put in the air at one time.

Informed of the president's decision to go ahead with Bolero, General MacArthur remained undaunted. He responded on 8 May with a long message to Marshall outlining the strategic situation as he saw it. According to MacArthur, the Japanese were concentrating in strength to move against Australia and the line of communication with the United States. There would be no offensive against India in the near future as the British feared, implying that British forces defending the western Indian Ocean were going to waste. The real threat was in the Pacific. MacArthur proposed to meet the enemy attack frontally in the South Pacific, while developing a flank threat either by an outright offensive or a feint against the Japanese communications. To do this, he wanted under his command two aircraft carriers to "balance" his naval forces. In addition he requested an increase in operational combat planes in Australia from 500 to 1,000. As a ground force he required three "first-class" American divisions. He did not consider the two American National Guard divisions allocated to him to be well trained. Marshall replied in the negative to all of MacArthur's suggestions.[86] Bolero had its uses against the commander of the Southwest Pacific as well as the Navy.

MacArthur and his commanders in the Southwest Pacific Area analyzed the operational results of their participation in the Coral Sea Battle. On 13 May he informed Marshall that his air units had achieved "complete coordination with naval forces." Such coordination between air and naval forces, MacArthur added, could be developed "without difficulty." In contrast there was great trouble in obtaining such cooperation in operations involving land, sea, and air forces. In that case, "the operation must be handled both as to planning and execution by the commander of the area in which the operation takes place."[87] In other words, MacArthur thought he should assume supreme command over any action in his area requiring cooperation between air, naval, and land forces. This meant the impending Japanese attempt to take Port Moresby, with possible attacks on northeast Australia. MacArthur was irritated over the fact that carrier forces glided through his area, participating in operations to defend key areas within SWPA, but not under his control.

MacArthur was certainly overly sanguine when he stated that his air units had attained complete coordination with the naval forces. Rear Admiral Crace and the sailors of Support Group did not agree with him. On 7 May three B-17's from Townsville mistook Support Group for Japanese transports and bombed them, fortunately with horrendously poor accuracy. Crace complained to Leary as soon as he reached port on 12 May. Leary brought the matter to Brett's attention and received assurances on 16 May that recognition of naval vessels by aviators would improve. The bomber crews complained that they had neither the training to recognize warships nor detailed preflight knowledge of friendly ship movements to determine where their own forces might be. Crace was not satisfied and complained so loudly that on 19 May Brett prohibited further discussion of the matter as it would create "especially fine material for Japanese propaganda."[88] The fact remains that there was very little coordination between air and naval operations aside from search missions. Rear Admiral Fletcher was unable to secure coordinated attacks on Japanese vessels until the mistaken identification on 9 May of a force pursuing Task Force 17.

On 14 May in a communication to MacArthur, Marshall discussed the War Department's ideas relating to the upcoming crisis in the Pacific.[89] He noted the Japanese concentration north of Truk and indicated that the planners believed the Japanese would strike the line of communication from Hawaii to Australia sometime between 25 May and 1 June. Because of the disparity in strength between the contending carrier forces, it was vital that the Pacific Fleet have support from land-based aircraft. As of yet the ultimate target for the Japanese attack was not known. The War Department planners hoped to retain the flexibility in deployment of the air strength to shift bombers to the point of danger. He informed MacArthur that 16 heavy bombers in the process of flying through the air ferry route to Australia were being halted in the South Pacific, specifically one provisional squadron (eight planes) at New Caledonia and the other at Fiji. Regarding the two squadrons of medium bombers, he ordered MacArthur to send the ground echelons already in Australia to New Caledonia to join the combat crews and aircraft slated to fly down from the West Coast via Hawaii.

Marshall described the intended deployment of the bombers. If the Japanese attacked MacArthur in Australia, then the bombers were to join him immediately; but if the enemy showed up east of New Caledonia, they would remain at New Caledonia and Fiji. If the enemy split the difference and operated in the Coral Sea, then MacArthur would receive eight B-17's, while the other eight remained based on New Caledonia. Marshall stated the basic strategy thusly:

> We are striving to have each of the island bases so well protected by ground forces and to have Army and Navy air strength so flexibly arranged that we can strike the enemy damaging blows wherever he may appear.[90]

Thus Marshall adopted the basic strategy he ridiculed in his 5 May memorandum for the president, that of preparing the island bases for attack. Unfortunately the amount of air strength in the South Pacific did not live up to his contention that the Japanese Striking Force would very likely suffer "damaging blows."

In the middle of May, CinCPac Naval Intelligence officers succeeded in piecing together a remarkably accurate picture of the mpending Japanese offensive in the Central and North Pacific reas. On 16 May General Emmons learned from Admiral Nimitz hat the Japanese objectives were most likely Midway and the Aleuians, with the possibility of raids on Oahu. Emmons reported this nowledge to the War Department.[91] The next day Admiral King old the Joint Chiefs of the depth of the Japanese offensive and alled for reinforcements for Hawaii and Alaska. On 18 May he ubmitted a memorandum to Marshall outlining the forecast of he ComInCh and CinCPac staffs regarding the course of the Japaese offensive. According to the latest information, the Japanese ad scheduled the opening attacks for 30 May or a little later. A najor objective of the enemy was the destruction of a large amount f the Pacific Fleet. Consequently King asked Marshall to reinforce he Hawaiian garrison and hold temporarily in Hawaii forces desined for other areas. King stressed the word temporarily, because he Japanese would supposedly follow up their Central Pacific drive with attacks beginning in the middle of June against Southwest ind South Pacific areas. Probable Japanese objectives included Port Moresby, the airfields in northeastern Australia, New Caledonia, and Fiji. This would necessitate a redeployment of strength to the southwest after the threat to the Central Pacific had been dealt with.[92]

The planners at the War Department acted quickly once they learned that Hawaii and Alaska were under direct threat of Japanese attack. Hitherto they had largely neglected those two areas. The Seventh Air Force in Hawaii had received very few reinforcements since the beginning of the war when the Japanese had struck a deadly blow to its strength during the Pearl Harbor attack. On 1 May the Seventh Air Force had only eighteen B-17 heavy bombers and fourteen obsolete B-18 bombers in operational condition, protected by about 140 fighters in working order. The Eleventh Air Force in Alaska consisted of 15 heavy bombers, 24 medium bombers and 54 fighters, supported by 30 fighters and 12 medium bombers from the Royal Canadian Air Force. The War Department on 18 May arranged to fly additional B-17 bombers to Hawaii, but no organized units. Sixteen of the bombers had crews temporarily furnished by a bomb group training on the West Coast, but the rest did not. On 20 May General Arnold decided to fly eight B-17's down to New Caledonia, half of the original 16 intended for temporary service in the South Pacific before proceeding on to the Southwest Pacific Area. In Hawaii, General Emmons was to hold the remaining eight B-17's and also the air echelons of the two medium bomb squadrons (26 bombers), four aircraft of which had reached Hawaii. By 31 May, the Seventh Air Force wielded a force of fifty-six B-17's, of which 44 were operational. However, the War Department had provided no new fighter units.[93]

To defend Alaska, Admiral Nimitz was forced to detach warships for the North Pacific Area to comprise Task Force 8 under Rear Admiral Robert A. Theobald. Task Force 8 consisted of two heavy cruisers, three light cruisers, 13 destroyers, and seven submarines. To reinforce the Eleventh Air Force, the War Department despatched seven B-17's as replacements, followed by two heavy bomb squadrons with 24 bombers, one medium bomb squadron with 16 bombers, and four fighter squadrons with a total strength of 115 fighters.[94] When aircraft were needed to defend what the War Department considered an important area, they despatched them with alacrity, in contrast to the lackadaisical manner in which they provided aircraft for the South Pacific.

In the midst of concern for the Japanese attack on Midway and the Aleutians, both Admiral King and General MacArthur sought to remind the War Department of the continuing danger to the Southwest and South Pacific. On 18 May, Rear Admiral John S. McCain arrived at Noumea and two days later assumed his post as Commander of Air Forces in the South Pacific Area. On 21 May he sent to King and Nimitz an estimate of the forces needed for his command. For immediate reinforcements to be sent "as soon as planes and personnel can be made available," McCain requested a total of 34 fighters, 24 medium bombers, and 24 heavy bombers from the AAF, as well as 31 dive bombers, six patrol planes, and six observation planes from the Navy. Eventual reinforcements for ComAirSoPac recommended by McCain totaled 135 fighters, 60 medium bombers, and 60 heavy bombers from the AAF and 25 fighters, 100 dive bombers, and 18 search planes from the Navy. McCain had real reason to worry about his command in the event of a strong Japanese attack. As of 18 May, the island chain between New Caledonia and Samoa had only 156 aircraft, of which the 96 fighters were the only combat worthy planes. There were no bombers other than 12 obsolete Marine Corps dive bombers at Samoa and 12 New Zealand Hudsons at Fiji.[95]

On 19 May, General MacArthur realized that the first phase of the Japanese offensive was directed toward Hawaii and Alaska. On that day he informed Admiral Nimitz that he was recommending to the Combined Chiefs of Staff, evidently through General Marshall, that elements of the British Eastern Fleet in the Indian Ocean be brought into the Southwest Pacific Area or create a diversion in the eastern Indian Ocean. He added: "I will assist your actions to the extent possible by direct support or through diversion. Number of planes here inadequate for direct reinforcement of SOPAC Area."[96] Thus MacArthur would not release his meager force of heavy bombers to fly to the South Pacific bases for the excellent reason that he needed them to defend Australia from the feared widespread Japanese advance. Japanese air units based in Papua and Rabaul kept steady pressure on the Southwest Pacific Area. This was the fatal flaw in the AAF's idea of strategic mobility for the bombers. Japanese threats, actual or potential, could freeze the bombers in Hawaii or Australia and prevent them from staging through the ferry route to the South Pacific.

MacArthur continued his pressure on the War Department for additional reinforcements to the Pacific despite Bolero. In this he served as an ally of Admiral King and the Navy, who were trying to achieve the same result. On 22 May Marshall tried to mollify MacArthur by pointing out the reasons behind the concentration of forces in Hawaii and added that if a Japanese threat developed against the Southwest Pacific Area, additional aircraft would fly down from Hawaii to Australia. Evidently this message failed to reassure him, for the next day he radioed Marshall his analysis of the situation and the measures he thought necessary to meet it. MacArthur noted that, "Lack of seapower in the Pacific is and has been the fatal weakness in our position since the beginning of the war."[97] He went on to suggest that the Combined Chiefs of Staff carefully weigh the needs of the Atlantic and Indian Ocean areas and then withdraw much of the naval strength there, sending it to the Pacific. Suitably reinforced, the Pacific Fleet would have the capacity to deal with the Japanese Navy once and for all.

General MacArthur's suggestions were in agreement with ideas being developed by the ComInCh planners. On 19 May the Joint Chiefs received the War Department schedule drawn up on 13 May detailing the allocation of forces to the Pacific, according to the current priority for Bolero. Two days later, King learned of Rear Admiral McCain's recommendations for air reinforcements to the South Pacific, which certainly would not be met in the War Department's present allocations. On 24 May King submitted to the Joint Chiefs a memorandum calling for another reassessment of policy for the Pacific. He outlined the Navy's progress to date in the Pacific, attributing success to the Navy's access to "timely information" through a partial reading of the Japanese naval cipher. King warned that such information might not continue in the future, and in that event given the weakness of Allied forces in the Pacific, "disaster in the PACIFIC AREA is probable."[98] Clearly worrying

King was the planned Japanese post-Midway offensive in the South Pacific, the scope of which was to some extent known to the Americans. To meet the threat, King proposed a concentration of air and seapower in the Australia-Fiji area to be completed by 1 July. To reinforce his own fleet units, King proposed that the British Eastern Fleet be moved from the western Indian Ocean to Ceylon as soon as possible, there to be joined by warships detached from the Atlantic, including carriers and battleships. The whole assemblage was to sail to the waters between Australia and Fiji by early July to join with the Pacific Fleet. One of King's staff later wrote that for his boss to call upon Royal Navy assistance for the Pacific meant that he was most worried indeed.[99]

From the War Department King requested vastly increased air support in the South Pacific to cover the combined Allied fleets. Such an increase in air strength in the region would require the build-up to take place "as rapidly as possible, giving this objective first priority (even over BOLERO)."[100] ComInCh planners forecast that the Southwest and South Pacific Areas together should have an air strength in July of 175 heavy bombers, 280 medium bombers, 26 light bombers, and 795 army fighters. AAF allocations according to JCS 48 and the War Department's 19 May schedule provided the two commands with 110 heavy bombers, 172 medium bombers, 87 light bombers, and 642 fighters, most of which were to be on station by 31 August 1942. King's concern for the air strength in the two areas was very real. The Southwest and South Pacific Areas together had in mid-May approximately 20 heavy bombers, 86 medium bombers, 15 light bombers, and 380 army fighters in operational condition. Because of Bolero the supply of aircraft to the Pacific, except to reinforce Hawaii and Alaska, was nearly nonexistent. King felt the new circumstances in the Pacific compelled a drastic change of policy, even to the detriment of Bolero. Because of the vast distances involved, action had to be taken quickly to reinforce the region Australia-Fiji.[101]

General Marshall was not impressed with King's alarums and resented another intrusion in the schedule for Bolero. Marshall replied to King's memorandum on 27 May.[102] He pointed out that he was willing to agree to such a naval concentration, strange since he would need naval support for his cherished Sledgehammer operation in September if final plans were approved by the British. However, Marshall stated categorically that he would not provide the AAF aircraft required to protect such a concentration of warships. He hearkened back to the president's decision of 6 May in favor of Bolero and restated his determination to follow through

ith that course of action. The AAF was anxious to begin its pre-
nvasion air offensive against Germany. Marshall noted the prepa-
ations which the War Department had made to meet the threat
n the North and Central Pacific. That was enough diversion
f effort to the Pacific. Nimitz and MacArthur would have to deal
vith the Japanese offensives largely using the resources at hand.
Marshall had the aircraft with which to reinforce the Pacific, but
hose to commit them to Britain. Events about to take place in
he Central Pacific were to bring about the end of the First South
'acific Campaign in a most surprising manner.

19
Midway—
Unexpected Solution
for the
South Pacific Problem

In the three weeks' grace given it through radio intercepts telling of Japanese intentions to attack Midway, the Pacific Fleet diligently prepared for what would be the decisive encounter of the Pacific War—the Battle of Midway. On 18 May Admiral Nimitz convened a conference among the CinCPac staff to assess the situation and determine the best course of action to take to meet Japanese attacks on Midway. On 21 May the staff produced a detailed situation estimate.[103] The immediate problem was twofold. CinCPac expected the Japanese to launch an offensive in the Central Pacific with Midway as its objective, with a great likelihood of a raid on Oahu. Secondly, the Japanese were going to attack the western Aleutians with the idea of capturing one or more islands to use as a foothold in the area. Regarding forces, CinCPac analysts believed on the basis of radio intelligence that the Japanese would employ in the Midway attack four fleet carriers, two to four fast battleships, eight to nine heavy cruisers, 15 to 20 destroyers, two submarine squadrons, and troops for an invasion force, totaling, according to carrier air strengths known to CinCPac, about 260 combat planes. The latest intercepts indicated that the Midway force would leave Saipan about 26 May or shortly thereafter, able o reach its objective by 3 June or thereabouts. The Aleutian attack force was believed to be weaker, only two carriers, one light and the other converted, with low plane strengths. In escort, the staff believed there might be three heavy cruisers, one light cruiser, 16 destroyers, and eight to ten submarines, as well as troops. According to schedule, the Aleutian force was to leave northern Japan about 25 or 26 May and reach the target area around 1 June.

In determining his strategy, Admiral Nimitz had to consider the forces available to him. The heart of his striking force was Halsey's Task Force 16 built around the *Enterprise* and the *Hornet*, expected to reach Pearl Harbor on 26 May. This would enable Nimitz to place the two carriers in position near Midway by 1 June. Fletcher's Task Force 17 with the *Yorktown* was the big question mark. Nimitz hoped the Pearl Harbor dockyard could patch up the damaged carrier in time to join Task Force 16 north of Midway. If not, he decided to send her immediately to the West Coast, as Pearl Harbor would not be safe enough if the Japanese attacked again. The two task forces would comprise three carriers, seven heavy cruisers, one light antiaircraft cruiser, and 14 destroyers, with 230 combat planes counting the presence of the *Yorktown*. Without the *Yorktown*, Halsey would have only about 155 aircraft, which would weaken him severely. The only other carrier available for service was the *Saratoga*, expected to leave San Diego on 5 June. She would not be able to arrive in time for the early stages of the action. On the West Coast also were the seven battleships of Task Force 1 under Vice Admiral Pye. They could sail for Pearl Harbor at any time. As his submarine force, Nimitz had the 19 submarines of Task Force 7 at his disposal. To handle the Aleutian defense, Nimitz utilized two heavy cruisers, three light cruisers, 13 destroyers, and seven submarines to form Task Force 8 under Rear Admiral Theobald. Theobald headed north to cooperate with Army forces already there.

Nimitz had a definite directive from King regarding the use of CinCPac's carrier and cruiser forces. On 17 May, ComInCh specified, as related previously, that attrition was to be used and that the striking forces were not to enter into "decisive action"[104] which might cause heavy damage to them. Nimitz fully agreed. Circumstances had changed since 22 April, when CinCPac issued the situation estimate for the South Pacific campaign involving the Coral Sea battle. In it, Pacific Fleet analysts had rated Japanese naval air power as "excellent against surface ships when not well protected from air attack."[105] On 21 May, one battle later, they noted that the Japanese "have amply demonstrated their ability to use their carrier air with great ability. We can no longer underestimate the naval air efficiency."[106] The loss of the *Lexington* and the possible crippling of the *Yorktown* brought about a change of attitude among the planners regarding the next encounter. They were no quite as sure of victory should the two fleets meet in battle as the were in April. It was not that Task Force 17 had not fought well it had. But with the Coral Sea came the full realization, for Cin CPac planners if not the Japanese, that no matter how well some one fights, there are bound to be casualties.

The odds confronting CinCPac at Midway according to his situation estimate really were no worse than what had appeared to face him in late April in the South Pacific. Then he was willing to meet the Japanese head-on, confident of victory. This time both King and Nimitz opted reluctantly for new tactics. Nimitz agreed with King that it would be foolish to meet the Japanese directly:

> Not only our directive from Commander-in-Chief, U.S. Fleet, but also common sense dictates that we cannot now afford to slug it out with the probably superior approaching Japanese forces. We must endeavor to reduce his forces by attrition—submarine attacks, air bombing, attack on isolated units. The principle of calculated risk is indicated. . . . If attrition is successful the enemy must accept the failure of his venture or risk battle on disadvantageous terms for him.[107]

The word "now" in the first sentence of the quote is significant. Previously there was the expectation in the Pacific Fleet that is could defeat the Japanese in battle, even with the odds somewhat against it. Now the Pacific Fleet would have to be much more careful, husbanding slim reserves, springing surprise attacks. Stealth rather than strength would have to be the answer. Nimitz did not prefer such tactics; in his situation estimate he listed them in the section detailing American weaknesses.

In accordance with the new policy, Nimitz decided to enhance the mobility and long-range striking capability of his forces. This meant the battleships were once more out of the picture. They were slow and could not operate efficiently with the carriers, and there were not sufficient escort vessels to have them operate independently of the carriers. They required heavy air support to protect them from air attack. They could not even stay in Pearl Harbor, as it was not safe from a second raid. The only logical course was for the battleships to remain on the West Coast. Instead, Nimitz put his faith in carrier striking forces combined with land-based air. He decided to deploy Task Force 16 northeast of Midway, where could offer support to Midway and operate on the right flank f any Japanese advance toward Midway or Oahu. Task Force 17 would join Halsey if the *Yorktown* could be repaired in time. He endeavored to bring the *Saratoga* to the Hawaiian area as soon as possible. Likewise air reinforcements as well as ground troops were sent to Midway. By 4 June, there were about 110 aircraft stationed on the island, including Marine fighters and dive bombers, Navy patrol flying boats and torpedo bombers, and Army B-17 heavy bombers. Nimitz counted on the Midway air force to observe and report enemy locations as well as attack the Japanese striking force. This was to help prevent entrapment of the warships, which ComInCh warned was part of the Japanese plan. In addition, there was to be a submarine line west of Midway-Hawaii in the hope that some of the submarines might have an opportunity to score against Japanese warships. To conceal the redeployment of his forces, CinCPac ordered the utmost care to be taken in preventing radio transmissions which might alert the Japanese to the change in emphasis to the Central Pacific. Surprise was to be a potent ally. To meet all eventualities, Nimitz ordered the Amphibious Force at San Diego, parts of the 1st and 2nd Marine Divisions plus an Army division, to go on 48-hour alert so that it could be used to retake Midway or other bases captured by the Japanese.[108]

On 26 May Task Force 16 entered Pearl Harbor to begin rapid reprovisioning in order to sail two days later. Vice Admiral Halsey suffered from a very severe skin disease, and Admiral Nimitz most reluctantly had to order him into the hospital. Halsey recommended that Rear Admiral Spruance, his cruiser commander, take control of Task Force 16. He would have the benefit of Halsey's own staff of aviators to compensate for the fact that he was not a pilot himself. Nimitz readily agreed with Halsey's nomination. Task Force 17 reached Oahu the next day, and the damaged *Yorktown* immediately underwent examination in dry dock to determine whether she could be prepared in time to take part in the battle. There was no question of complete repairs. All the naval yard authorities could do would be to patch the holes in the hull, shore-up the damage from the bomb hit, and reprovision the ship whose stores had run very low after 101 days at sea. Very quickly Nimitz ascertained that the *Yorktown* indeed would be able to sail in a few days. There now came the question of appointing a new tactical commander for the two task forces in place of the ill Halsey. Nimitz immediately chose Rear Admiral Fletcher.[109]

Fletcher had come in for criticism of his performance in the Coral Sea, especially from Admiral King. King still remembered the 29–30 March mistaken sighting of Task Force 17 off Rabau On 11 May in a signal to Nimitz, King expressed his displeasu that Fletcher had not used his destroyers for night attacks on th enemy, especially since he had adequate numbers of them afte the junction of the three task forces.[110] Fletcher did not learn o this until 16 May; then he sent a long message to CinCPac outlir ing the reasons why he did not make a night attack. Briefly sun marized, they were: the need to keep the destroyers to screen th task force, uncertainty over the location of the enemy, and fue restrictions given the tight logistical situation forced on Task Forc 17. Fletcher concluded with the statement, "Acting on my bes judgment on the spot, no opportunity could be found to use de stroyers in night attacks on the enemy except the attacks by Sup port Group which I ordered."[111] Nimitz himself was more sanguin over the results achieved by Fletcher during the battle. On 16 Ma he radioed MacArthur, "From present knowledge believe Fletcher' operations were remarkably well-timed and executed at the loca tion where enemy was most vulnerable and he little subject t attack by enemy shore-based air."[112]

When Fletcher arrived at Pearl Harbor on 27 May, he sut mitted a long letter to Nimitz detailing his actions in the South Pacific including the 29 March incident and the Coral Sea.[113] Nim itz subsequently had a long talk with Fletcher and wrote King or 29 May of his conclusions:[114] "Both of these matters have beer cleared up to my entire satisfaction and, I hope, to yours." Nimit continued: "Fletcher did a fine job and exercised superior judg ment in his recent cruise to the Coral Sea. He is an excellent seagoing, fighting naval officer and I wish to retain him as a tasl force commander for the future." He again requested promotior for Fletcher and a decoration as well. He noted that Fletcher woulc be in tactical command of the Striking Force of three carriers CinCPac closed with the statement, "We are actively preparing tc greet our expected visitors with the kind of reception they deserve and we will do the best we can with what we have."[115]

The Battle of the Coral Sea had a number of effects on the Imperial Navy and its participation in the Midway Operation. Most were detrimental. Pre-eminent and, in the light of subsequent events, crucial was the inability of the 5th Carrier Division to joir Vice Admiral Nagumo's Striking Force bound for Midway. Bomb damage to the *Shokaku* had rendered the big carrier inoperable for two to three months in the opinion of Combined Fleet experts. She arrived at Kure on 17 May, and the time needed to repair her was revised to one month. Combined Fleet hoped to have her eady for the July invasion of Fiji and New Caledonia. Japanese nd Americans alike have contrasted the time of repair between he *Shokaku* and the *Yorktown*, criticizing the Japanese for "lacka-laisical" efforts in readying the *Shokaku* for battle. This is not ntirely fair because the American high-explosive bombs had caused nore damage with heavy fires to the *Shokaku* than the single bomb iit to the *Yorktown*. With the *Zuikaku*, however, it was a case of iot having reserve air crews sufficiently trained to fill out the ship's arrier air group. By the time the *Zuikaku* reached the homeland, here was only about a week before the sailing of Striking Force. Iad the trained aviators been on hand, there was no reason the *uikaku* could not have sortied with Nagumo. As it was, the *Zui-taku* had to work up a new set of aviators and missed the Battle f Midway. Thus Fletcher's carriers at the Coral Sea had effectively educed Nagumo's Striking Force by one-third, perhaps 130 combat iircraft.[116]

The Coral Sea also contributed to a heightening of Japanese overconfidence, called by two Japanese officers "Victory Disease."[117] Combined Fleet believed that the MO Operation cost the Pacific Fleet at least one and very likely two carriers sunk, along with one nonexistent battleship sunk on 7 May. Believing as they did that they had already sunk the *Lexington* in January, this left two, possibly three, operational carriers in the Pacific Fleet to face their four fleet carriers, which were supported indirectly by four light or converted carriers. The Coral Sea victory, as they saw it, had been accomplished by the first-line naval aviators of the 5th Carrier Division, but Combined Fleet considered them inferior to the elite aircrews of the 1st and 2nd Carrier Divisions of Striking Force. Obviously the Japanese thought they could triumph over the Pacific Fleet without the participation of Rear Admiral Hara's 5th Carrier Division. Coral sea served to expand even more Japanese confidence in the ability of Striking Force to crush the American carriers.[118]

Five days after South Seas Force had located Task Force 16 in the South Pacific, Combined Fleet issued the final orders for the Midway Operation. The Japanese expected to encounter in the Midway-Hawaiian area after the landings two to three American fleet carriers, two to three converted carriers, four to five heavy cruisers, 30 destroyers, and 25 submarines. Despite the indications from South Seas Force, Combined Fleet still reckoned with the probability of encountering American carriers at some point in the Midway Operation. The two carriers spotted on 15 May east of Tulagi could easily have returned to Pearl Harbor by early

June. Of course, the Japanese planners believed that the American would not be forewarned about the Japanese descent on Midway and would not be ready for the attack.[119]

Beginning about 25 May, CinCPac initiated an elaborate scheme of radio deception in the Southwest Pacific.[120] Using the seaplane tender *Tangier* and her patrol bombers, communications officer simulated the presence of a carrier task force by broadcasting conversions sounding like traffic between aircraft and fighter director officers. This was the kind of traffic which appeared on the air during the Battle of the Coral Sea, and CinCPac's radio deception officer knew the Japanese listened closely to it. There evidently was also some involvement in this by the heavy cruiser *Salt Lake City*, lent by Halsey to Leary's ComSoWesPacFor. The faked aircraft radio communications strongly indicated to the Japanese the presence of an American carrier task force in the Southwest Pacific. Nimitz intended the operation to convince the Japanese that he had not moved his carriers to the Central Pacific, and this impression would greatly assist the surprise counterattack Nimitz planned to spring at Midway.

The Naval General Staff's analysts in Tokyo fell completely for CinCPac's radio deception. They informed Admiral Yamamoto that the Americans must be totally unaware of the impending attack on Midway; otherwise they would surely have withdrawn their carriers from the South Pacific to the Hawaiian area. After 30 May, Yamamoto on board his flagship *Yamato* was not so sure. His own radio intelligence officers had detected increased radio traffic between aircraft in the Hawaiian area. This indicated to them the possible sortie of an American carrier task force from Pearl Harbor. Indeed, they had picked up the departure on 30 May of Rear Admiral Fletcher's Task Force 17. Despite this information which the Naval General Staff also received, analysts in Tokyo felt sure because of signals intercepted from the Solomons area that American carriers remained in the South Pacific. Unfortunately for Nagumo, he was not aware of the Pearl Harbor transmissions, but remained a recipient of the Naval General Staff's soothing intelligence bulletins indicating the Americans were not prepared for the Midway attack. Not wishing to break radio silence, Yamamoto did not pass his doubts on to Nagumo. Japanese authors have criticized the Naval General Staff's attitude as "a tendency for wishful thinking."[121] The Americans, however, had served up a most palatable and reasonable bait to their opposite numbers in Tokyo, and the Japanese swallowed it whole.

As previously shown, the Japanese did not concentrate their forces into one or two powerful striking forces, but scattered them among several widely separated commands. Nagumo's Striking Force of four fleet carriers, two fast battleships, two heavy cruisers, and a destroyer squadron approached Midway from the northwest. The actual invasion force, based around Vice Admiral Kondo's Second Fleet, came at Midway from the southwest. Kondo's forces consisted of one light carrier, two fast battleships, eight heavy cruisers, two destroyer squadrons, and transports. The initial Aleutian attack force comprised two light carriers, three heavy cruisers, one destroyer squadron, and transports to invade Attu and Kiska. CinCPac Intelligence had very closely determined the composition of these frontline forces. However, they did not fully realize the existence of Yamamoto's reserve force, divided into Main Force under his direct command and Guard Force under Vice Admiral Takasu, commander of First Fleet. Main Force consisted of three battleships, the small light carrier *Hosho,* and a destroyer squadron, and took station about 600 miles west of Nagumo. Takasu's Guard Force numbered four battleships and a destroyer squadron. Yamamoto positioned this unit about 500 miles north of him to provide support for the Aleutians invasion. Light cruisers accompanied the destroyer squadrons in all the forces. ComInCh in one of his messages to CinCPac had indicated that there was evidence that First Fleet might support the Midway Operation from the rear, but evidently the radio intercepts regarding this force were incomplete.[122] It is more likely that because First Fleet had remained in Japan, there was far less radio communication with its units as the commanders used telephone lines hooked up to the flagships through buoys. Adding the reserve force of seven battleships makes the odds for Midway look much worse than they appeared to Admiral Nimitz, who did not know they would be involved in the operation.

The results of the Battle of Midway are common knowledge.[123] The Japanese premised their plans on achieving surprise over the Pacific Fleet and entrapping it as it sortied to the relief of Midway. Because the Americans were warned, they were able to avoid detection and strike the heavier blow. CinCPac foiled the second Japanese flying boat reconnaissance raid intended for Oahu, Operation "K," by patrolling the islet upon which the aircraft would refuel. Secondly, the Pacific Fleet departed from Pearl Harbor several days before the Japanese submarine lines took up position to the north and west of Oahu. Task Force 16 left Pearl Harbor on 28 May and Task Force 17 two days later. Fletcher and Spruance effected rendezvous on 2 June at a point 325 miles northeast of Midway, Fletcher took tactical command of both task forces, giving him three carriers with 227 combat aircraft, seven heavy cruisers, one light antiaircraft cruiser, and 14 destroyers, with a fleet train of two fleet oilers and two destroyers. According to current doctrine, he separated the two task forces by a distance of about ten miles, instructing Spruance to stay within visual sighting range. Then the two task forces settled down to await the appearance of the Japanese, expected early on 4 June. The general operating plan for that day was for Task Force 17 to handle the preliminary search, while Task Force 16 kept its two air groups ready for immediate launch. The *Yorktown* could then launch part of its strength with the first attack or serve as a reserve. The plan was predicated on surprising the Japanese, but Fletcher was prepared for other eventualities.

On 3 June two events occurred which demonstrated to Nimitz the validity of his intelligence data on Japanese intentions. In the Aleutians, the Japanese 2nd Carrier Striking Force of the light carriers *Ryujo* and *Junyo* launched an air strike on Dutch Harbor, indicating that the Japanese carriers committed to the offensive were not all in one large, powerful group. Secondly, a PBY Catalina flying boat on search from Midway spotted the Japanese transport convoy about 600 miles southwest of the island, right on schedule. Because this confirmed CinCPac's information, the next expected Japanese action would see Vice Admiral Nagumo's 1st Carrier Striking Force of four fleet carriers close on Midway from the northwest to a distance of about 200 miles and launch one or more air strikes on the island. Because it appeared that the Japanese had not discovered that the Pacific Fleet was ready for them, Nimitz felt especially optimistic about Fletcher's chances of really dealing them a heavy blow. On the night of 3 and 4 June, Fletcher maneuvered so as to be about 200 miles north of Midway at dawn. The air staffs hoped to catch the Japanese with a surprise air strike while they were reservicing their planes after attacking Midway.

At dawn on 4 June, Fletcher readied the carriers for the expected strike on the Japanese carriers. He sent search planes to cover the sector directly north of him in case the Japanese approached from that direction. The search was negative. At 0603 came word from a PBY flying boat based out of Midway that he had sighted two Japanese carriers. Other reports indicated that the Japanese had launched aircraft as expected against Midway. Fletcher ordered Spruance at 0607 to "Proceed southwest and attack enemy carriers when definitely located."[124] Spruance endeavored to send his entire air striking force, 116 aircraft, against the reported enemy osition, gambling that all four carriers were there. Fletcher, on the other hand, felt there was a chance that the carriers had split. CinCPac's operational plan for Midway had noted the possibility that at some point the Japanese carriers might split, one or two to attack Midway, the others to search for the American fleet. Fletcher decided to delay the launching of his strike group until the other Japanese carriers had been located. He did not want to repeat the unfortunate action of 7 May, when he sent his entire strike force against the wrong target.

Historians have covered the Midway air battles in minute detail, and only a bare outline is required here. Nimitz's high expectations regarding the land-based aircraft, particularly the Marines, proved to be erroneous. Because of the heavy fighter opposition and the inexperience of the aircrews, the Midway-based aircraft were unable to score a single hit on the Japanese carriers.[125] Spruance's two air groups took almost an hour to take off and form up. After 45 minutes passed the air groups had still not departed, and Spruance ordered the *Enterprise* dive bombers to proceed on their own. When the two air groups finally did leave the area of Task Force 16, at about 0800, they were divided into five separate groups, none of which made a coordinated attack with the other. Most of the *Hornet* group, 35 dive bombers and ten fighters, never made contact at all. The two torpedo plane squadrons, Torpedo Eight and Torpedo Six, found the Japanese first and attacked, only to be chopped to ribbons by Japanese Zero fighters. Only Lieutenant Commander C. Wade McClusky's famous decision to follow a Japanese destroyer led the *Enterprise* dive bombers to the target. There they destroyed two Japanese carriers, the *Akagi* and the *Kaga*, inflicting mortal damage with their bombs.

The *Yorktown* air group was there as well. Fletcher had waited until about 0830 waiting for additional sighting reports on the Japanese carriers. When no other reports came in, he decided to launch part of the air group, six fighters, 17 dive bombers, and 12 torpedo planes, keeping a squadron of 17 dive bombers in reserve. This proved to be a very wise decision. The *Yorktown* group departed at about 0900 and was the only air group of the three to stay together for coordinated attacks. The *Yorktown*'s experience at Coral Sea had done her good service because of the increased efficiency with which the air officer and the air group commander handled the group. The torpedo planes of Torpedo Three fell victim to an overwhelming concentration of 40 or more Zeros, leaving the field clear of fighters to McClusky and the *Yorktown* dive bomber commander, Lieutenant Commander Maxwell F. Leslie.

Leslie's SBD dive bombers hit the *Soryu* three times and started heavy fires which doomed the ship. The attacks of the *Yorktown* group and McCluskey's *Enterprise* dive bombers were virtually simultaneous, despite the fact that McClusky had left an hour earlier.

Three of Nagumo's four carriers were out of action and engulfed in fire. The fourth, the *Hiryu*, succeeded in launching two air strikes that morning and early afternoon which hit the *Yorktown* with three bombs and two torpedoes, leaving her listing severely and without power. After several attempts at salvage, a Japanese submarine sank her on the morning of 6 June. Shortly before the first Japanese attack, Fletcher launched 10 dive bombers of the 17 in reserve to locate targets missed on the first strike. One of these aircraft later spotted the *Hiryu* and reported her position. That afternoon Spruance launched a second strike which accounted for the last of Nagumo's four carriers, mortally damaging the *Hiryu*. With the damage sustained by the *Yorktown*, Fletched had to shift his flag to a heavy cruiser. He magnanimously turned over tactical command of the American Striking Force to Spruance, who still had two fully operational flattops. Thus Spruance led Task Force 16 in the subsequent two days of battle, which saw the destruction of one Japanese heavy cruiser and an abortive attempt by Admiral Yamamoto to draw Spruance into a trap. Spruance had prudently refused to unleash his forces in a wild, headlong pursuit of the Japanese which might have resulted in a night battle against superior odds. The later knowledge that elements of the Japanese First Fleet were in support of Nagumo's force only served further to justify Spruance's decision.

By nightfall on 6 June, the Battle of Midway was over, and with it Japanese superiority in carrier strength in the Pacific. All four of Nagumo's carriers had slipped beneath the waves. It was a strategic and tactical victory of immense proportions, and vindicated Admiral Nimitz's belief that if the Pacific Fleet could engage the Japanese carriers under favorable circumstances, it would emerge victorious. Both Fletcher and Spruance performed well in battle, and Fletcher's prior experience at Coral Sea had served him handsomely in making his command decisions. The *Yorktown* air group acted as a reserve, filling in at crucial points and providing search aircraft when especially needed. The *Yorktown* flyers had also helped themselves in that they had helped damage the *Shokaku* and aided in cutting up the *Zuikaku*'s air group at the Coral Sea. Without this there might have been no victory at Midway. The absent Japanese 5th Carrier Division could easily have turned the scales the other way.

20
The End of the "Defensive-Offensive" Campaign

The Battle of Midway provided immediate relief for the South Pacific problem, as the Imperial Navy no longer had the requisite superiority in carriers to force its way into the South Pacific. For the first time in the Pacific War, the Pacific Fleet possessed with its four fleet carriers more carrier strength than the Imperial Navy's two fleet carriers and three light carriers. The Battle of Midway essentially concluded the First South Pacific Campaign because of its far-reaching effects on Allied and Japanese grand strategy. The next time the two powers shifted their focus to the South Pacific, it was the United States which had the initiative. Still of interest to this study are the effects of Midway on the region and also the outcome of General Marshall's efforts to follow through on Bolero and Sledgehammer, an offensive in 1942 against Northwest Europe.

After Midway, Admiral Yamamoto painfully realized that the battle had indeed been decisive, but with disastrous results for Japan. On 11 June Imperial General Headquarters postponed for two months the execution of planned invasions of New Caledonia, the Fijis, and Samoa. A month later, they quietly shelved the operations for good. The only area in which the Japanese contemplated further attacks was eastern New Guinea, which is ironic because that was originally the sole objective for South Seas Force. On 1! June the Army Section of Imperial General Headquarters ordere Lieutenant General Hyakutake's Seventeenth Army to concentrat on an overland offensive across the Papuan peninsula to captur Port Moresby. Out of necessity because of a lack of sea power, th Japanese opted to send troops over the Owen Stanley Mountains t attack Port Moresby from the north. This entailed landing at Bun and Gona on the northern coast of Papua to utilize them as jumping off points for the hike to Port Moresby. Japanese soldiers from Rabaul accomplished this on 21 July, and soon advance element had pushed to the high passes in the Owen Stanleys.[126]

After the Battle of the Coral Sea, Vice Admiral Inoue's Fourth Fleet worked on preparations to construct a series of interlocking mutually supporting air bases in the Solomons and eastern New Guinea. South Seas Force also resolved to attempt again the cap ture of Ocean and Nauru at a favorable time in the future. This they accomplished finally in August 1942. Inoue knew he would have to defend the Solomons against the expected Allied counter offensive on the approaches to Rabaul. South Seas Force decided to begin construction an an airfield on the north coast of Guadal canal. On 8 June naval troops from the Tulagi garrison crossed Sealark Channel and occupied points on Guadalcanal's northern coast. In late June and early July, naval garrison troops and two construction battalions from Rabaul landed on the island. On 16 July they began work on the airfield itself. Simultaneously, other labor troops worked to make operational an emergency field at Buka to assist in staging aircraft from Rabaul to Guadalcanal 560 miles distant. Plans envisioned stationing aircraft at Guadalcanal beginning in early August. By the end of the month, most of the 25th Air Flotilla was to operate from there.[127]

On 14 July the Combined Fleet underwent another massive re-organization. This included the activation of Eighth Fleet head-quarters at Rabaul under Vice Admiral Mikawa Gunichi. Mikawa superseded Vice Admiral Inoue as chief naval commander in the Rabaul area. His tasks were to continue Inoue's program of con-structing air bases, with the primary objective of protecting Rabaul from the anticipated Allied counteroffensive. Mikawa controlled four heavy cruisers of the 6th Cruiser Division, plus the heavy cruiser *Chokai* as his flagship and two light cruisers of the 18th Cruiser Division. There were the usual destroyers and support ves-sels. Mikawa assumed formal command of Eighth Fleet at the end of July.

Mikawa found Seventeenth Army totally concerned with plans for its impending Port Moresby offensive. On 28 July Imperial General Headquarters issued the final directive for the Port Moresby attack. Three days later, Eighth Fleet and Seventeenth Army signed the "Army-Navy local agreement." Major General Horii's South Seas Detachment with an additional infantry regiment was in the process of forcing its way across the Owen Stanley Mountains, despite miserable jungle terrain and Australian opposition. Hyakutake estimated that his troops would be in striking distance of the target by late August. To cooperate with the final attack, the Navy was to land an infantry battalion from Seventeenth Army at a point just east of Port Moresby. Seven fast patrol boats and a few destroyers were to rush the troops to the debarkation point, supported by aircraft from the 5th Air Attack Force. Eighth Fleet was to land garrison and base troops at Samarai to build a seaplane base and relay station there. Thus the Navy's participation in the second attempt on Port Moresby was greatly reduced, limited mostly to air support. Actually, the Navy would soon have troubles of its own defending the lower Solomons. United States Marines landed on Guadalcanal on 7 August, inaugurating the Second South Pacific Campaign. The combined Army-Navy assault on Port Moresby did not take place, and the Japanese never captured that base.[128]

If Admirals King and Nimitz were worried about the outcome of the Midway and expected South Pacific battles, this concern was not evident in the president and his closest advisors. At the end of May, Soviet Foreign Minister Vyacheslav M. Molotov traveled to Washington to confer with the president on grand strategy and aid to the Soviet Union. Roosevelt was especially anxious to demonstrate to the Soviets the extent of Allied commitment to the Second Front in Europe. To reassure the Communists, on 31 May the president told Molotov that "we expect the formation of a second front this year."[129] Molotov understandably took this to mean an Allied landing on the European continent. It is evident that the president believed that Sledgehammer was feasible. In his draft of the communique to Churchill concerning the Molotov meetings, Roosevelt specified August 1942 as the latest date for a landing in France. Marshall was not so sanguine, but did little to disabuse his chief's enthusiasm over the prospects of Sledgehammer. This was despite estimates showing a great shortage of landing craft and the presence in France of strong German forces.[130]

At the end of May, Admiral Nimitz offered a very modest proposal for an offensive move in the South Pacific. On 28 May he suggested to General MacArthur that the 1st Raider Battalion, an elite Marine Corps outfit, land on Tulagi and destroy the base before withdrawing. Likely as not, CinCPac considered the raid as a diversion or spoiling attack. The Solomons fell under the jurisdiction of MacArthur's Southwest Pacific Area. He vetoed the idea indicating that there was too little strength. MacArthur preferred outright conquest of the place if he could secure the necessary forces. King was not ready to commit Marines to such an audacious undertaking because of the expected build-up of Japanese strength in the South Pacific following the Midway Operation. All he wanted for the present was a raid.

After the tremendously gratifying victory at Midway, the entire situation concerning the South Pacific changed radically. MacArthur was the first to suggest that the Allies take immediately an offensive stance in the South Pacific. On 8 June he outlined in a communication to the War Department a proposal for the direct invasion of New Britain. The specific objective was Rabaul. MacArthur wanted to take the big step quickly, before the Japanese recovered from the shock of Midway. He indicated that he required one amphibious division and two aircraft carriers. Because Rabaul was in the Southwest Pacific Area, MacArthur assumed he would have complete control over offensive operations in the New Guinea–New Britain–Solomons region. All the War Department had to do, according to MacArthur, was to talk the Navy into releasing one of its two Marine divisions and two aircraft carriers, and Rabaul would be his.

Strangely enough, MacArthur's proposal looked very attractive to the War Department planners, including General Marshall himself. Suddenly they were in favor of attacking Rabaul, cutting off the Solomons, and pushing the Japanese back to Truk. On 12 June Marshall made a formal suggestion to King that he support MacArthur's operation against Rabaul. The War Department believed that the Southwest Pacific Area could accomplish the task with one Marine division to be supplied by CinCPac and three infantry divisions from Australia to follow up. Marshall promised to beef up air power in the Southwest Pacific Area by reducing the number of aircraft based in Hawaii. He asked for three aircraft carriers to support the invasions. Marshall desired a decision as soon as possible, as his planners recommended that the initial landings take place in early July. This attitude represented an enormous change on the part of the War Department. At the same time that he pushed vigorously for premature offensives in northern Europe, Marshall attempted equally dangerous moves in the Southwest

Pacific. The War Department certainly underestimated Japanese strength in the area; perhaps they had grossly understimated it all along.[131]

Admiral King was eager for an offensive in the South Pacific, but one that would take place on his terms. Winging directly to Rabaul certainly was not one of them. ComInCh turned the question over to his staff, and they came up with specific objections. First and foremost was the question of risking aircraft carriers in very narrow waters close to a powerful enemy base. They could easily be sunk or damaged by land-based aircraft, particularly as they were out of range of virtually all land-based air support except for a few heavy bombers. A few successful air attacks on the part of the 5th Air Attack Force at Rabaul, and Japan might again enjoy superiority in the number of aircraft carriers. King much preferred the gradual type of advance though the lower Solomons, as previously described to the president and the Joint Chiefs. The second great objection lay in the fact that MacArthur as Supreme Commander of the Southwest Pacific Area would command the operation, including naval forces. There was little chance that the Navy would place its precious carriers under MacArthur's control.[132]

King refused to concede to MacArthur direction of the counteroffensive in the lower Solomons. After several weeks of debate, Marshall and King came to an understanding. On 2 July they signed a directive outlining the general offensive against the New Britain–New Ireland area. There were three tasks. The first fell to Vice Admiral Ghormley as ComSoPac. He was to seize Santa Cruz, Tulagi, and "adjacent positions,"[133] which proved to be Guadalcanal. Tasks two and three were to come under MacArthur's Southwest Pacific Area. Task two was the occupation of the rest of the Solomons and Lae-Salamaua on the northern Papuan coast. Task three was the actual invasion of New Britain and New Ireland. The directive specified that the offensive was to begin in early August. It was a great victory for King's strategy of gradual advances. The next day, ComInCh spelled out the mission of the South Pacific Area in inaugurating the offensive. Ghormley, who had assumed command in late June, was to occupy the Santa Cruz Islands, capture Tulagi, Florida, and Guadalcanal in the Solomons, occupy Funafuti in the Ellice Islands, and reinforce the Espiritu Santo garrison. On 7 August the 1st Marine Division landed on Tulagi and Guadalcanal to begin the Second South Pacific Campaign. The long and hard struggle to hold Guadalcanal vindicated King's insistence on the step-by-step advance in the Solomons.

Remaining to be discussed is the fate of General Marshall's Bolero-Sledgehammer plan, the one he used as the major excuse to deny reinforcements to the Pacific when the Japanese exerted the most pressure. In early June, Churchill made known to Roosevelt British misgivings regarding the efficacy of Sledgehammer. The principal objections were the lack of landing craft and the strength of expected opposition. The Germans had the power to crush a weak landing force without having to divert large numbers of troops from the Russian Front. Churchill gradually converted Roosevelt to this viewpoint. Marshall reacted by threatening in early July to renounce American efforts for immediate operations against the Germans and concentrate in the Pacific for the defeat of Japan. He violently opposed Churchill's alternate plan of landing in Northwest Africa, the Gymnast plan, soon to be christened Torch. Roosevelt, however, would not permit even the thought of leaving the British to fight alone in the European theater. By the end of July, he approved American participation in Torch which led to the invasion of North Africa in November 1942.[134] The concept of Sledgehammer was abandoned totally. It is fortunate that Marshall's stubborn insistence on the execution of a totally unfeasible plan did not cause the loss of valuable positions in the Pacific, not to mention the striking power of the Pacific Fleet. King and Nimitz triumphed in the Pacific despite the Army's lack of interest and cooperation.

PART IV

CONCLUSION

21
The Roots
of Strategic Victory
and Defeat
in the Pacific

Within the high commands of Japan and the United States, three groups of planners interacted to determine basic strategy employed in the Pacific War. They were the Army, the naval supreme command, and the fleet commanders. Remarkably, each of the three groups mirrored the viewpoint of its enemy counterpart regarding the best course of action in the Pacific Area. There were also a number of very significant differences which ultimately proved to be decisive for American victory. Strategy as proposed by the three planning staffs in each country revolved around the three alternatives of the defensive posture of limited commitment in the Pacific, the idea of acquiring or denying to the enemy strategic positions, and the belief that the enemy's fleet was the prime danger to be dealt with above all. Before analyzing Japanese and United States strategy in the "Defensive-Offensive" campaign of early 1942, it is necesary to outline the viewpoint of each of the planning staffs.

Both the leaders of the U.S. Army and the Imperial Army largely controlled the course of grand strategy in their respective supreme headquarters. Indeed, in Japan Premier Tojo was himself a general, while General Marshall as Chief of Staff served as President Roosevelt's principal military advisor and as chairman of the

Joint Chiefs of Staff. Similarly the Army leaders of the two countries actively sought to restrict the operations of their navies in the Pacific because they considered the decisive theater of war to be elsewhere. Marshall saw Germany as the principal foe of the Allies and hoped to attack her directly by landing troops in 1942 in northwest Europe. Japanese generals wanted to commit the vast bulk of their forces on the East Asian continent to knock China out of the war and invade Soviet Siberia. Thus both services acted as a brake to prevent the extension of effort in the Pacific area proper by denying troops, aircraft, and shipping for operations that they considered unnecessary to the furtherance of their continental aims. The Japanese Army desired no widespread commitments in the Pacific outside of the economically rich Dutch East Indies and Southeast Asia. They wanted the Imperial Navy to hold the Pacific defensive perimeter while they consummated their ambitions in East Asia. There could be no operations which required the use of even moderate numbers of Army troops and resources, such as large-scale invasions. They expected the Navy to remain on the defensive, but aggressively counterattacking any American thrusts toward vital areas. This was traditional Japanese strategy which saw the decisive area of confrontation in the Japanese defensive perimeter.

General Marshall and his colleague General Arnold desired that the United States limit its effective defense of the Pacific to two areas, Alaska and Hawaii. Only at the president's urging did the two render some assistance to Australia and the line of communication through the South Pacific to the West Coast. In early 1942 after casting about for some sort of strategic plan, Marshall decided to direct as much effort as possible into attacking German holdings in western Europe. He succeeded in demonstrating to Roosevelt that the probable turning point of the war lay in taking the pressure off the Soviets by a Second Front in Europe. Despite overwhelming signs that such an attack would be unfeasible because of German strength in France and the dearth of Allied landing craft, Marshall persisted in curtailing reinforcements for the Pacific in the face of the alarming Japanese advances toward Australia and the South Pacific. Marshall used his strategy to deny additional forces for the Pacific and also to hinder British efforts to divert American attention to northwest Africa. It appears that Marshall would brook no deflection from what he considered his main effort and scorned "diversionist" operations which he thought would dissipate his troops into sideshow secondary theaters.

The two naval supreme commands, the Naval Section of Japan's Imperial General Headquarters and Admiral King's ComInCh headquarters, were of the opinion that the acquisition or denial to the enemy of strategic positions in the Pacific was paramount. It was on the initiative of members of the Naval General Staff, vigorously seconded by Vice Admiral Inoue's Fourth Fleet, that Japan pushed into the South Pacific to secure valuable island positions. This was at first to block expected Allied counteroffensives from the direction of Australia and the South Pacific. In early 1942 successes in the East Indies led to proposals by the Naval General Staff to attack Australia directly. The Navy had to back down at the angry insistence of the Army. Instead, the naval planners settled for operations designed to cut off Australia from the United States, possibly to force her out of the war. This would be accomplished by invading New Caledonia, Fiji, and Samoa, key positions along the line of communication from the United States to Australia. Thus the Naval General Staff departed from traditional Japanese strategy by wishing to extend offensive operations deep into the South Pacific rather than waiting behind the defensive positions in the Mandates for the big decisive battle.

Admiral King from the very beginning of his tenure as ComInCh took great interest in the South Pacific and the necessity of holding vital strategic positions and acquiring others. It was intolerable to him that the United States would allow the Japanese to move into the vacuum that was the South Pacific. It was necessary to block the Japanese advance in order to assume the initiative and counterattack. The South Pacific was the one area where the Allies could meet the advancing enemy on near-equal terms. Alone among the Joint Chiefs of Staff, King continually urged that United States forces help in the defense of Australia and the line of communication to the West Coast. He knew it was the Navy which would take the beating during the subsequent counteroffensives if the Japanese succeeded in consolidating their hold in the South Pacific. If Australia was lost or left isolated, the road back for the Allies would be a hard and bloody one indeed. King was willing to buck prevailing opinion in Washington for a Germany-first strategy in order to prevent such a calamity from happening in the Pacific. He therefore advocated soon after the outbreak of the war that the United States hold the island bases in the South Pacific to deny them to the enemy and also to build them into staging points for the offensives he hoped to launch. The South Pacific became the battleground for strategic position because the vast and empty Central Pacific effectively limited the spheres of influence between America and Japan King backed up his intentions by using significant portions of the Pacific Fleet for the defense of the South Pacific. Secondly he agitated for the establishment of important bases at Efate, Tongatabu the Ellice Islands, and New Caledonia.

If the South Pacific drew the attention of the rival naval supreme commands, the two fleet commanders, Admiral Yamamoto of Combined Fleet and Admiral Nimitz of the Pacific Fleet, looked to each other's striking forces as the principal concern. Admiral Yamamoto risked his career by threatening to resign unless his superiors agreed to his attack on Pearl Harbor to destroy the carriers and battleships of the Pacific Fleet. Even though the surprise raid was only partially successful, Yamamoto still felt he had gained the time to use his carriers in the conquest of the Dutch East Indies. Consequently, Vice Admiral Nagumo's magnificent Striking Force spent the early months of 1942 in the East Indies and the Indian Ocean. By March 1942, however, widespread American carrier strikes on outlying Japanese positions had demonstrated to Yamamoto that he had to draw the Pacific Fleet into decisive battle in order to destroy the American carriers. He feared American war production potential and hoped to smash the Pacific Fleet and bring a negotiated peace favorable to Japan. Yamamoto adopted the Midway plan as a thrust against a position strategically vital to the Americans but of little value to Japan because of its untenable position. The whole scheme was begun for the opportunity to entrap in the open the Pacific Fleet with Combined Fleet's superior forces. Thus Yamamoto in his haste to destroy the Americans proposed to offer decisive battle far outside Japan's defense perimeter, relinquishing the inherent strategic and tactical advantages to be accrued if the battle were fought in the Marshalls or the Carolines. He had full confidence in the ability of Combined Fleet to defeat the Americans in this decisive battle.

It took the Pacific Fleet time to recover from the shock of Pearl Harbor and formulate a strategy other than strictly a defense of positions east of 180° longitude. There was no question of becoming directly involved in the defense of the Philippines or the Dutch East Indies because the Pacific Fleet lacked the strength to project its forces in those areas in the face of overwhelming Japanese carrier and land-based air power. The Pacific Fleet planners felt that the primary responsibility of the fleet was to protect Hawaii, Alaska, and Samoa from Japanese attack. To do this required that the majority of available forces remain in the Central Pacific ready to repulse any Japanese attacks. Thus CinCPac was most concerned with the capabilities of the Japanese carrier striking force rather than dispersing his forces in the South Pacific to hold that area as well. The impetus for Pacific Fleet operations in the South Pacific came directly from ComInCh.

Given the three competing strategic proposals within the Japanese high command, it is interesting to analyze their interaction and the resultant course of Japanese strategy in the Pacific. An outstanding feature of Japanese strategic planning was the Army's success in preventing any operations in the Pacific requiring heavy troop commitments. Indeed the Army's contribution to Pacific operations east of the Dutch East Indies proper amounted to only about one and a half divisions. The second prime factor was the inability of the Naval General Staff to override the veto of Admiral Yamamoto regarding strategic policy. Yamamoto refused to take a secondary role in the determination of strategy in the Pacific and succeeded in pressing both his Pearl Harbor and Midway plans onto the reluctant Naval General Staff. Thus the Naval General Staff was crippled in two aspects in executing plans to increase Japanese holdings in the South Pacific in order to eliminate or neutralize Australia. Neither the Army nor Admiral Yamamoto expressed much interest in South Pacific operations.

Because of the Naval General Staff's inability to force through its own strategic policy, Japanese operations in the South Pacific suffered defeat. After the easy conquest in January of Rabaul, subsequent Japanese offensive operations were hesitant and spaced too far apart. The Japanese failed to follow up quickly and decisively their initial success at Rabaul. Given the nature of Allied opposition in the area before the commitment of American carriers, there was little to prevent the speedy conquest of eastern New Guinea and the Solomons had the Japanese allocated available forces and moved with determination. Japanese procrastination gave Admiral King time to send American carriers to support Allied positions and harass further Japanese advances in the region. Beginning with the March attack on Lae and Salamaua, American carrier forces dealt with every Japanese operation south of Rabaul, severely damaging ships from the Lae-Salamaua and Tulagi Invasion Forces and thwarting the Japanese conquest of Port Moresby and Nauru-Ocean. Thus hesitant Japanese moves into the South Pacific pointed out clearly to leaders like Admiral King how weak the Allies were in that area. Thus the lack of a clear-cut strategy in the South Pacific served to bring about the undoing of Japan's hold in the area and left the southern flank prey to attacks from Australia and a step-by-step advance through the Solomon Islands toward Rabaul.

Admiral Yamamoto and the staff of Combined Fleet controlled the strategic operations of their powerful Striking Force. Because of a lack of interest in South Pacific operations, they offered little support to Vice Admiral Inoue and his South Seas Force in their efforts to secure the approaches to Rabaul. In light of his definite worries about the eventual danger of the Pacific Fleet to Japan's defensive perimeter, it is surprising that he did not take note of the increasing signs that the U.S. Navy was utilizing a significant portion of its strength in the South Pacific, and that the United States was concerned over the South Pacific and Australia perhaps even enough to offer the decisive battle he desired so much. Astute members of the Naval General Staff had deduced as much, but were unable to win over Combined Fleet. In February 1942, Yamamoto possessed the carrier strength to lend to South Seas Force to accomplish many of its missions. However, he was more concerned about American carrier raids in the Central Pacific and despatched the 5th Carrier Division from the Dutch East Indies to the waters south of the homeland to conduct defensive patrols until the middle of March. After that the massive raid into the Indian Ocean took the services of five of the six Japanese fleet carriers and most of Second Fleet. Again some of these forces could have gone to South Seas Force for the conquest of eastern New Guinea and the Solomons. The Port Moresby Operation was delayed mainly because of a lack of forces in Fourth Fleet weakened by the Lae-Salamaua raid. Because of the approval of Combined Fleet's Midway plan, the Port Moresby Operation turned into another sideshow, to be fitted into the schedule according to the requirements of more important events Combined Fleet had planned. South Seas Force would have to make do with what Yamamoto could spare. Obviously Combined Fleet expected little Allied opposition to the MO Operation and because of this, Japan suffered a major strategic check, the first since the start of the war.

The vacillation of Japanese strategy between the acquisition of strategic positions and Yamamoto's concept of victory through decisive battle meant ultimately that Japan achieved neither objective. Yamamoto reversed the traditional Japanese strategy of making the defensive perimeter strong and then seeking decisive battle. When that battle did occur at Midway, Combined Fleet's defeat indeed proved decisive because Japan had not completed her defensive perimeter and lacked the means to take vital strategic positions and hold them. When the Allied counteroffensive took place, it occurred in the very area that Combined Fleet had neglected, and Japan payed the full penalty for that mistake.

United States strategy in the Pacific during the first six months of the war can be characterized succinctly in Admiral King's two categories, the "defensive" and the "defensive-offensive." The defensive phase lasted from the Pearl Harbor attack on 7 December 1941 into February 1942. During that period, the Pacific Fleet generally operated to defend its prewar bases, Hawaii, Midway, and Samoa, with an abortive attempt to retain Wake Island. CinCPac remained poised with forces in the Central Pacific to meet a possible second Japanese raid on the Hawaiian Islands. The only operation of note outside of the Central Pacific was the reinforcement of Samoa, which Admiral Nimitz covered with two carriers. The operations of the Pacific Fleet followed the precept that Hawaii was paramount and had to be guarded by the fleet at all costs. There was no thought of relieving the Philippines or committing significant Pacific Fleet forces to the defense of the Dutch East Indies. Rather, the idea was to hold what they already possessed.

Admiral King initiated the "defensive-offensive" phase when he ordered Pacific Fleet forces into the South Pacific to defend key positions along the line of communication to Australia and to expand into the South Pacific vacuum to garrison new bases. Task Force 11's attempted raid on Rabaul in late February inaugurated a new stage of American involvement in the South Pacific. King had two reasons for providing American forces for the region. Firstly, he hoped to deny to the Japanese strategically vital islands which would give the enemy a lodgment in the South Pacific. Secondly, he wanted to obtain bases for use as staging points in an early counteroffensive toward Rabaul. At any rate the idea of remaining strictly on the defensive was unthinkable to King, and the South Pacific was the one area where the United States could expand to meet the enemy before they could consolidate their conquests into near impregnable bases. It was the only area where Allied land-based air power could support the fleet in offensive operations. Thus there were two facets to King's South Pacific operations: use of Pacific Fleet units, especially carriers, to defend the island bases and keep the enemy off balance by offensive stabs, and the allocation of base troops and aircraft to construct additional bases and garrison them.

In opting for operations in the South Pacific, King encountered two opponents, the Army and his own Pacific Fleet. His attempt to increase American strength in the South Pacific met with the bitter opposition of the Army which longed to fight the so-called real war in Europe. They blocked his every request to increase air and ground forces from Hawaii to Australia. Unfortunately for King, he had to petition the Joint Chiefs of Staff for troops and air units which the Navy did not possess in order to safeguard the island bases. The Army leaders succeeded in convincing the president tha Bolero and Sledgehammer were both feasible and absolutely neces sary to the final victory. Neither point was entirely true. Genera Marshall and the Army planners used the president's approval o their plans as the excuse to deny needed reinforcements to the Pacific. They remained unwilling to increase their allocation o forces to the South Pacific even in the face of King's repeated de mands and despite the fact that King could show proof of Japanese plans to invade the bases he wished to defend. The Navy ultimately solved the problem of the defense of the Pacific through its victory at Midway, but it was not due in any great measure to Army assistance.

The Army's failure to provide necessary forces, especially air craft, placed the defense of the Pacific squarely on the Pacific Fleet. Most island garrisons were not capable of defending themselves against possible Japanese carrier raids. At first the Pacific Fleet staff was quite loathe to commit their forces out of the Central Pacific, on the belief that the Japanese possessed the capability o launching very severe attacks on Hawaii. King prodded the Pacific Fleet into providing carrier support for vital troop movements to New Caledonia. He sealed CinCPac's commitment to the South Pacific through the allocation of fleet forces for the construction o advanced bases at Efate, Funafuti, and Tongatabu. In March, King directed that CinCPac deploy his carriers so that one or preferably two were always on patrol in the South Pacific. On 27 April he issued a basic directive which instructed Admiral Nimitz to retain no fewer than two carriers in the South Pacific until further notice.

King had to overcome the Pacific Fleet's reluctance to commit large forces a great distance away from Hawaii. The staff viewed with suspicion King's efforts to divide their forces between the Central and South Pacific areas. They changed their ideas as their radio decript analysts and intelligence officers began again to predict accurately Japanese intentions and movements. Such prediction was nothing new, as intelligence had operated with much the same tools before the war, but it took time for the shock of Pearl Harbor to wear off. By March, Admiral Nimitz knew enough about Japanese strategic deployment to shuttle his carriers confidently back and forth to the South Pacific, and even approve of King's idea for a raid on the Japanese homeland.

With the increasing effectiveness of combat and radio intelligence came the knowledge in early April that the Japanese planned to invade Port Moresby and probably inaugurate widespread atacks in the South Pacific as well. This required a decision on the part of CinCPac and his staff as to how to meet the Japanese offensives. Radio intelligence had provided the tremendously important hints as to Japanese strategic deployment, but it did not really affect the tactical situation. To stop the Japanese, the Pacific Fleet would have to commit its carriers to the fight, risking their destruction by probably numerically superior forces. Nimitz and his staff were fully aware that Japan's naval strength lay in her carrier forces. Destroy or cripple Vice Admiral Nagumo's Striking Force, and the United States could assume the initiative in the Pacific. Nimitz saw the impending South Pacific battles as the first remotely favorable opportunity he had to engage the enemy carriers in battle with a reasonable chance of success. Consequently, he advised committing all four available carriers in the South Pacific, a heretofore unprecedented move. Thus, the Coral Sea campaign did not merely represent an attempt to blunt an attack on Port Moresby; rather, Nimitz meant it as an actual contest of strength between the Japanese and American forces. He did not intend that his commanders attack foolhardily, but he desired them to use favorable opportunities to strike at the Japanese and whittle down their strength. He had great confidence in the superior quality of the Pacific Fleet's personnel and ships over that of the enemy. Therefore, Nimitz saw the defense of the South Pacific bases as a way of accomplishing his mission of destroying the Japanese carrier forces and also complying with King's directives to hold the South Pacific. In contrast to Yamamoto, Nimitz did not see the two basic alternatives as mutually contradictory.

As events transpired, the staff had vastly overestimated the extent of Japanese forces and objectives in the South Pacific, although they had sized up the actual Port Moresby attack force very well. To those not familiar with the basic strategic decisions underlying the campaign, Task Force 16's dash to the south looks merely like an effort to concentrate overwhelming strength against the Port Moresby attack forces. This viewpoint ignores the wider conception of the South Pacific offensive held by the American planners at that time. Thus the importance of the Coral Sea campaign remains unappreciated. Coral Sea could easily have been as decisive as Midway, had the Japanese actually committed forces there in the magnitude which Nimitz thought. It is supposed that before Midway Nimitz finally decided to use his carriers in battle in a desperation move to stop Combined Fleet. Actually Nimitz opted to do that very same thing in the South Pacific, not in desperation but in quiet confidence.

The Battle of the Coral Sea took place. Task Force 17 blunted the Japanese attack on Port Moresby, but at the cost of the carrier *Lexington*. The expected Japanese follow-up to the MO Operation failed to materialize. CinCPac deduced that the next Japanese objectives were actually in the Central Pacific, specifically Midway Island, and that the Japanese would come in great strength. Nimitz never lost sight of the fact that the Central Pacific was still the most vital area he had to defend. Nor did he want to lose an opportunity to cause attrition to the Japanese Striking Force. There was some difficulty over interpretation of radio intelligence between ComInCh and CinCPac. Nimitz tactfully arranged to disengage his carriers from South Pacific operations in order to concentrate them near Midway to deal with a greater threat. Fully realizing the impact of radio intelligence, Nimitz concealed his own redeployment and initiated radio deception to lead the Japanese to believe American carriers had remained in the South Pacific. The Pacific Fleet's carriers had been bloodied and were more wary, but no less aggressive in meeting at Midway the threat only just envisioned in the South Pacific. This was a major encounter with the powerful Japanese carrier forces. The Pacific Fleet won a victory at Midway which was beyond the wildest expectations of the Americans, and which tended to mask the real concern of King and Nimitz regarding the situation in the South Pacific.

Even as they readied to do battle at Midway, King and Nimitz were aware of Japanese intentions to invade Port Moresby, New Caledonia, Fiji, and Samoa after the completion of the Midway offensive. It appears that the two commanders expected the Midway confrontation to be at best a drawn battle with a temporary check to the Japanese and losses on both sides as in the Coral Sea, and certainly not a stunning victory, the destruction of all four Japanese fleet carriers present for the loss of one American carrier. Despite his doubts regarding the outcome of the Battle of Midway, King was willing to fight once more in the South Pacific to protect vital bases along the line of communication to Australia. He solicited assistance from the Army, but received only a rebuff. Only the victory at Midway saved the United States from another tough defensive-offensive campaign in the South Pacific. After Midway, the U.S. Navy no longer had to remain on the defensive.

The telling difference between United States and Japanese naval strategy in the Pacific during the period under consideration here was one of consistency and clearly defined goals. There was no supreme commander in the Imperial Navy analogous to the position of ComInCh held by Admiral King. The Naval General taff was relatively powerless to execute its strategy in the face of Admiral Yamamoto's intransigence. Strangely enough, while Japan enjoyed success after success in the Dutch East Indies and Southeast Asia, the Imperial Navy's planners had not settled on basic strategy for the Second Operational Stage. Both the Naval General Staff and Combined Fleet after a few months settled on rival strategic plans. Consequently, there was some delay, particularly as the Japanese executed the almost meaningless Indian Ocean operation instead of turning immediately eastward to confront the United States. These delays gave the Allies time to regroup and deploy forces into the South Pacific. Finally, the Navy adopted Admiral Yamamoto's Midway plan which saw Combined Fleet attack the Pacific Fleet in the area in which it was the strongest, near Hawaii. In contrast to Japanese strategic vacillation, Admiral King had early set his sights on the South Pacific and worked tirelessly to strengthen the American presence there. Admiral Nimitz discovered that he could accomplish both of his primary tasks while defending the South Pacific. Radio intelligence provided tremendous advantages to the U.S. Navy, but victory depended upon having naval leaders willing to use the new source of information to the fullest and risk battle with superior forces. This Admirals King and Nimitz did splendidly.

Notes

**Part I
The Strategic Situation**

1. Fujiwara Akira, "The Role of the Japanese Army," in Dorothy Borg and Shumpei Okamoto, *Pearl Harbor as History: Japanese-American Relations 1931–1941*, 194–195.
2. Asada Sadao, "The Japanese Navy and the United States," in Borg and Okamoto, 235–243.
3. General Douglas MacArthur, *Reports of General MacArthur*, Vol. II, Part 1, 52–58, with full organizational charts.
4. U.S. Army, Far East Command, Military History Section, *The Imperial Japanese Navy in World War II*.
5. *MacArthur Reports*, II, Part 1, 59–71.
6. Asada in Borg and Okamoto, 255.
7. Mitsuo Fuchida and Masatake Okumiya, *Midway: the Battle That Doomed Japan*, 20–24; John Toland, *The Rising Sun*, 149–156, 168–172.
8. Text of "Combined Fleet Top Secret Operations Order No. 1, November 5, 1941," in U.S. Congress, 79th Cong., 1st Sess., *Pearl Harbor Attack*, Part 13, 431–484, quote from p. 438.
9. *MacArthur Reports*, II, Part 1, 51–52, including verbatim statements by members of Imperial General Headquarters.

10. *Ibid.*, 126–127, citing statements from Fourth Fleet staff officers.

11. U.S. Army, Far East Command, Military History Section, Japanese Research Division, *Japanese Monographs*, No. 143, "Southeast Area Operations Record, Part I (January–May 1942)," 1–2.

12. Synopsis of Orange War Plans in Admiral James O. Richardson, *On the Treadmill to Pearl Harbor*, 251–281.

13. Maurice Matloff and Edwin M. Snell, *Strategic Planning for Coalition Warfare 1941–1942*, 32–35.

14. Samuel Eliot Morison, *History of United States Naval Operations in World War II*, Vol. III, *The Rising Sun in the Pacific*, 42–47; Julius A. Furer, *Administration of the Navy Department in World War II*, 178–180; Richardson, 307–333.

15. Full text of Rainbow Five, WPL-46, 26 May 1941 in *Pearl Harbor Attack*, Part 18, 2877–2941. See also George C. Dyer, *The Amphibians Came to Conquer*, Vol. I, 157, 162–165, and Grace P. Hayes, *The History of the Joint Chiefs of Staff in World War II, The War Against Japan*, Vol. I, 11–13.

16. For Pearl Harbor attack, see Morison, III, 80–142.

17. Message SecNav to AlNav 071930 of December 1941, copy in War Plans, CinCPac Files, "Captain Steele's Running Estimate and Summary, 7 December 1941 to 31 August 1942," hereafter *CINCPAC Greybook*, 5. Messages are cited by the standard form of originator to addressee followed by the date and time the message was sent. For full titles, see the list of abbreviations.

18. Message OpNav to CinCLant 081700 of December 1941 in *CINCPAC Greybook*, 5.

19. Message OpNav to CinCPac, CinCAF 090139 of December 1941 in *CINCPAC Greybook*, 6.

20. "Briefed Estimate of the Situation, December 10, 1941," full text in *CINCPAC Greybook*.

21. The entries for 12 to 25 December 1941 in the *CINCPAC Greybook* provide a summary of the Wake Island relief expedition; see also Morison, III, 223–254 for the fall of Wake Island.

22. *CINCPAC Greybook*, 17 December 1941.

23. Furer, 126–127; Ernest J. King and W. M. Whitehill, *Fleet Admiral King: A Naval Record*, 350–353.

24. See *CINCPAC Greybook* for appended statements of Vice Admiral Pye and some of the staff; also Message CinCPac to OpNav 280417 of December 1941 on p. 120.

25. Message OpNav to CinCPac 091812 of December 1941 in *CINCPAC Greybook*, 6–7.

26. Message OpNav to CinCPac 142346 of December 1941 in *CINCPAC Greybook*, 50; Message OpNav to CinCPac 170115 of December 1941 in *CINCPAC Greybook*, 70.

27. "Task Forces, U.S. Pacific Fleet, Estimate of the Situation, December 24, 1941," text in *CINCPAC Greybook*.

28. *Ibid.*

29. Message ComInCh to CinCPac 301740 of December 1941 in *CINCPAC Greybook*, 121.

30. Message ComInCh to CinCAF 312300 of December 1941 in *CINCPAC Greybook*, 122.

31. Mattloff and Snell, 114.

32. For the Arcadia Conference, see *Ibid.*, 97–123; Robert Sherwood, *Roosevelt and Hopkins: An Intimate History*, 444–478; Richard W. Steele, *The First Offensive 1942*, 46–80.

33. Dyer, I, 233–234.

34. *Ibid.*

35. King and Whitehill, 364; Hayes, 76–79.

36. Mattloff and Snell, 114–119.

37. Message OpNav to CinCPac 291431 of December 1941 in *CINCPAC Greybook*, 121; Message ComInCh to CinCPac 021718 of January 1942 in *CINCPAC Greybook*, 122; "Employment of Carrier Task Forces in January, January 2, 1942 with corrections to January 24, 1942," text in *CINCPAC Greybook*.

38. *CINCPAC Greybook*, entries for 8 January and 13 January 1942; Message CinCPac to ComInCh 090445 of January 1942 in *CINCPAC Greybook*, 142; Morison, III, 260–261.

39. Message ComInCh to CinCPac 191815 of January 1942, in *CINCPAC Greybook*, 178.

40. Morison, III, 193–206, 271–280.

41. Asada in Borg and Okamoto, 237.

42. *MacArthur Reports*, II, Part 1, 125–126.

43. Japanese Self-Defense Agency, War History Office, *Senshi Sosho. Nantohomen Kaigun Sakusen Gato Dakai Sakusen Kaishi Made (War History Series. Southeast Area Naval Operations until the Guadalcanal Counteroffensive)*, Vol. I, 175–176. Hereafter *Senshi Sosho*.

44. Text in U.S. Army, Far East Command, Military History Section, *Imperial General Headquarters Navy Directives*, 20.

45. *Japanese Monographs*, No. 143, 13–14.

46. *Senshi Sosho*, 163–164.

47. *Ibid.*, 165.

48. "Appreciation of the Pacific Situation as at 15th January 1942," in *CINCPAC Greybook*.

49. Mattloff and Snell, 114–115.

50. Message ComInCh to CinCPac 202150 of January 1942 in *CINCPAC Greybook*, 179; Message CinCPac to all CTF (Action CTF-11) 212217 of January 1942 in *CINCPAC Greybook*, 180, and also entry for 23 January 1942.

51. Message CinCPac to all CTF (Action CTF-8) 280311 of January 1942 in *CINCPAC Greybook*, 193.

52. Message ComInCh to CinCPac 241740 of January 1942 in *CINCPAC Greybook*, 185; Message ComInCh to CinCPac 261721 of January 1942, 192; Message ComInCh to CinCPac 292110 of January 1942, 203.

53. Message ComInCh to CinCPac 271945 of January 1942 in *CINCPA* *Greybook*, 193.
54. *CINCPAC Greybook*, entries 25 and 28 January 1942.
55. Message ComInCh to CinCPac 292200 of January 1942, Messag ComInCh to CinCPac 311606 of January 1942, in *CINCPAC Gre book*, 197, 205.
56. U.S. Navy, Office of Naval Intelligence, *Early Raids in the Pacif February 1 to March 10, 1942*, 1–34; Morison, III, 261–265.
57. Alfred D. Chandler, ed., *The Papers of Dwight David Eisenhowe The War Years*, Vol. I, 101–103 with text of MacArthur to Marsha Radio No. 201 of February 1942 and Marshall to MacArthur, Radi No. 1024 of 8 February 1942.
58. *CINCPAC Greybook*, 7 February 1942; Message ComInCh t CinCPac 062352 of February 1942, 221.
59. *CINCPAC Greybook*, text of "Briefed Estimate of the Situation, February 1942."
60. Message ComInCh to CinCPac 092245 of February 1942, in *CINCPA Greybook*, 222.
61. *CINCPAC Greybook*, entries of 10–12 February 1942.
62. Message ComInCh to ComANZAC, CTF-11 122200 of February 194 Message CTF-11 to ComInCh 140022 of February 1942, in *CINCPA Greybook*, 222, 223.
63. Sources for 20 February raid, "Action Report, Cruise of Task Forc Eleven from January 31 to March 26, 1942," (Vice Admiral Wilso Brown) in Classified Operational Archives; *Early Raids in the P cific*, 35–40; *Senshi Sosho*, 88–92.
64. For Wake Island Raid, see *Early Raids in the Pacific*, 41–52.
65. *Japanese Monographs*, No. 143, 15–17; No. 96 "Eastern New Guine Invasion Operations (March–September 1942)," 3–5.
66. Message CinCPac to ComInCh 251209 of February 1942 in *CINCPAC Greybook*, 255; entry for 24 February 1942.
67. Message CTF-11 to CinCPac 260458 of February 1942, in *CINCPAC Greybook*, 255.
68. Message ComInCh to CTF-11, 17, ComANZAC 261630 of February 1942, in *CINCPAC Greybook*, 255–256.
69. *Ibid.*
70. *Early Raids in the Pacific*, 53–55.
71. Message CinCPac to ComInCh 280559 of February 1942, Message ComInCh to CTF-11 021615 of March 1942, in *CINCPAC Greybook* 257, 274; Vice Admiral Brown's Action Report.
72. Vice Admiral Brown's Action Report; *Japanese Monographs* No. 96 4–5, No. 143, 17–18; *Early Raids in the Pacific*, 57–68.
73. *CINCPAC Greybook*, 11 March 1942.
74. *Senshi Sosho*, 163–165; *MacArthur Reports*, II, Part 1, 130–131.
75. *MacArthur Reports*, II, Part 1, 131–132; Fuchida and Okumiya, 54–55
76. *MacArthur Reports*, II, Part 1, 132, with a statement by Rear Ad miral Yano.

77. *Ibid.*, 132–133; Fuchida and Okumiya, 54–55.
78. *Senshi Sosho*, 164–165.
79. Fuchida and Okumiya, 48–51 with an account of Combined Fleet planning.
80. *Ibid.*, 52–53; for the activities of Striking Force, see *Japanese Monographs*, No. 113, "Task Force Operations (November 1941–April 1942)."
81. Fuchida and Okumiya, 38, 66; *CINCPAC Greybook*, entries of 1–2, 12–13 March 1942.
82. Fuchida and Okumiya, 53–54, 66.
83. Detailed account of the meetings in *Ibid.*, 56–61.
84. *Senshi Sosho*, 166–167 for extracts.
85. Fuchida and Okumiya, 62; Inoue was the only real opponent of the Midway operation among the fleet commanders.
86. Hayes, 79; King and Whitehill, 356–357, 366; Furer, 132–135.
87. Mattloff and Snell, 147.
88. Dyer, I, 240–241; King and Whitehill, 382.
89. Mattloff and Snell, 154–155.
90. Full text in *Eisenhower Papers*, I, 149–155.
91. *Ibid.*, 151.
92. King and Whitehill, 382.
93. Hayes, 119–120; Sherwood, 501–503, 508–509; Winston S. Churchill, *The Hinge of Fate*, 155–156. Churchill wanted to use Australian troops in the defense of Burma, but Curtin refused.
94. Full text of memo in King and Whitehill, 384–385.
95. *Ibid.*; Steele, 103–104.
96. *CINCPAC Greybook*, 17 February 1942.
97. *Ibid.*, 21 February 1942.
98. *Ibid.*
99. *Ibid.*, 27 February 1942.
100. Message ComInCh to CinCPac 222200 of February 1942, in *CINCPAC Greybook*, 252.
101. Message CinCPac to CTF-17 130339 of March 1942, Message ComInCh to ComANZAC, CTF-17 131535 of March 1942, in *CINCPAC Greybook*, 288.
102. Message CTF-17 to CinCPac 132141 of March 1942, Message CinCPac to CTF-17 160217 of March 1942, in *CINCPAC Greybook*, 291, 292.
103. Cited in Steele, 104.
104. *Ibid.*, 105.
105. Mattloff and Snell, 161.
106. *Ibid.*, 161; Hayes, 163–164.
107. W. F. Craven and J. L. Cate, *The Army Air Forces in World War II*, Vol. I, *Plans and Early Operations (January 1939 to August 1942)*, 436–437.
108. Dyer, I, 248–249.
109. *CINCPAC Greybook*, 19 March 1942.
110. *Eisenhower Papers*, I, 189–191.

111. Dyer, I, 249; Mattloff and Snell, 210–211.
112. Louis Morton, *Strategy and Command: The First Two Years (Unite States Army in World War II, The War in the Pacific)*, 241.
113. *Ibid.*, 251.
114. *Ibid.*, 247–249; for the full text of the directive to MacArthur, se pp. 614–616.
115. Message ComInCh to CinCPac, ComANZAC, ComSoWesPacFo 041725 of March 1942, Message CinCPac to ComInCh 070451 o March 1942, in *CINCPAC Greybook*, 276, 280.
116. Message CTF-17 to ComANZAC 210833 of March 1942, in *CINCPA Greybook*, 313; also entries for 28 and 29 March 1942.
117. Message CTF-17 to ComInCh 292346 of March 1942, Messag ComInCh to CTF-17 301930 of March 1942, in *CINCPAC Greyboo* 322. The "292346" signal number means that the message was sen on the 29th day of the month (March) at 2346 hours, Greenwic Central Time.
118. Letter Fletcher to Nimitz, 28 May 1942 in Miscellaneous Corre spondence of Fleet Admiral Nimitz, Classified Operational Archives Report by Fletcher dated 23 June 1942, "Operations of Task Forc 17 in the Coral Sea March 16 to April 20, 1942—Statements to clarif erroneous impressions gained at CINCPAC Headquarters," also i Classified Operational Archives.
119. Minutes of 25 April 1942 Conference at San Francisco between Ad mirals King and Nimitz, in King Papers, Classified Operationa Archives.
120. 23 June 1942 report, "Operations of Task Force 17 in the Coral Se March 16 to April 20, 1942 . . . ," submitted by Fletcher.
121. Messages, ComInCh to CinCPac 031905, 032123, 032017, 031922 o April 1942, in "Commander-in-chief, U.S. Pacific Fleet Messages, Se cret and Confidential Chronological File," on microfilm from Classi fied Operational Archives. Contains the text of the basic directive to CinCPac.

Part II
The Battle of the Coral Sea

1. *Senshi Sosho*, 167, 169; see also Walter Lord, *Incredible Victory*, 11, for an estimate of the reputation of the 5th Carrier Division.
2. Primary course for the planning of the MO Operation is *Senshi Sosho*, which has the text of key orders.
3. *Ibid.*, 170, 172–174.
4. *Ibid.*, 221–222; *MacArthur Reports*, II, Part 1, 134–135.
5. *Senshi Sosho*, 175.
6. *Ibid.*, 176–185 for full text of order.
7. *Ibid.*, 197–224.
8. *Ibid.*, 187–188, 224; Fuchida and Okumiya, 66–70.

9. *Senshi Sosho*, 185–186, 189. See also the postwar interview of Hara in "Supplemental Report of Certain Phases of the War against Japan, derived from interrogations of senior naval commanders at Truk," 1945, also known as "Truk Report," in Classified Operational Archives.

10. *Senshi Sosho*, 186–187; for the text of Takagi's orders, see 189–191.

11. *Ibid.*, 223. See also *Japanese Monographs*, No. 143, 18–19.

12. *Senshi Sosho*, 193–194, 223.

13. *Ibid.*, 194–202 for summaries of the orders.

14. *Japanese Monographs*, No. 120, "Outline of Southeast Area Naval Air Operations, Part I (December 1941–August 1942)," 14–26; *Senshi Sosho*, 202–218.

15. *Senshi Sosho*, 176–178, 192; quote from 176.

16. *Ibid.*, 189.

17. "War Diary, 25th Air Flot. (Bismarck Area Base Air Force), 1st April to 11th May 1942," WDC 161725, 4, in Classified Operational Archives.

18. *CINCPAC War Diary*, 9 April 1942, in Classified Operational Archives.

19. Basic sources for United States naval radio intelligence are Clay Blair, *Silent Victory*, 73–76, 87–92, 111–119; David Kahn, *The Codebreakers*, 561–570; Lord, 17–23, 27–28. These sources are based mainly on interviews with former naval cryptanalysts.

20. The Japanese name for their naval cipher was "Naval Code Book D"; see *Japanese Monograph* No. 118, "Operational History of Naval Communications (December 1941–August 1945)"; Kahn, 586–587.

21. Kahn, 564–567.

22. *CINCPAC Greybook*, 26 May 1942.

23. The author has benefited greatly in his understanding of the use of radio and combat intelligence through the help of Rear Admiral Edwin T. Layton (Retired).

24. See the message lists "Commander-in-chief, U.S. Pacific Fleet Messages, Secret and Confidential Chronological File" for the daily numbered intelligence bulletins.

25. *MacArthur Reports*, I, Part 1, 22–23.

26. *CINCPAC War Diary*, 3 April 1942.

27. *CINCPAC Greybook*, 10 April 1942.

28. Message CinCPac to CTF-17 142027 of April 1942, in CinCPac Message File.

29. *CINCPAC Greybook*, 2 April and 10 April 1942.

30. Morison, III, 389; for Tokyo Raid, see Morison, III, 389–398, Craven and Cate, I, 438–444, and Fuchida and Okumiya, 66–71.

31. Message OpNav to Comb 150249 of April 1942 in CinCPac Message File. Comb is short for "Combined Addressees," the intelligence distribution network. *CINCPAC Greybook*, 15 April 1942.

32. Message ComANZAC to ComInCh, CinCPac 110641 of April 1942, in *CINCPAC Greybook*, 347; also 16 April 1942 entry.

33. *CINCPAC War Diary*, 17 April 1942; *CINCPAC Greybook*, 17 Apr 1942.

34. *CINCPAC Greybook*, 17 April 1942.

35. *Ibid.*, 18 April 1942; Message CinCPac to CTF 11, 17 192109 of Apr 1942 in CinCPac Message File.

36. *CINCPAC War Diary*, 18–19 April 1942, quote from 19 April; *CINCPAC Greybook*, 18 April 1942; Messages Com 14 to Com 170054 of April 1942 and 170115 of April 1942, both in CinCPac Message File. Com 14 is the 14th Naval District, the originator of the Hypo Messages.

37. "Estimate of the Situation, April 22, 1942," in *CINCPAC Greybook*

38. *Ibid.*

39. *Ibid.*

40. *Ibid.*

41. See the operation plan for the Kamchatka fisheries raid in *CINCPAC Greybook*.

42. "Estimate of the Situation, April 22, 1942."

43. Samuel Eliot Morison, *History of United States Naval Operations in World War II*, Vol. IV, *Coral Sea, Midway and Submarine Actions May 1942–August 1942*, 15.

44. *Ibid.*, 16.

45. Messages, CinCPac to CTF-11 and 17 220345 of April 1942, 25035 of April 1942, and 260327 of April 1942, all in CinCPac Message File

46. King and Whitehill, 376–377; for conference, see minutes in King Papers, Classified Operational Archives; also Edwin P. Hoyt, *How They Won the War in the Pacific*, 74–77.

47. CinCPac Operation Plan No. 23-42, 29 April 1942, in Classified Operational Archives.

48. Messages, Com 14 to Comb 270246 of April 1942 and 282146 of April 1942, both in CinCPac Message File.

49. CinCPac Operation Plan No. 23-42, 29 April 1942.

50. Morison, IV, 263; Craven and Cate, I, 428–435, IV, *The Pacific Guadalcanal to Saipan*, 10–13; Annex to Task Force 17 Operation Order No. 2-42, appended to Rear Admiral Fletcher's action report "The Battle of the Coral Sea, May 4–8, 1942," dated 27 May 1942 in Classified Operation Archives.

51. Message Com 14 to Comb 300316 of April 1942, in CinCPac Message File.

52. Messages Com 14 to Comb 010810 of May 1942, Com 14 to Comb 302350 of April 1942, CinCPac to all CTF 010311 of May 1942, all in CinCPac Message File.

53. Message Com 14 to OpNav 011108 series of May 1942 in CinCPac Message File.

54. *Ibid.*

55. *Ibid.*

56. *CINCPAC Greybook*, 1 May 1942.

57. Dudley McCarthy, *South-West Pacific Area—First Year Kokoda to Wau*, 66.
58. Samuel Milner, *Victory in Papua*, 25.
59. McCarthy, 25–26, 43–45.
60. *Ibid.*, 82.
61. Milner, 28–29; Mattloff and Snell, 212–214; Hayes, 178–181.
62. Letter King to Marshall, 28 April 1942; Message Col. J. R. Deane to General MacArthur, 30 April 1942, both in King Papers, Classified Operational Archives.
63. Messages CinCPac to CTF-17 250357 of April 1942, CTF-17 to CinCPac 152126 of May 1942, both in CinCPac Message File.
64. For Allied air activities in the Coral Sea, see Craven and Cate, I, 478–481; U.S. Army Air Forces, Historical Division, *The AAF in Australia to the Summer of 1942 (Army Air Forces Historical Studies No. 9)*, 119–136. Douglas Gillison, *Royal Australian Air Force 1939–1942*, records the histories of the RAAF squadrons. See also the daily ComSoWesPacFor intelligence bulletins (in CinCPac Message File) for daily mission summaries.
65. Japanese air operations are covered in *Senshi Sosho*, 208–212, and *Japanese Monographs*, No. 120, 17–18.
66. The best Japanese account of the Battle of the Coral Sea is in *Senshi Sosho*, 227–326. This narrative is based on virtually all surviving operational documents and includes diaries and personal recollections of key commanders and staff officers.
67. *Japanese Monographs*, No. 143, 19.
68. *Senshi Sosho*, 229–230.
69. Important American sources for the Battle of the Coral Sea include the action reports for Task Force 17 (in Classified Operational Archives); U.S. Naval War College, *The Battle of the Coral Sea, May 1 to May 11 Inclusive, 1942, Strategical and Tactical Analysis*; Morison, IV, 10–64, based largely on the War College analysis.
70. Text of order appended to Task Force 17 Action Report, dated 27 May 1942.
71. *Ibid.*
72. *Ibid.*
73. *Senshi Sosho*, 235.
74. Message CinCPac to CTF-17 020641 of May 1942, in CinCPac Message File.
75. Schedule of tanker arrivals: Messages CinCPac to CTF-17 260327 of April 1942, CinCPac to CTF-17 072209 of May 1942, ComSoWesPacFor to CTF-17, 44, 071219 of May 1942, in CinCPac Message File.
76. Task Force 17 Action Report, 27 May 1942, 3.
77. For Tulagi Attack, see USS *Yorktown* Action Report, "Action at Tulagi," dated 11 May 1942, in Classified Operational Archives; *Senshi Sosho*, 230–234.
78. U.S. Naval War College Analysis—*Coral Sea*, 41.

79. Message ComSoWesPacFor to CTF-17 040950 of May 1942, in CinCPac Message File.

80. Message ComSoWesPacFor to CTF-17 030745 of May 1942, in CinCPac Message File.

81. *Senshi Sosho*, 233–235.

82. Message CinCPac to CTF-17 050329 of May 1942, in CinCPac Message File.

83. Message CinCPac to CTF-17 050345 of May 1942, in CinCPac Message File.

84. Task Force 17 Action Report, 27 May 1942, 4–5; Task Group 17. Action Report (Rear Admiral Aubrey W. Fitch), "The Battle of the Coral Sea, May 7–8, 1942," dated 18 May 1942, 1.

85. For Crace's activities, see Task Force 44 Action Report, "Attack by Torpedo Bombers and High Level Bomber Aircraft," dated 21 May 1942; G. Hermon Gill, *Royal Australian Navy*, Vol. II, 1942–1945, 47–49.

86. *Senshi Sosho*, 239–241.

87. *Ibid.*, 245–246, 273–274.

88. *Ibid.*, 242, 271–272.

89. *Ibid.*, 276–278.

90. Message ComSoWesPacFor to CTF 17 062239 of May 1942, in CinCPac Message Files; Task Force 17 Action Report, 27 May 1942, 5–6.

91. *Senshi Sosho*, 286.

92. Task Force 44 Action Report, 21 May 1942; Gill, II, 49–50; Craven and Cate, I, 450.

93. Message CTF-17 to CinCPac 071024 of May 1942, in CinCPac Message File.

94. *Senshi Sosho*, 296, 299–300.

95. For 8 May Battle, see Task Force 17 Action Report, 27 May 1942, 9; U.S. Naval War College Analysis—*Coral Sea*, 81–112; *Senshi Sosho*, 303–328.

96. Message CinCPac to CTF-17 072209 of May 1942, in CinCPac Message File.

97. Message CTF-17 to CinCPac 080252 of May 1942, in CinCPac Message File; Task Force 17 Action Report, 27 May 1942, 9.

98. Message CTF-17 to CinCPac 080252 of May 1942, in CinCPac Message File.

99. Message CTF-17 to ComSoWesPacFor 080137 of May 1942, CTF-17 to ComSoWesPacFor 080244 of May 1942; summary of AAF air operations in Message MacArthur to Marshall, Melbourne to C/S, AG No. 719, 13 May 1942, retransmitted ComInCh to CinCPac, 142100 series; all in CinCPac Message File.

100. *Senshi Sosho*, 326–327.

101. Fourth Fleet Secret Radio Message No. 396, 8 May 1942, text in *Ibid.*, 324.

102. Combined Fleet Operational Radio Message No. 140, 8 May 1942, text in *Ibid.*, 327.

103. *Ibid.*, 327, for text of South Seas Force Operational Radio Message No. 174, 8 May 1942.

104. Message CinCPac to CTF-17 080703 of May 1942, in CinCPac Message File.

105. Official loss statements in Fuchida and Okumiya, 105, and Task Force 17 Action Report, 27 May 1942, 11.

106. U.S. Naval War College Analysis—*Coral Sea*, 103–104.

107. Message CinCPac to CTF-17 090117 of May 1942, in *CINCPAC Greybook*, 452.

108. Gill, II, 51–53.

109. U.S. Naval War College Analysis—*Coral Sea*, 105; *CINCPAC Greybook*, 9 May 1942.

110. Message CinCPac to ComInCh 090207 of May 1942, in *CINCPAC Greybook*, 452.

111. *CINCPAC Greybook*, 9 May 1942.

112. *Senshi Sosho*, 328–330.

Part III
Strategic Aftermath of the Coral Sea Battle

1. Fuchida and Okumiya, 72.

2. For a detailed account of Midway planning, see *Ibid.*, 80–88.

3. *MacArthur Reports*, II, Part 1, 133–134.

4. *Senshi Sosho*, 329–330; *Japanese Monographs* No. 34, "Southeast Area Operations Record, Volume 1 (May 1942–January 1943)," 5–7.

5. *Imperial General Headquarters Navy Directives*, I, 39.

6. *MacArthur Reports*, II, Part 1, 134; Fuchida and Okumiya, 89, 95.

7. *Japanese Monographs* No. 34, 6–9; Saburo Hayashi and Alvin D. Coox, *Kogun: The Japanese Army in the Pacific War*, 43–44.

8. Sherwood, 515–516; quote from Mattloff and Snell, 217.

9. Mattloff and Snell, 182–187; Steele, 110–114.

10. Sherwood, 521–543; Mattloff and Snell, 187–190; Steele, 115–120. For General Sir Alan Brooke's reaction to the Sledgehammer plan, see Arthur Bryant, *The Turn of the Tide 1939–1943*, 358–359.

11. Dyer, I, 252–253; Morton, 292–293.

12. The best discussion of JCS 48 in relation to air power is in Craven and Cate, IV, 13–17.

13. Dyer, I, 255.

14. Mattloff and Snell, 217–218.

15. *Eisenhower Papers*, I, 280.

16. *Ibid.*, 281.

17. Dyer, I, 255–256 with full text of memo.

18. *Ibid.*

19. Extract in *Eisenhower Papers*, I, 281.
20. *Ibid.*
21. Text in Mattloff and Snell, 219; see Hayes, 168–173 for an overview of the controversy.
22. Craven and Cate, IV, 18.
23. *Eisenhower Papers*, I, 269; Mattloff and Snell, 223; Craven and Cate, IV, 19–20.
24. *Eisenhower Papers*, I, 296–298 for text of the War Department memo to the Joint Chiefs, 13 May 1942.
25. *CINCPAC Greybook*, 3 and 4 May 1942.
26. Message Com 14 to Comb 030002 of May 1942, in CinCPac Message File.
27. Messages Com 14 to Comb 031812 of May 1942, 040816 of May 1942, in CinCPac Message File.
28. Message Com 14 to Comb 042302 of May 1942, in CinCPac Message File.
29. *CINCPAC Greybook*, 5 and 6 May 1942.
30. Message Com 14 to Comb 070306 of May 1942, in CinCPac Message File.
31. Message Com 14 to Comb 090054 of May 1942, in CinCPac Message File.
32. *Ibid.*
33. Message Com 14 to Comb 090114 of May 1942, in CinCPac Message File.
34. Message Com 14 to Comb 092236 of May 1942, in CinCPac Message File.
35. *CINCPAC Greybook*, 8 May 1942.
36. For the Ocean-Nauru Operation from the Japanese viewpoint, see *Senshi Sosho*, 251–255.
37. Task Force 16's general activities are covered in Vice Admiral Halsey's War Diary for Task Force 16, 30 April–18 May 1942, in Classified Operational Archives.
38. Messages CinCPac to CTF-16, 17 080235 of May 1942, CinCPac to CTF-16, 17 100045 of May 1942, in CinCPac Message File.
39. Message CTF-16 to CinCPac 101850 of May 1942, in CinCPac Message File.
40. Message CinCPac to CTF-16 120041 of May 1942, in CinCPac Message File.
41. Message CTF-16 to ComSoWesPacFor 120137 of May 1942, in CinCPac Message File.
42. Message CinCPac to all CTF 120429 of May 1942, in CinCPac Message File.
43. Message CTG-17.2 to CTF-16 120400 of May 1942, in CinCPac Message File.
44. Message CTF-16 to CTG-17.2 122333 of May 1942, in CinCPac Message File.

45. Message ComSoWesPacFor to CTF-16 140115 of May 1942, in CinCPac Message File.
46. Task Force 16 War Diary, 14 May 1942.
47. Message CinCPac to all CTF 100111 of May 1942, in CinCPac Message File.
48. *CINCPAC Greybook*, 9 May 1942.
49. Message Belconnen to Comb 110140 of May 1942, in CinCPac Message File.
50. Lord, 20–23; Blair, 234.
51. Message CinCPac to ComInCh 102347 of May 1942, in *CINCPAC Greybook*, 463.
52. *CINCPAC Greybook*, 12 May 1942.
53. Message ComInCh to CinCPac 121245 of May 1942, in *CINCPAC Greybook*, 456.
54. *Ibid.*
55. Message ComInCh to CinCPac 121950 of May 1942, in *CINCPAC Greybook*, 464.
56. Messages CinCPac to ComInCh 140639, 140741, 140829, 140853 of May 1942, in CinCPac Message File.
57. *Ibid.*
58. *Ibid.*
59. *Ibid.*
60. Message CinCPac to CTF-16 140319 of May 1942, in CinCPac Message List.
61. Task Force 16 War Diary, 14 May 1942.
62. Information on the secret despatch was obtained from Rear Admiral Layton. For Halsey's activities, see Task Force 16 War Diary, 14–15 May 1942.
63. Task Force 16 War Diary entry, 15 May 1942.
64. Message, CTF-16 to CTG-17.2 150445 of May 1942, in CinCPac Message File.
65. Fleet Admiral William F. Halsey and J. Bryan, III, *Admiral Halsey's Story*, 105–106.
66. *Ibid.*
67. *Ibid.*
68. *Ibid.*
69. For example, Morison, IV, 62 covers the Ocean-Nauru Operation and Task Force 16's operations in a footnote.
70. *Senshi Sosho*, 255–256, details South Seas Force reaction to Halsey's appearance in the South Pacific.
71. Message ComInCh to CinCPac 152130 of May 1942, in *CINCPAC Greybook*, 468.
72. Message CinCPac to ComInCh 160325 of May 1942, in CinCPac Message File.
73. Message CinCPac to CTF-16 160307 of May 1942, in CinCPac Message File.

74. Message CinCPac to CTF-16 170937 of May 1942, in *CINCPAC Greybook*, 491.
75. Quoted in Halsey and Bryan, 106.
76. Message CinCPac to ComInCh 170407 of May 1942, in *CINCPAC Greybook*, 490.
77. *Ibid.*
78. Message ComInCh to CinCPac 172200 of May 1942, in *CINCPAC Greybook*, 489–490.
79. *Ibid.*
80. Personal communication.
81. Message CinCPac to ComSoWesPacFor for MacArthur 170537 of May 1942, in *CINCPAC Greybook*, 469–470.
82. Message ComSoWesPac to CinCPac 190345 of May 1942, in *CINCPAC Greybook*, 493.
83. Morison, IV, 252–254, 263n.
84. Mattloff and Snell, 223–224; Morton, 280–281; *Eisenhower Papers*, 299.
85. *Eisenhower Papers*, I, 299–300.
86. *MacArthur Reports*, I, 38–39.
87. Message Melbourne to C/S (MacArthur to Marshall), No. AG 719, 13 May 1942, retransmitted to ComInCh to CinCPac 142100 series of May 1942 in CinCPac Message File.
88. Albert Harkness, *Command History, U.S. Naval Forces in the Southwest Pacific Area in World War II*, Part I, *Retreat in the Southwest Pacific*, 99, and see also 80, 193–194 (available from Classified Operational Archives); Task Force 44 Action Report dated 21 May 1942; Morison, IV, 38–39.
89. *Eisenhower Papers*, I, 301–302.
90. *Ibid.*
91. Mattloff and Snell, 224.
92. *Eisenhower Papers*, I, 311.
93. Craven and Cate, I, 452–455; *Eisenhower Papers*, I, 314.
94. Craven and Cate, I, 462–465, IV, 10–13.
95. Message ComAirSoPac to CinCPac 210900 of May 1942, in *CINCPAC Greybook*, 522.
96. Message ComSoWesPac to CinCPac 190345 of May 1942, in *CINCPAC Greybook*, 493.
97. Dyer, I, 256.
98. *Ibid.*, 256–257; Mattloff and Snell, 226.
99. Dyer, I, 257.
100. Mattloff and Snell, 226.
101. *AAF in Australia to the Summer of 1942*, 106–141; see sources cited *supra*, Part II, note 50.
102. Mattloff and Snell, 226; Hayes, 183–185; Forrest C. Pogue, *George C. Marshall: Ordeal and Hope 1939–1942*, 324.
103. "Estimate of the Situation, May 21, 1942," text in *CINCPAC Greybook*.

104. Message ComInCh to CinCPac 172220 of May 1942, in *CINCPAC Greybook*, 489–490.
105. "Estimate of the Situation, April 22, 1942," text in *CINCPAC Greybook*.
106. "Estimate of the Situation, May 21, 1942," text in *CINCPAC Greybook*.
107. *Ibid.*
108. *Ibid.*
109. Letter Nimitz to King, 29 May 1942 in Miscellaneous Correspondence, Fleet Admiral Nimitz, in Classified Operational Archives; Thomas B. Buell, *The Quiet Warrior: A Biography of Admiral Raymond A. Spruance*, 120–122.
110. Message ComInCh to CinCPac 111245 of May 1942, in CinCPac Message File.
111. Message CTF-17 to CinCPac 160200 of May 1942, in CinCPac Message File; *CINCPAC Greybook*, 15 May 1942.
112. Message CinCPac to ComSoWesPac 170537 of May 1942, in *CINCPAC Greybook*, 469–470.
113. Letter Fletcher to Nimitz, 28 May 1942, in Miscellaneous Correspondence of Fleet Admiral Nimitz, Classified Operational Archives.
114. Letter Nimitz to King, 29 May 1942, in Miscellaneous Correspondence, Fleet Admiral Nimitz, Classified Operational Archives.
115. *Ibid.*
116. Fuchida and Okumiya, 106, 243.
117. *Ibid.*, 245.
118. *Ibid.*, 109–110.
119. U.S. Navy, Office of Naval Intelligence, *The Japanese Story of the Battle of Midway*, 2–3. This is the translated version of Vice Admiral Nagumo's official report.
120. Personal communication from Rear Admiral Layton. There is a hint of this radio deception in *CINCPAC Greybook*, 25 May 1942.
121. Fuchida and Okumiya, 129–130.
122. Message ComInCh to CinCPac 172220 of May 1942, in *CINCPAC Greybook*, 489–490.
123. General studies of the Battle of Midway include Fuchida and Okumiya, Morison, IV, 68–184, and Lord; the best from the standpoint of operations is the U.S. Naval War College, *The Battle of Midway including the Aleutian Phase, June 3 to June 14, 1942, Strategical and Tactical Analysis*.
124. U.S. Navy War College, *The Battle of Midway . . .* , 122.
125. Craven and Cate, I, 459–462, discuss the failure of the B-17's to hit anything.
126. *Japanese Monographs*, No. 34, 9–11; *MacArthur Reports*, II, Part 1, 138–139.
127. Toshikazu Ohmae, "The Battle of Savo Island," in Raymond O'Connor, *The Japanese Navy in World War II*, 76–78. Ohmae was an officer on the staff of Vice Admiral Mikawa's Eighth Fleet.

128. *Ibid.*, 77–79; *Japanese Monographs* No. 34, 11–23.
129. Sherwood, 563.
130. For Molotov's visit, see Sherwood, 556–579, Mattloff and Snell, 231–232, and Steele, 136–141.
131. Mattloff and Snell, 258–260; Morton, 293–298.
132. Dyer, I, 258–261; Morton, 298–301.
133. Morton, 619, for the background to Guadalcanal landings, and see 301–304, 619–620 for the text of the agreement; also Mattloff and Snell, 261–265, and Dyer, I, 269–276.
134. Mattloff and Snell, chapters XI, XII, XIII; Steele, 143–179.

Bibliography

Documents

The principal source of documents has been the U.S. Navy's Classified Operational Archives, headed by Dr. Dean C. Allard. Part of the Naval History Division, the Classified Operational Archives offers a wealth of after-action reports, war diaries, message logs, letters, and some captured Japanese documents. One outstanding source for the planning and operations of the Pacific Fleet is the *CINCPAC Greybook*, also known as "Captain Steele's Running Estimate and Summary, 7 December 1941 to 31 August 1942." The War Plans section on the CinCPac staff compiled this massive war diary, which includes in addition to detailed daily entries, the text of important messages, situation estimates, and operational plans. Captain Vincent R. Murphy had charge of the work until about May 1942, when Captain J. M. Steele took over the diary. Mention must also be made of the key message list entitled, "Commander-in-chief, U.S. Pacific Fleet Messages, Secret and Confidential Chronological File." The daily messages, with some exceptions, to and from CinCPac headquarters are here recorded on microfilm. The author especially studied the messages from 14 April to 16

May 1942, culling out from the several thousand routine messages key communications relating to the intelligence background of the Coral Sea and Midway campaigns. The Operational Classified Archives also includes portions of the papers of Fleet Admirals Ernest J. King and Chester W. Nimitz. See the Notes for specific documentary citations.

Unpublished Sources

In addition to the documents themselves, a number of unpublished studies proved most useful:

Harkness, Lieutenant (j.g.) Albert. *Command History, U.S. Naval Forces in the Southwest Pacific Area in World War II*. Part I. *Retreat in the Southwest Pacific* (available from the Operational Classified Archives).

Hayes, Lieutenant Grace P. *The History of the Joint Chiefs of Staff in World War II, The War Against Japan*. Volume I. *Pearl Harbor to TRIDENT*. Washington, D.C.: The Joint Chiefs of Staff, 1953 (available through the National Archives).

U.S. Army, Headquarters Far East Command, Military History Section. *Imperial General Headquarters Navy Directives*. Tokyo, 1951 (available through the National Archives).

————. *The Imperial Japanese Navy in World War II*. Tokyo, 1952 (available through the National Archives).

U.S. Army, Headquarters Far East Command, Military History Section, Japanese Research Division. *Japanese Monographs*.

No. 34, "Southeast Area Operations Record, Volume I (May 1942–January 1943)." Covers operations of 17th Army in preparing for the Fiji–New Caledonia–Samoa and Port Moresby attacks.

No. 45, "History of Imperial General Headquarters, Army Section (1941–1945)."

No. 96, "Eastern New Guinea Invasion Operations (March–September 1942)."

No. 113, "Task Force Operations (November 1941–April 1942)." Covers activities of Nagumo's Striking Force from Pearl Harbor through the raid in the Indian Ocean.

No. 118, "Operational History of Naval Communications (December 1941–August 1945)."

No. 120, "Outline of Southeast Area Naval Air Operations, Part I (December 1941–August 1942)."

No. 143, "Southeast Area Operations Record, Part I (January–May 1942)." Covers the operations of Horii's South Seas Detachment up through the Coral Sea Battle.

(The *Japanese Monographs*, which are available through the National Archives, were a product of General MacArthur's headquarters in

Japan. They were written by former Japanese officers based on such documents as were then available or sometimes memory. As such they are uneven in quality.)

U.S. Army Air Forces, Historical Division. *The AAF in Australia to the Summer of 1942 (Army Air Forces Historical Studies* No. 9), 1944 (available from the Albert Simpson Historical Center, Maxwell Air Force Base, Alabama).

U.S. Navy, Office of Naval Intelligence. *Early Raids in the Pacific February 1 to March 10, 1942.* Washington, D.C.: Office of Naval Intelligence, 1943 (available from the Naval History Division; excellent resume of the early carrier strikes in the Pacific).

_____. *The Japanese Story of the Battle of Midway (A Translation).* Washington, D.C.: Office of Naval Intelligence, 1947 (Vice Admiral Nagumo's official report for Midway; available from the Naval History Division).

U.S. Naval War College. *The Battle of the Coral Sea, May 1 to May 11 Inclusive, 1942, Strategical and Tactical Analysis.* Newport: U.S. Naval War College, 1947.

_____. *The Battle of Midway including the Aleutian Phase June 3 to June 14, 1942, Strategical and Tactical Analysis.* Newport: U.S. Naval War College, 1948.

(Both War College studies are available through the Naval History Division and are extremely useful summaries with excellent maps. The volume on Midway especially brings together widely scattered documents for the most detailed account of the battle.)

Service Histories

The student of the Pacific War is fortunate to have at his disposal a number of excellent service histories. Strategic planning as well as operational details are well covered in the relevant volumes of the series *The United States Army in World War Two*:

Mattloff, Maurice, and Snell, Edwin M. *Strategic Planning for Coalition Warfare 1941–1942 (United States Army in World War Two: The War Department).* Washington, D.C.: Government Printing Office, 1953.

Milner, Samuel. *Victory in Papua (United States Army in World War Two, The War in the Pacific).* Washington, D.C.: Government Printing Office, 1957.

Morton, Louis. *Strategy and Command: The First Two Years (United States Army in World War Two, The War in the Pacific).* Washington, D.C.: Government Printing Office, 1962.

The activities of the Army Air Forces appear in that service's official history:

Craven, W. F., and Cate, J. L. *The Army Air Forces in World War II.*

Volume I. *Plans and Early Operations (January 1939 to August 1942)*. Chicago: University of Chicago Press, 1948.

_____. *The Army Air Forces in World War II*. Volume IV. *The Pacific: Guadalcanal to Saipan (August 1942–July 1944)*. Chicago: University of Chicago Press, 1950.

Rear Admiral Samuel Eliot Morison's monumental *History of United States Naval Operations in World War II* is described as a "semiofficial history," but functions as the Navy's service history for World War II. The volumes specifically related to this study are:

Volume III. *The Rising Sun in the Pacific 1931–April 1942*. Boston: Little, Brown, 1948.

Volume IV. *Coral Sea, Midway and Submarine Actions May 1942–August 1942*. Boston: Little, Brown, 1949.

The earliest volumes of Morison's history reflect the fact that they were written soon after the end of the war, without access to many key documents and new Japanese sources.

Great Britain and Australia have produced official histories of value to this work. The British series is multi-service:

Kirby, Major General S. Woodburn, et al. *The War Against Japan*. Volumes I and II. London: Her Majesty's Stationery Office, 1957–1958.

In contrast, the Australians have written detailed studies from the viewpoint of each of the services:

Gill, G. Hermon. *Royal Australian Navy*. Volume I, 1939–1942. Volume II, 1942–1945 (*Australia in the War of 1939–1945*, Series 2). Canberra: Australian War Memorial, 1957, 1968.

Gillison, Douglas. *Royal Australian Air Force 1939–1942* (*Australia in the War of 1939–1945*, Series 3). Canberra: Australian War Memorial, 1962.

McCarthy, Dudley. *South-West Pacific Area—First Year, Kokoda to Wau* (*Australia in the War of 1939–1945*, Series 1, Volume V). Canberra: Australian War Memorial, 1957.

Wigmore, Lionel. *The Japanese Thrust (Australia in the War of 1939–1945*, Series 1, Volume IV). Canberra: Australian War Memorial, 1957.

The Australian histories are especially useful as a balance to the American histories of the war in the Southwest Pacific.

Japanese Histories

In recent years the Japanese Self-Defense Agency has inaugurated an ambitious program of official histories covering Japanese operations in the Pacific War. They are based largely on documents, personal interviews, memoirs, and other sources hitherto untapped by historians. Filling an enormous gap regarding Japanese operations in the South Pacific before the Guadalcanal Campaign is the following volume of this series:

Japanese Self-Defense Agency, War History Office. *Senshi Sosho. Nantohomen Kaigun Sakusen Gato Dakai Sakusen Kaishi Made (War History Series. Southeast Area Naval Operations until the Guadalcanal Counteroffensive).* Volume One. Tokyo: Asagumo Shimbun, 1971.

It is unfortunate that there is no program for translating these volumes into English in order to make them available to American historians of the Pacific War.

Other Published Sources

Blair, Clay, Jr. *Silent Victory.* Philadelphia: J. B. Lippincott, 1975. A detailed history of United States submarine operations in the Pacific War, but with much excellent information on codebreaking secured from interviews with Navy codebreakers.

Borg, Dorothy, and Okamoto, Shumpei. *Pearl Harbor as History: Japanese-American Relations 1931–1941* New York: Columbia University Press, 1973. Contains articles by Japanese and American scholars on a number of subjects, including the armies and navies of the two powers. Especially noteworthy is the article by Asada Sadao entitled "The Japanese Navy and the United States," pp. 225–259.

Bryant, Arthur. *The Turn of the Tide 1939–1943.* London: Collins, 1957. Based on the papers of Field Marshall Viscount Alanbrooke, Chief of the Imperial General Staff.

Buell, Thomas B. *The Quiet Warrior: A Biography of Admiral Raymond A. Spruance.* Boston: Little, Brown, 1974. Excellent discussion of command decisions at the Battle of Midway.

Chandler, Alfred D., ed. *The Papers of Dwight David Eisenhower. The War Years,* Volume I. Baltimore: The Johns Hopkins Press, 1970. Contains the text of many key documents regarding War Department planning and operations in early 1942.

Churchill, Winston S. *The Hinge of Fate.* Boston: Houghton Mifflin, 1950.

Dyer, Vice Admiral George C. *The Amphibians Came to Conquer: The Story of Admiral Richmond Kelly Turner.* Two volumes. Washington, D.C.: Government Printing Office, 1971. Turner was chief of War Plans on Admiral King's staff in early 1942. The author was himself on the ComInCh staff and provides valuable insights on the thinking of Turner and his boss regarding the South Pacific.

Fuchida, Mitsuo, and Okumiya, Masatake. *Midway: the Battle That Doomed Japan.* Annapolis: United States Naval Institute, 1955. Superb study by two former Japanese naval officers on the background and execution of the Midway operation.

Furer, Rear Admiral Julius A. *Administration of the Navy Department in World War II.* Washington, D.C.: Government Printing Office, 1959.

Halsey, Fleet Admiral William F., and Bryan, J., III. *Admiral Halsey's Story.* New York: Whittlesey House, 1947.

Hayashi, Saburo, and Coox, Alvin D. *Kogun: The Japanese Army in the Pacific War.* Quantico: The Marine Corps Association, 1959. Very useful summary of Japanese Army strategic policy.

Hoyt, Edwin P. *How They Won the War in the Pacific: Nimitz and his Admirals.* New York: Weybright and Talley, 1970.

Ito, Masanori. *The End of the Imperial Japanese Navy.* New York: Dutton, 1962.

Kahn, David. *The Codebreakers: the Story of Secret Writing.* New York: Macmillan, 1967. A pioneering study of codebreaking with valuable information on the decipering of the Japanese naval code.

King, Fleet Admiral Ernest J., and Whitehill, Commander W. M. *Fleet Admiral King: A Naval Record.* New York: W. W. Norton & Company, 1952.

Lord, Walter. *Incredible Victory.* New York: Harper & Row, 1967. A fine study of the Battle of Midway. The author's careful analysis cleared up a number of controversial points regarding the battle.

MacArthur, General Douglas. *Reports of General MacArthur.* Two volumes in four parts. Washington, D.C.: Government Printing Office, 1966. A compilation by historians on the general's staff, the first volume is a narrative of operations in the Southwest Pacific Area. The second volume, largely written by former Japanese officers, is a very valuable account of the Japanese opposition to MacArthur. There are a large number of quotes by key Japanese commanders and staff officers.

O'Connor, Raymond. *The Japanese Navy in World War II.* Annapolis: United States Naval Institute, 1969. A collection of a number of important articles by former Japanese naval officers which had been published in the Institute's *Proceedings.*

Pogue, Forrest C. *George C. Marshall: Ordeal and Hope 1939–1942.* New York: Viking, 1966. A sympathetic biography of the Chief of Staff.

Richardson, Admiral James O., with Vice Admiral George C. Dyer. *On the Treadmill to Pearl Harbor: The Memoirs of Admiral James O. Richardson.* Washington, D.C.: Government Printing Office, 1973. Excellent for the prewar activities of the U.S. Navy and especially well-documented.

Sherwood, Robert. *Roosevelt and Hopkins: An Intimate History.* New York: Harper, 1948.

Smith, Vice Admiral William Ward. *Midway: Turning Point of the Pacific.* New York: Crowell, 1966. An account of Coral Sea and Midway by Rear Admiral Fletcher's cruiser commander.

Steele, Richard W. *The First Offensive 1942: Roosevelt, Marshall and the Making of American Strategy.* Bloomington: Indiana University Press, 1973. Penetrating analysis of Marshall's plans for an early offensive in

Northwest Europe. The author concludes that implementation of Sledgehammer would have been disastrous, but does not consider the implications of Marshall's tie-up of valuable resources for the Pacific.

Toland, John. *The Rising Sun.* New York: Random House, 1970.

U.S. Congress, 79th Congress, 1st Session. *Pearl Harbor Attack: Hearings before the Joint Committee on the Investigation of the Pearl Harbor Attack.* 38 parts. Washington, D.C.: Government Printing Office, 1946. Many valuable documents including translations of Japanese orders are contained in voluminous exhibits.

Index

231

India, 50, 52, 128
Indian Ocean Raid, 43–44, 69, 78, 200
Inoue, Vice Admiral Shigemi: commander of Fourth Fleet/ South Seas Force, 9; and First Operational Stage, 9–11; and invasions planned for South-west Pacific, 23–27; to capture Ocean and Nauru, 27; invades Lae and Salamaua, 35–36; attacked at Lae and Salamaua, 39–40; requests carrier support, 40–42; plans for MO Operation, 46–47, 65–74; and Battle of the Coral Sea, 97, 99, 103, 105–106, 110; cancels invasion of Port Moresby, 112–113, 115–116, 124; and RY Invasion, 68, 116, 141–144, 158–159; post-Coral Sea plans of, 186; assessment of strategy of, 197, 200
Ito, Vice Admiral Seiichi, 46

Jaluit Island, 16, 17, 30
Japanese Army, 1–2, 5–6, 8–9, 11, 41, 43, 122, 123, 124–125, 186, 187, 195–196, 199; units: 4th Infantry Regiment, 125; 35th Brigade, 125; 41st Infantry Regiment, 125; 124th Infantry Regiment, 125; 144th Infantry Regiment, 11, 125
Japanese Navy, air flotillas: 24th, 24, 27, 33–34, 35–36, 67; 25th, 65, 67, 69, 70, 72, 78, 186
Japanese Navy, divisions: 1st Battleship, 91, 124; 2nd Battleship, 91, 124; 3rd Battleship, 137–139; 4th Cruiser, 91; 5th Cruiser, 66, 69, 81, 88, 90, 143–144, 145, 147, 159; 6th Cruiser, 71, 91, 144, 145, 147, 158, 186; 8th Cruiser, 139; 18th Cruiser, 186; 1st Carrier, 65, 66, 179; 2nd Carrier, 17, 65, 139, 179; 3rd Carrier, 159; 5th Carrier, 43–44, 66, 68–70, 79, 81, 88, 90, 100, 104, 105, 107, 108, 143, 178–179, 184, 200
Japanese Navy, fleets: First, 7, 137–139, 181, 184; Second, 7–8, 69, 80, 122, 124–125, 139, 181; Fourth, 7, 8, 9–11, 23, 35, 39, 40, 88, 99, 124–125, 137–138, 186; Sixth, 7–8, 69, 138; Eighth, 124–125, 186–187; First Air, 7–8, 137–139; Eleventh Air, 7–8, 42, 47, 81
Japanese Navy, submarine squadrons: 1st, 123; 3rd, 123; 5th, 123; 8th, 69, 74
Johnston Island, 18, 21, 29, 42
Joint Board, 14, 16, 48
Joint Chiefs of Staff, 48, 51, 52, 54–55, 57–58, 60, 126–136, 165–166, 169, 171, 189, 196, 201–202
Joint Staff Plans Committee, 128–130, 131
Jomard Passage, 66, 74, 104, 105–106, 108
Junyo, 182

Kaga, 42, 43, 47, 65, 66, 75–76, 77, 78, 80, 82, 91, 102, 138, 139; sunk, 183
Kajioka, Rear Admiral Sadamichi, 71, 105–106, 107, 108
Kakuta, Rear Admiral Kakuji, 123
Kamchatka, 85
Kanazawa, Rear Admiral Masao, 70–71
Kashima, 97
Kasuga Maru, 80, 82, 115
Katori, 69, 138
Kavieng, 74, 141
Kawaguchi, Major General Kiyotake, 125
Kawai, Captain Iwao, 71
Kikuzuki, 141
Kilinailau Islands, 145, 147
Kimmel, Admiral Husband E., 14, 15, 16, 17
King, Admiral Ernest J.: appointed CinCLant, 14; becomes ComInCh, 17; basic directive of, to CinCPac and CinCAF, 19; and Arcadia Conference, 20–21; requests garrisons for Bora Bora and New Caledonia, 19, 20; wants early action in the

Vanikoro, 146–149, 156
Vila, 144

Wailupe, 75
Wake Island, 11–12, 15, 16–17, 29, 32–34, 35, 44
War Department. *See* Arnold, Lieutenant General Henry H., Eisenhower, Brigadier General Dwight D., and Marshall, General George C.
Wasp, 151, 153
Watanabe, Commander Yasuji, 44–45, 46
Wavell, General Sir Archibald, 19, 31, 57
Wotje, 30

Yamada, Rear Admiral Sadatoshi, 72, 96, 98, 106, 158
Yamamoto, Admiral Isoroku: commander of Combined Fleet, 8; Pearl Harbor attack plan of, 9; plans for invasion of Mid-way, 42–46, 121–123; orders Inoue to pursue American forces in the Coral Sea, 113; and post-Midway plans for South Pacific, 124–125; and Battle of Midway, 180, 181; assessment of strategy of, 198, 200, 204–205
Yamaoka, Commander Mineo, 71
Yamato, 46, 180
Yano, Rear Admiral Shikazo, 40, 42, 99
Yazawa, Colonel Kiyomi, 125
Yorktown, 15–16, 18, 21, 30, 32, 37–38, 54, 59, 72, 78, 83, 99, 101, 102, 103, 107, 108, 110–111, 114–115, 135, 151, 152, 153, 161, 165, 175, 176, 177, 179, 182, 183; sunk, 184

Zuikaku, 43, 66, 80, 82, 100, 110, 112, 113, 143–144, 145, 179, 184

240